Beyond Words

Beyond Words

Discourse and Critical Agency in Africa

⌒ ANDREW APTER ⌒

The University of Chicago Press
Chicago and London

Andrew Apter is professor of history and anthropology and chair of the interdepartmental program in African studies at the University of California, Los Angeles. He is the author of *Black Critics and Kings: The Hermeneutics of Power in Yoruba Society* and, most recently, *The Pan-African Nation: Oil and the Spectacle of Culture in Nigeria*, both published by the University of Chicago Press.

The University of Chicago Press, Chicago 60637
The University of Chicago Press, Ltd., London
© 2007 by The University of Chicago
All rights reserved. Published 2007
Printed in the United States of America

16 15 14 13 12 11 10 09 08 07   1 2 3 4 5

ISBN-13: 978-0-226-02351-9 (cloth)
ISBN-13: 978-0-226-02352-6 (paper)
ISBN-10: 0-226-02351-6 (cloth)
ISBN-10: 0-226-02352-4 (paper)

Library of Congress Cataloging-in-Publication Data

Apter, Andrew H. (Andrew Herman)
    Beyond words : discourse and critical agency in Africa / Andrew Apter.
    p. cm.
    Includes bibliographical references and index.
    ISBN-13: 978-0-226-02351-9 (cloth : alk. paper)
    ISBN-10: 0-226-02351-6 (cloth : alk. paper)
    ISBN-13: 978-0-226-02352-6 (pbk. : alk. paper)
    ISBN-10: 0-226-02352-4 (pbk. : alk. paper)
    1. Ethnology—Africa—History.   2. Ethnology—Africa—Philosophy.
3. Discourse analysis—Africa.   4. Culture—Semiotic models.   5. Social
problems—Africa.   6. Africa in popular culture.   7. Africa—Colonization.
8. Arfica—Social conditions.   9. Africa—Civilization.   I. Title.
GN308.3.A35A78 2007
306.096—dc22

                                                      2006103502

⊗ The paper used in this publication meets the minimum requirements of the American National Standard for Information Sciences—Permanence of Paper for Printed Library Materials, ANSI Z39.48-1992.

Contents

Illustrations

Figures

Tables

Preface

The essays collected in this volume represent my long-standing engagement with ritual-language genres in Africa, connecting a set of specialized concerns within anthropological theory to the broader politics of discourse in African studies. As I look back over my various forays and interventions, with the inevitable revisionism that hindsight affords, I would like to think that they not only return to the classic topoi of Africanist ethnography for material and inspiration but also point forward to renewed arenas of sociolinguistic analysis and critical exegesis. In some ways, the "project" I am pursuing may appear irrelevant to a continent plagued by regional conflict, genocide, and the AIDS pandemic, producing refugees, orphans, and child soldiers in epidemic proportions. For those struggling in the devastated areas and conflict zones, it probably is irrelevant. But in the larger, even global dimensions of Africanist research—as I shall argue—explorations of critical agency in Africa oppose the very conditions in which Africa is pathologized and the mechanisms by which the "Dark Continent" is continually reinscribed.

It is impossible to acknowledge the many mentors and influences that have shaped my interest in language and discourse, but a number stand out as especially formative. To my undergraduate coadvisers Rulon S. Wells and Sheyla Benhabib I owe a "pragmaticist" approach to logic and semiotics as well as an intensive introduction to critical social theory. At Cambridge University, where I shifted from philosophy to social anthropology, I worked through the traditional "functionalist" canon, all the while retaining my interest in modes of devolution, joking relationships, and the dialectics of fission and of rituals of rebellion. I also took classes with Stephen Levinson, whose emerging focus on sociolinguistics and pragmatics was propelling formal concerns with syntactic structures into dynamic arenas of social interaction. When I returned to Yale for graduate study, this interest in pragmatics was further encouraged by Susan Bean and was tolerated by M. G. Smith—my dissertation adviser—whose more "structural" approach to political anthropology subordinated language to the bedrock of corporation theory. Although M. G.'s model of power and authority (as a dialectic of segmentary politics and hierarchical administration) informed my fieldwork on Yoruba orisha worship (even if I abstracted the subversive dimensions of power sui generis beyond his comfort zone), it was always with the aim of reincorporating discourse, not only in ritual idioms of possession and incantation, but as a sanctified hermeneutics of power that is context specific and opposed to authority. Yoruba deep knowledge is powerful, I have argued, when it negotiates and revises authority structures—highlighting the politics of symbolic revision.

My interest in Yoruba ritual as an indigenous form of critical practice developed within its own revisionary process—from dissertation into book (Apter 1992). I realize now that several signal texts were catalysts in readjusting my interpretive focus. John L. Comaroff's "Talking Politics: Oratory and Authority in a Tswana Chiefdom" (1975) identified critical functions of code convergence and divergence in negotiating political authority within competitive political arenas, outlining an *indigenous* incumbency model that established rhetorical conditions of political evaluation. Tswana praises, he showed, were indeed critical practices that mobilized shifting coalitions and loyalties on the ground. The second text was Karin Barber's "Yoruba *Oríkì* and Deconstructive Criticism" (1984), something of a Copernican revolution in literary theory because it relocated the insights of rhetorical analysis—particularly the critique of narrative and textual closure—within the oral literary practices of Yoruba praise-singers and their paradigmatically intertextual strategies. Barber showed that deconstructive criticism had homegrown varieties in West Africa, unmaking and remaking the very field of social relations through their oratorical terms of engagement. If this move toward vernacular critical traditions was expanded and amplified in her first monumental ethnography (Barber 1991a), it was theoretically elaborated by Henry Louis Gates Jr., whose *The Signifying Monkey* (1988) established a Yoruba genealogy for African American textual strategies based on operations of "tropological revision" glossed by the social poetics of "signifyin(g)." What Gates posited as a "myth of origins" I could document ethnographically, focusing on how deep-knowledge claims, activated by ritual, revised the symbolic charters of political authority.

The same year that Gates published his theory of "Afro-American" literary criticism, V. Y. Mudimbe posed a fundamental challenge to the Africanist academy at large. In *The Invention of Africa: Gnosis, Philosophy, and the Order of Knowledge* (1988), Mudimbe examined the discursive conventions that "invented" Africa as an object of knowledge and that generated a "colonial library" of projections and illusions that have persisted even when explicitly disavowed. Central to his exposition is how African philosophy, defined as gnosis, or secret knowledge, represents the limit of this ideological horizon. Attempts by Placide Tempels and Marcel Griaule and their followers to penetrate the veil and learn the secrets of deep knowledge in Africa only further mystified the illusions which they tried to overcome. Mudimbe's critique was not limited to Western scholars but extended to African intellectuals who continued to write within this ethnophilosophical vein.

I was inspired by the power of Mudimbe's deconstructive project, not only for its dazzling exposition of colonial discourse in Africanist scholarship, but because my own research was so directly implicated. His was a challenge I *had* to confront, since my focus on secrecy and deep-knowledge claims was buried so deeply within the colonial library. My "solution" was to recast deep knowledge as unstable and indeterminate—less a hidden transcript of secret knowledge than a discursive space of critical negation, an unmaking and revising of official truths and meanings that could be mobilized to make a political difference. Deep-knowledge claims invoked by ritual belonged to indigenous forms of critical practice. They were ritually charged because they were politically dangerous, safeguarding possibilities of critical agency. If Mudimbe was correct in debunking Western fantasies of cracking African codes, he was less successful in appreciating how they work on the ground. Foreclosed from his position was how ritual-language genres and practices could recast participation frameworks, performance contexts, and relations of hierarchy and rank between social actors—how a ritual discourse could build a rival up or bring an incumbent down, or oppose representatives of colonial authority—not what deep knowledge meant but how it worked. Mudimbe's challenge could be met on methodological grounds by recasting ethnophilosophy as ethnopragmatics.

Thus, I returned to narrower concerns with indexicality, deictic reference, pronominal shifting, and metapragmatic function, those dimensions of linguistic performance and practice that shape and transform the interactive contexts in which they are embedded. My exposure to this more technical terrain owes much to my colleagues Michael Silverstein and Bill Hanks during my years at the University of Chicago, whose explorations of "discursive semiosis" and "referential practice" have helped me understand how ritual language works and how its performativity is framed by cultural idioms of ritual power. While I have drawn on their ideas in developing a reflexive concept of critical agency, I am also indebted to the metadiscourse community at UCLA, particularly Alessandro Duranti, whose work on the grammar and politics of agency has allowed me to elaborate its critical dimensions and relate discourse to broader sociopolitical contexts. More recently, valuable discussions with Sherry Ortner have helped me rethink the diachronic dimensions of agency.

Within the broader community of UCLA Africanists, I have benefited from a rigorous array of critical perspectives: from Françoise Lionnet and Dominic Thomas, whose work on discourse and the politics of African literature is remapping Francophone horizons; from Ghislaine Lydon and her pathbreaking research on Arabic texts and textuality in Africa; from Chris Ehret and his uncanny explorations of early African history in semantic reconstructions and linguistic protoforms; and from the linguists Tom Hinnebusch and Russell Schuh, whose technical interests in formal analysis are matched by an extraordinary commitment to African-language instruction. And final thanks to the James S. Coleman African Studies Center and its director, Allen F. Roberts, for sustaining, with such energy, a commitment to Africa that goes beyond words.

Research on Yoruba ritual-language genres (chapter 4) was supported by the American Philosophical Society and the American Council of Learned Societies, for which I am grateful. Earlier versions of chapters 1–6 appeared in the following journals: "*Que Faire?* Reconsidering Inventions of Africa," *Critical Inquiry* 19, no. 1 (1992): 87–104; "In Praise of High Office: The Politics of Panegyric in Three Southern Bantu Tribes," *Anthropos* 78 (1983): 149–68; "In Dispraise of the King: Rituals 'Against' Rebellion in South-east Africa," *Man*, n.s., 18 (1983): 521–34; "Discourse and Its Disclosures: Yoruba Women and the Sanctity of Abuse," *Africa* 68, no. 1 (1998): 68–97; "Griaule's Legacy: Rethinking '*la Parole Claire*' in Dogon Studies," *Cahiers d'Études Africaines* 40, no. 177, issue 1 (2005): 95–129; and "Africa, Empire, and Anthropology: A Philological Exploration of Anthropology's Heart of Darkness," *Annual Review of Anthropology* 28 (1999): 577–98. Permission to reprint them is greatly appreciated.

Introduction

How can we write about "indigenous" Africa without reviving the ghosts of the "Dark Continent," Europe's projected alter ego in the era of imperial expansion? How can we transcend what Mudimbe has called the colonial library—the grand narratives, tribal tropes, distorted images, and "natural" histories that forged "the foundations of discourse about Africa" (1988, xi) and that, as Mbembe (2001) so vividly demonstrates, remain firmly entrenched in the postcolony?

The study of discourse and critical agency in *Beyond Words* represents an extended answer to this challenge, which has been posed by a number of subaltern scholars in various registers over the years, perhaps most radically by Mafeje's consignment of Africanist anthropology to the dustbin of history (Mafeje 1998). It is a challenge that any Western approach to an Africa beyond words and images should acknowledge, given the series of tenacious negations—not-civilized, not-human, not-rational, not-moral, not-white, not-healthy, and, finally, not even historical—that continue to deform Africa's place on the margins of modernity (see also Desai 2001). To be sure, progress has been made in demystifying Africanist discourse, but the gains have also involved the loss of important sociocultural territory. From the standpoint of critical theory, the deconstruction of Africanist discourse exposed the rhetorics of racism, the topologies of tribalism, the evolutionary narratives of progress and loss, the invocations of authentic tradition, for what they were—inventions of an imperial imagination—but could say nothing of what lay beyond this ideological horizon. I am by no means opposed to deconstructive criticism and endorse the power of its negative dialectic, but in clearing the slate for less innocent research it has not told us how to proceed.

One way of avoiding this cul-de-sac was pursued in Africanist anthropology by turning the colonial library on itself as it emerged from the civilizing missions in Africa and informed the development of colonial culture. Emphasizing empire and modernity over "traditional society," the distinction was recast dialectically within the colonial encounter itself—not as a precolonial situation dominated from without, but as two opposed domains that emerged historically within the same sociopolitical formation (Jean Comaroff and John Comaroff 1991, 212; Mamdani 1996; Ranger 1983). The "traditional" society of the traditional Africanist monograph—the world of "the Nuer," "the Tallensi," "the Dogon," or "the Swazi"—was no longer viable as an autonomous object of knowledge but concealed and congealed the historical conditions that produced, indeed invented, the cultural terrain of the colonized, one that was naturalized into "native" administration, showcased in world's fairs, codified by customs, and contrasted with Western modernity.[1] The insights of this new historical anthropology are indisputable and illuminate the dynamic character of "tribal" ethnogenesis, the zones of interaction between Africans and Europeans, the poetics and politics of domination and resistance, and of course the fundamental modernity of "traditional" Africa as a domain of ethnographic recovery (Amselle 1985, 1998; Piot 1999). In a sense, we have learned that traditional Africa is "always already mediated" by the European encounter and its modes of surplus extraction, ranging from the naked appropriation of human capital and the primitive accumulation of raw materials to the more refined arts of moral persuasion; hence, to indulge in the problematic territory of tradition is to risk complicity with its mythic origins. How then do we establish an Afrocentric ground of cultural inquiry that neither reinvents a fictitious past nor emerges in opposition to European overrule? Is such a middle ground between the Scylla of tradition and the Charybdis of empire even possible or desirable?

Many issues are at stake in answering this question, which inevitably returns to the unequal relations of material production underlying the unequal relations of intellectual production in African studies and academia at large (Depelchin 2005, 1–24). No amount of critical scholarship is likely to make much of an impact on this larger global situation, but it illuminates the backdrop of my narrow angle of attack—a focus on discourse and critical agency in Africa.

Briefly stated, I begin with critical discourses generated in Africa, largely in ritual contexts, where powers are activated, ancestors invoked, reputations negotiated, and histories recalled, and where sociopolitical relations are reproduced and transformed within idioms of purification and renewal. I return, not to the models of colonial anthropology—tribal traditions with set-piece rituals—but to dynamic arenas of discursive interaction and political negotiation where "tradition" makes sense in local languages, as a rhetorical

---

1. For a concise critique of such structural-functional models in Africanist studies, see Piot 1999, 10–11. For an extended critique, see Kuklick 1991. For an extended defense, see Goody 1995.

resource invoked by Africans rather than one imposed by ethnographic convention. Whether culled from "old" monographs in the work of other scholars or derived from the "here" and "now" of my own Yoruba fieldwork in Nigeria, the texts and "text-artifacts" (Silverstein 1996, 81, 82, 87, 90) that I explore in these studies represent critical traditions of linguistic play and performance, combining poetic figures and allusions with pragmatic features and functions. Since one of the hallmarks of Africanist ethnography is the marked significance that language holds throughout the continent, represented by elaborate forms of oratory (Finnegan 1970; Leiris 1992; Schapera 1965; Barber 1991a), specialized roles like that of the king's linguist, and indigenous theories that account for the power of speech (Amuka 2000; Calame-Griaule 1965; Zahan 1963), my goal is to recast these ideas and institutions as characteristic forms of vernacular criticism. Although my "sample" of cases is mostly secondary and admittedly small, drawing on material from western and southeastern Africa, it illustrates a widespread awareness not merely of the role of language in shaping sociopolitical structures and ritual events but of an associated form of critical agency, one that brings its grammatical and sociopolitical forms into "intersecting frames" (Irvine 1996, 135) of structural alignment.

To characterize "critical agency" in relation to discourse we can start with a basic distinction between linguistic and sociopolitical agency. Clearly, both kinds of agency engage important issues in philosophy, linguistics, and social theory that could be explored, but to carve out an analytical space for critical agency I will begin with the work of Ahearn (2001) and Duranti (2004). Each develops a general concept of agency as the capacity for effective social action that, following Giddens (1986, 88, 92, 93), has the "transformative capacity" to "make a difference" and is therefore to some degree powerful. For Ahearn (2001, 112) "agency refers to the socioculturally mediated capacity to act," a concise definition that places the manifold forms of sociocultural mediation—including grammar and discourse—at the forefront of investigation. Crucial to this point of departure, however, is the importance of socially significant action, that which transforms a structure, changes a situation, or influences an outcome to make some sort of difference. Duranti (2004, 453) offers a working definition that delineates the basic properties of the sociocultural field: "Agency is here understood as the property of those entities (i) that have some degree of control over their own behavior, (ii) whose actions in the world affect other entities' (and sometimes their own), and (iii) whose actions are the object of evaluation (e.g. in terms of their responsibility for a given outcome)." Agents can be individual or collective, persons or institutions, simple (in some sense acting "alone") or complex (acting with or on behalf of others); hence, for Duranti they are "entities." With some degree of autonomy, agents are always implicated in webs of sociality because their actions are evaluated by others, implying forms of recognition and reflexivity that I will address in due course.

It is clear from these definitions that sociopolitical agency is both context dependent and historically situated: first, because it "goes against" the structural grain of the system in which the agent is embedded; and, second, because (a) the system itself is historically conditioned, and (b) the agent's actions are diachronic and processual, like the logic of practice to which agency belongs (Bourdieu 1990), unfolding through strategies and tactics toward specific goals, with intended and unintended consequences. But if agency transforms these structural and historical "fields," what forms does it take, and in what degrees? Ahearn (2001, 113–17) warns against monolithic notions of agency as resistance, manifest in struggles against colonial or patriarchal domination, because "oppositional agency" is only one form among many. Thus, she invokes Ortner (2001, 79), who complements the oppositional agency of power with the more quotidian "agency of intentions—of projects, purposes, desires," as well as MacLeod (1992, 534), whose idea of "complex and ambiguous agency" confounds stark oppositions between collaboration and resistance.[2] To this we could add what Kratz (2000, 137 et passim), following Hobart (1990, 96), calls the "complex agency" of multiple actors in Okiek marriages, as well as the "secret agency" (Shaw 2000) of hidden and indirect action in the "deep" Temne arts of sorcery and divination.

For Ahearn (2001, 122n5), the exploration of "different kinds of agency" both avoids the pitfalls of reductionism and replaces gradient notions of relative degree with typological considerations of modality and form. Helpful as this perspective is in expanding the range of agentive activities, it loses sight not only of the principle of power underlying all of their variations but also of the degrees of agency, which, if not sociologically quantifiable, are recognized by social analysts and actors alike.[3] By combining Duranti's emphasis

2. See Ortner n.d. See also John Comaroff and Jean Comaroff 1997 for a cogent statement of the gray zone between overt domination and resistance that informs their study of colonization in nineteenth-century Bechuanaland, "founded on an intricate mix of visible and invisible agency" (28). Critics like Peel (1995) who fault the Comaroffs for neglecting Tswana "narratives" of agency miss the point that discursive agency, situated in public contexts, is for the most part *nonnarrative* precisely because it engages metapragmatic strategies that are highly context specific.

3. Such an awareness of how agency imposes upon others is built into the concepts of the Face Threatening Act (FTA) developed by Brown and Levinson (1978) and of "the mitigation of agency" developed by Duranti (2004, 465–67) as universal dimensions of politeness phenomena.

on power and "the *degree* of agency that is attributed to a given entity" (Duranti 2004, 454; his emphasis) with Ahearn's expansive attention to form, we can sketch a structural framework of power and authority to illuminate the dialectics of sociopolitical agency in practice.

The model I have in mind, derived from M. G. Smith (1956, 1975), identifies power and authority as fundamental principles that are dialectically implicated in all sociopolitical systems and relations. Authority relations, representing the administrative logic of a top-down chain of executive commands, are hierarchical and asymmetrical—as such they include or subsume the subordinate units which they regulate, defining the official order as legitimate, that is, sanctioned by collective values that are in some sense moral, jural, and even religious. Political relations, by contrast, are equivalent and symmetrical, representing the segmentary logic of power competition as actors and coalitions vie against each other to influence the regulation of public affairs—the making of decisions before they are executed. In his original conceptual breakthrough, Smith (1956) liberated the principles of fission and fusion, of segmentary opposition and hierarchical inclusion, from the African lineage systems and "segmentary societies" in which they were embedded by recognizing their structural characteristics as specific modalities of politics and administration, principles equally at work in complex polities with specialized bureaucracies, in political parties, and even in the inner circles of authoritarian regimes. In its pure, "abstract" form, power operates *ultra vires*, outside the authority structures that seek to regulate and domesticate its labile potencies (Smith 1975, 85). It is ultimately revisionary and revolutionary because it "opposes" authority, seeking to dismantle its hierarchic relations through radical leveling. Power sui generis is thus dangerous, polluted, and illegitimate. Since it violates the strictures and structures that channel it through legitimate means and ends, power is often culturally framed in idioms of pollution—transgressing the moral order, confounding what should be kept apart, and dividing what should be combined and united. If in vertical terms power is associated with the people, from "below," contra the hierarchical organization of authority relations, in horizontal terms this subversive capacity is nearly universally associated with "leftness" and disorder (transformation), opposed to the "rightness" and normative order of the conservative status quo (reproduction).

Unlike Smith, however, I am less interested in a structural theory of politics as such than in the more abstract dialectics of power and authority as they inform the micropractices of social and discursive agency. Whereas authority and its hierarchic relations of administration highlight the structure of institutions, offices, and symbolic codes at all levels of corporate organization, power and its segmentary political relations inhere in people and persons. Again, as the rich anthropological record attests (Jackson and Karp 1990), cultural idioms of personhood and selfhood may be complex and variable, whether framed as the autonomous individuals of bourgeois society or as individuated aspects of larger sodalities (a lineage, caste, or revolutionary proletariat), but people and persons, not institutions, have power.[4] As we shall see, the distinction between incumbent and office, person and position, is central to effective agency as it mediates and negotiates power and authority.[5]

I hope to have established that any kind of agency must be powerful in its capacity to make a difference as effective action, regardless of the level of "authority" and form of inequality that it opposes. If in resistance movements and revolutions agency emerges in full glory contra the established system of domination, not all agency must be so exalted to be powerful and oppositional. But in a more abstract sense, all forms of agency, however complicit or ambiguous, work against the sociopolitical grain to some degree, whether engaged in the quotidian concerns of "serious games" (Ortner n.d.), in poaching "à la perruque" in the workplace (de Certeau 1984, 24–28), in the inspiration of religious revival (Jean Comaroff 1985), in overt political and ideological resistance movements, or in the misguided violence of alienated psychopaths who go on killing sprees and take their own lives. This latter example of running amok is of course extreme, representing one end of a power-authority continuum where the agent's power is completely destructive and illegitimate, but most forms of agency combine power and authority and in fact operate by renegotiating their relative proportion, maximizing agentive power within the cloak of legitimate authority to make the desired difference. The point at which an agent violates the rules of the game may represent the limits of the entity's power, or it may index the agent's power to "rewrite" the rules. Thus, if power comes from "below," it can be exercised from "above" precisely when it transforms authority by revising its strictures—by changing procedural rules to influence a vote, the term limits on an office to remain in "power," or criteria of eligibility for high office or by declaring a state of emergency. Power without authority is destructive. Authority without power is ineffective.

The dialectic of power and authority derived from M. G. Smith (1956) extends beyond the confines of institutional politics to the interactive spheres of language and discourse. If the negative notion of power as antistructure appears counterintuitive at first, it is because "power" is so often equated

4. For a philosophical discussion of the historicity of the modern Western "self," see Taylor 1989.

5. See the distinction made by Schegloff (1987) between "participants (that is, persons) and parties (roles and alignments)," cited in Irvine 1996, 133.

with authority, as in the power of the state or of a ruling class. Such power is cast as hegemonic, as domination opposed by the arts of resistance (Scott 1990), but I would argue that vertical domination in this view represents an authority system with enough power to keep resistance—the power of rivals, of the people—in check. In our view, the power of agency in such hierarchical contexts derives less from the structure or system of inequality and more from the impulse toward leveling and symmetry—a power that rearranges hierarchy by bringing the very relationship between structure and agency into focus. Here we approach the "critical" dimension where the agent engages its very conditions of possibility, but before moving on to this central concept we can illuminate power and authority in discourse by revisiting a classic article in historical sociolinguistics.

First published in 1960, Brown and Gilman's "The Pronouns of Power and Solidarity" brought politics into grammar by focusing on "you." The essay ranges broadly over time and space, rooting the European development of two second-person singular pronouns of address—one formal and polite (V), the other informal and familiar (T)—in the Latin distinction between *vos* and *tu* and pursuing why the second-person plural in so many languages became a respectful form of singular address: *vous* in French, *lei* in Italian, *usted* in Spanish, even "ye" in English (before "thou" and "ye" were assimilated to "you"). Where broad changes in use are associated with major historical transformations like the decline of feudalism, the impact of the French Revolution, and the spread of modern democratic ideologies, specific forms of pronominal address are related to power and status differentials between "superiors" and "inferiors" over a broad range of social classes and roles. These include monarchs and subjects, parents and children, nobles and commoners, officers and soldiers, teachers and students, elders and juniors, even customers and waiters, whose unequal relations are lexically marked by the "power semantic" of V. In a complementary and dynamically evolving dimension, the T, or "solidarity semantic," indicates symmetrical relations of equality: membership in the same social class or occupational group, or position of equivalent status and rank. Whatever the cultural and historical variations on this distinction, not to mention its more situated discursive contexts, Brown and Gilman identified two significant dimensions in what would later become the study of shifters and indexicals (Silverstein 1976b): vertical relations of hierarchy, inequality, and social distance marked by the formal V, and horizontal relations of equality and social proximity indicated by the informal T. Whereas the V form conveys respect, formality, and inequality between interlocutors, the T form conveys familiarity, equivalence, and equality. As Brown and Gilman noted, the "two-dimensional semantic" was not always stable, since a superior could use the T or V form to a subordinate but would receive only the V form in return. In these cases we might say the "power semantic" had context-dependent reciprocal and nonreciprocal forms (rather than propose a semantic shift from conflict to equilibrium), but for now, the V and T forms discussed by Brown and Gilman help to clarify two important relationships.

First, we can redefine power and solidarity with the V axis representing hierarchical authority and the T axis representing the leveling logic of segmentary power relations. The V form indicates not the "power" of a superior over an inferior in this reformulation but the authoritative position he or she occupies within the structure of unequal relations; as such, the position emphasizes the status, office, or role over and above the person who occupies it. We could even say that the formality of the honorific indexes the formality of the "system" itself. Second, the T form, by contrast, is powerful because it emphasizes familiarity between equals—members of the same social group, class, or category who are "at ease," even "joking," with no need to stand on ceremony. Such power is not necessarily that of A determining B's actions but of A bringing B to the same level, the power of *égalité* and *fraternité*, of camaraderie and comradeship. In effect, the power of the solidarity "semantic" is that of affective bonds between people rather than jural relations between offices and roles, between persons outside offices in their ideal form, acting on the system. Recast as the pronouns of authority and power, Brown and Gilman's V and T pronouns help us clarify the critical dimensions of discursive agency: first, in terms of the formality of hierarchic authority (V) and the informality of segmentary power (T); and second, in terms of the "role distance" (Goffman 1961, 143) they establish between person and "position," incumbent and office, or what inclusively distinguishes agency and structure.[6] It is obvious but still worth emphasizing that the power of these pronouns (and, as we shall see, other shifters and deictics) does not simply reflect gradient authority relations but actively produces them in the speech acts of address.

We are now in a position to examine linguistic or discursive agency as the power to negotiate authority relations through a variety of grammatical and oratorical forms. Admittedly, my understanding of the strictly grammatical forms of agency is extremely limited, not only in the ergative-absolutive and stative-active languages with which I am unfamiliar, but also in the nominative-accusative languages like English in which agents are subjects of

---

6. The mistaken identification of power with authority (high status) also weakens the predictive power of Brown and Levinson's work (1978), which cannot account for the "power" X gains over Y by indexing Y's superior status. For a similar point about the "coercive effect of verbal formulae," see Duranti 1992, 92, drawing on Irvine 1974.

transitive verbs acting on objects, including other agents (Duranti 2004, 460; Ahearn 2001, 120–21). These forms, called "semantic" and "participant" roles, are designated by categories such as Agent, Actor, Experiencer, Object, Patient/Undergoer, and Instrument that may be variably marked in certain languages, and if I neglect this dimension of what Duranti (2004, 459–65) calls "the encoding of agency" in favor of its pragmatic dimension, what he calls "the performance of agency" (2004, 455–59), it is more by necessity than design since most of my data are in English and French translations (except for chapter 4 below, on Yoruba insults and curses, which I gathered from the field). Nevertheless, from Ahearn's essay (2001, 122–23) and building on Dixon (1994) and the "animacy hierarchy" of Silverstein (1976a, 122), we can highlight the general predominance of the agentive "I" over descending pronominal and nominal forms:

> [F]rom the universal grammatical principles underlying all languages, we know that the most salient person in a linguistic interaction is the speaker, 'I.' . . . The second most salient person is the addressee, 'you.' Both 'I' and 'you' are more salient, and therefore more likely to be found in the Agent position, than the absent participants in the interaction, ranked in the following order: third person pronouns, proper nouns, common nouns referring to humans, common nouns referring to animate nonhumans, and common nouns referring to inanimate objects. (Ahearn 2001, 123)

Thus, grammatical agency in its most formal dimensions appears primarily grounded in the act of speaking itself—in the active, transitive modes of a speaking "I," followed by a "you" who is addressed, followed by a third person, and so on.

Although the agentive "I" appears universally grounded in a speaking subject that acts on other persons and things, it is not merely encoded as a semantic role but functions (like all shifters) indexically as a "duplex sign" anchoring the grammatical "I" within the social field of the speech act itself. Duranti (2004, 455) calls this performative dimension of such I-witnessing agency its "self-" or "ego-affirming" level, primary as an existential condition of the second, "act-constituting" level of linguistic or discursive agency. Such an ego-affirming function may appear redundant, but it further establishes three important conditions beyond that of existential quantification. First, it relates the social agent to the speaking subject, regardless of the "identity" of the speaker. In ritual-language genres of spirit possession, for example, a speaker's identity can shift between that of devotee and her deity to radically reframe the communicative context (Apter 1992, 136–47), but such shifting of the self would not be possible without ego-affirming agency in the "first place." A second important condition established by ego-affirming agency, contrary to the methodological individualism it might seem to imply, is the minimally dyadic relation between interlocutors. Performative agency is always other-oriented; it has another self-affirming agent built into its primary field—hence, the importance of greetings, which for Duranti (2004, 456–57) acknowledge the agency of "significant" others. The minimal "unit" of self-affirming agency is thus a social dyad, not a muttering monad. Finally, ego-affirming agency carries a critical potentiality that is central to the focus of this book and that is partially captured by the concepts of reflexivity and recursion when the "I" sees itself as the agent of the speech act.[7] Ego-affirming agency is a necessary if insufficient condition of critical agency, a concept we can now develop by turning to the broader pragmatics of "act-constituting agency" (Duranti 2004, 457–59).

Perhaps the best way to approach critical agency in Africa is from within its ritual languages and oratorical genres. Ruth Finnegan was the first scholar to perceive the relevance of performative utterances to discourse in Africa, developing a perspective in two perspicacious articles that together set the agenda for much of what I am trying to pursue. In "How to Do Things with Words: Performative Utterances among the Limba of Sierra Leone," Finnegan (1969b) focused on performatives like accepting, announcing, pleading, and greeting as important oratorical and illocutionary acts that illuminated much about not only Limba social interaction but also their ideas about formal speaking itself. Two core ideas in this seminal essay are worth highlighting. First is Finnegan's emphasis on the contractual and *transactional* dimensions of performative utterances in contexts of dispute settlement, marriage negotiations, funerals, and gift-giving that implicate actors in wider structures of reciprocity.[8] Finnegan (1969b, 549) even likens the spirit of the Maussian gift (that which generates a "return," a counterprestation) to the efficacy of illocutionary force: "The utterance or interchange of 'illocutionary acts' is in many ways analogous to the act of giving or receiving a gift." The political dimensions of these transactional dynamics—many of which combine prestations with performatives—emerge most clearly in the "thanking" and "honoring" between chiefs and their followers, a dynamic arena that "points to the reciprocal, even quasi-contractual, nature of authority among the Limba, where the relationship must be continually acknowledged on both sides, and

---

7. Whereas the dialectical relations between discursive "texts" and their situated "contexts" are thematized and developed in Duranti and Goodwin 1992, the reflexive and metapragmatic forms and functions through which these dialectical relations operate are more specifically foregrounded in Lucy 1993b.

8. For a pathbreaking analysis of transacting status in Wolof greetings, see Irvine 1974.

the mutual responsibilities and interdependence constantly voiced in verbal relationships" (1969b, 543). A second core idea that follows from this trans-actional negotiation of political authority is the widening of the contexts in which performatives perform—beyond, that is, the "isolated linguistic forms" (or Austin's [1962] minimal specification of their "felicity conditions") to "the locally accepted procedures, and the relationships and whole social situation involved" (Finnegan 1969b, 551).[9]

In "Attitudes to Speech and Language among the Limba of Sierra Leone," Finnegan (1969a) developed the more reflexive dimensions of Limba discourse by focusing on indigenous understandings of linguistic forms and functions. These are represented by ethnolinguistic glosses of "deep," "fine," "clean," "broad," "straight," "good," and "sweet" talk (1969b, 64), use of the quotative *na-* to introduce reported speech (66), and a highly elaborated concept of "speaking" (*gbonkoli*) that amounts to a linguistic philosophy of moral and social action rooted in "an attitude of self-conscious awareness to language" (65). The importance of these insights, however, lies, not in the identification of an ethnolinguistic theory as such, an achievement already claimed by Calame-Griaule (1965) for the Dogon, but in showing how Limba ideas about language focused on "the 'performative' function of speaking" (Finnegan 1969a, 74); how, in brief, the Limba philosophy of speaking *constitutes* a theory of performative utterances.[10] Following Finnegan in a similar vein, Ray (1973, 32) returned to the language of Dinka and Dogon ritual and argued that "the Dogon explicitly recognize the causal or perlocutionary aspect of their poetic praise formulae, and employ these forms in ritual contexts in order to manip-ulate spiritual agents for specific ends." Note that the indigenous ideas about illocutionary force in these Limba and Dogon examples do not amount to fully developed theories of linguistic practice on abstract conceptual terrain. Indigenous ideas of the power of language (like *gbonkoli* in Limba, *nyama* in Dogon, and, as we shall see, *àṣẹ* in Yoruba) are still endowed with mystical substance and agency (as are notions of mind and meaning in much Western philosophy), but this is precisely the point. By using powerful language to perform illocutionary acts of honoring, praising, cursing, blaming, and so on in order to negotiate power and authority relations and rearrange the so-cial world, and by *reflecting on* those ritually sanctioned powers of language

9. This broadening of sociolinguistic context has become a multidimensional and highly technical research agenda, with roots in ethnomethodology and the sociology of language. See, e.g., the editors' introduction and the contributions in Duranti and Goodwin 1992.

10. One might fruitfully compare the Limba quotative *na-* with the Mayan quotative *ki-*, which "maximally foregrounds the emergent pragmatic value of the quoted utterance as action or expression" (Lucy 1993a, 99).

that make a difference in important sociolinguistic transactions, speakers as actors exercise critical agency—they self-consciously relate their language forms to the very contexts which they help to produce and transform.[11]

What kinds of self-conscious awareness of language structure and use are involved in such critical agency, and in what degrees of critical reflexivity, are difficult questions of philosophical and psychological complexity which I prefer to avoid on methodological grounds. I am content with establishing a more preliminary framework for gathering evidence of how it works. We can certainly update the performative verbs available to Finnegan and Ray with innovative work on pronominal shifters (Silverstein 1976b), deictic reference (Hanks 1992, 1993), participant frameworks (Irvine 1996), and corporeal fields (Hanks 1990) to enrich the interactive contexts of critical agency, but what do these additional perspectives reveal?

The interpretive focus in *Beyond Words* is on ritual language in its basic performative and pragmatic dimensions to understand the politics of praising, blaming, invocation, and evaluation through the discursive negotiation of political authority.[12] There is more to this process than a simple transactional perspective suggests because part of the power of critical agency involves remapping the social terrain of the participant framework itself (accomplished, for example, by inclusive versus exclusive pronominal shifting). The linguistic work of vernacular criticism not only manipulates the distance between incumbent and office, indexing the "power" of the person or the "authority" of the position, but does so reflexively, by dynamically reshaping the relations among participants as the speech events unfold. In fact, both dimensions of discursive interaction are "functionally" related, in that maximizing role distance (power) corresponds with the leveling of the framework (emphasizing the "*communitas*" of the people), whereas minimizing the role distance (authority) corresponds with structuring the framework (emphasizing the "system," the hierarchical relations and role alignments). Moreover, we can observe this firsthand in the field or infer it from translated text-artifacts by the presence of metapragmatic discourse, as when a praise-singer or priestess mentions a speech act (such as "denying," "calling," "praising," "cursing") or quotes other indexical expressions within a ritualized speech act, thereby "transposing the indexical ground of reference" (Hanks 1992, 56) to reframe

11. If pushed for a definition, I would say: "Grounded in linguistic performance and reflexivity, critical agency refers to a speaker's self-conscious deployment of discourse to transform the sociopolitical relations within which he or she is embedded."

12. For the relationship of grammatical agency to praising and blaming in Samoan political discourse, see Duranti 1990, 1994.

context. This reflexive capacity of critical agency to reshape and transform the system from within is perhaps most formally expressed by the "metapragmatic indexicality" of specific ritual-language forms, a concept developed by Silverstein (1993, 47) that refers to "the indexical signaling of something about indexical signaling."

I emphasize these more abstract metapragmatic forms and functions because they foreground the reflexive dimensions of critical agency in ritual discourse. They help us identify critical agency and account for its capacity to transform the arenas in which it operates. They also help us explain a common characteristic of secret ritual languages in Africa, one that surprised ethnographers like Michel Leiris, who discovered that the "deepest" forms of Dogon ritual speech are context dependent and have little exegetical meaning (Leiris 1992). In the chapters that follow, I explore why this is of such critical importance to the politics of discourse in Africanist anthropology.

The first chapter, "*Que Faire?*" sets the larger problematic of representing "indigenous" African words and worlds by meeting the fundamental challenges of Mudimbe (1988) and Hountondji (1983) and their diatribes against ethnophilosophy with the revisionary strategies of Yoruba deep knowledge as a space of vernacular criticism. The terrain is thereby cleared for recasting ethnophilosophy as a more dynamic and empirically grounded *ethnopragmatics* to establish ritual domains of critical agency and practice in Africa. In chapters 2 to 5 I explore these domains in a variety of southern and West African cases, examining the pragmatic dimensions of ritual-language genres in relation to their critical functions.

Chapter 2, on the politics of panegyric, engages Ruth Finnegan's pathbreaking work on African oral literature to develop her counterintuitive insight that praise-poetry among southern African peoples can be ritually deployed as political criticism (Finnegan 1970, 142). It also compares John Comaroff's "indigenous incumbency model" (Comaroff 1975) of the Tswana with variations in Zulu and Xhosa praise-texts that bring out the formal dimensions of praising as a socially and institutionally located speech act. Comaroff's analysis is crucial to my study because his concepts of "code convergence" and "code divergence" establish the dynamic relationship between role distance and political evaluation. Chapter 3 reveals a corollary relationship between ritualized insults, or "dispraises," against the Swazi king and increased political support for his person. Reading Max Gluckman's famous analysis of the Swazi Ncwala as a "ritual of rebellion" (Gluckman 1954) against Tom Beidelman's counterargument that it served as a purification rite

(Beidelman 1966), I revise both interpretations in a unified approach to dispraise as a type of joking. Analyzed as a speech act, such joking explains why
the Swazi king is both powerful and polluted when separated from his office.[13]

This capacity of discourse to reshape sociopolitical relations and contexts
is highlighted in the fourth chapter, which draws upon my own Yoruba fieldwork and is thus empirically more complex and dense. Focusing on ritualized
songs of abuse, I show how political tensions are channeled into gendered discourses of sexual abandon and social criticism. It is here that the return of the
sexually and politically repressed (including repressed historical memories) is
given active voice by Yoruba women, who target and ostracize malefactors in
the community. The chapter thus addresses "classic" issues raised by Evans-
Pritchard (1965) concerning ritualized obscenities in Africa, but it locates his
emphasis on their "canalizing functions" within shifting frames of deictic
reference.

The fifth chapter engages Marcel Griaule and his controversial approach
to Dogon secret knowledge. Reading the politics of Dogon *connaissance* in
relation to Yoruba deep-knowledge claims, I reanalyze Dogon ritual language
in terms of its salient pragmatic dimensions, relocating the body at the center
of a corporeal field (Hanks 1990, 85) rather than as the cipher of a symbolic
code. Griaule (1952, 1996) was correct to recognize the importance of Dogon
connaissance, I argue, but he failed to grasp its unstable content as a context-
specific oppositional discourse.

In the sixth and final chapter, I return to the larger challenge of the opening
theme—the relationship of Africanist anthropology and empire—in a "philological" exploration of the discipline's colonial past. This history cannot be e-
rased, I argue, but it can be incorporated into more critical perspectives by
examining the politics of vernacular discourses, by turning on itself as an anthropology of colonialism, and by focusing on the nationalization and even
indigenization of colonial culture by African intellectuals (Apter 2005). I
thereby show how ritual languages in Africa carry significant illocutionary
force in local worlds and speak to the larger challenges of representing Africa
both within and beyond the academy.

13. Although subsequent studies have emphasized the need to historicize the rituals and
text-artifacts of these praises and "dispraises" (Opland 1983; Vail and White 1991; Lincoln 1987),
I would argue that the very legibility of the more structural dimensions I engage, mediated as
they are by history and translation, provides strong evidence of their underlying existence. For
the dangers of reading too much historical significance into the Swazi *simemo* songs, see Apter
1988.

⌒ 1 ⌒

Que Faire?

The subaltern cannot speak.
GAYATRI CHAKRAVORTY SPIVAK

At the African Studies Association (ASA) meetings of November 1989, V. Y. Mudimbe's *The Invention of Africa: Gnosis, Philosophy, and the Order of Knowledge* won the prestigious Melville J. Herskovits Award. Mudimbe's book is a landmark achievement, developing a critique of Africanist discourse in the spirit of Edward Said's *Orientalism* by posing as its central problem "the foundations of discourse about Africa."[1] Its publication revitalized what is currently recognized as the African humanities, and it is within this fertile and polemical field of inquiry that questions of African philosophy, vernacular strategies, and constructed identities converge. The debate I wish to examine developed at a panel session at the same ASA meetings organized on Mudimbe's book. The participants included leading figures in the field: Kwame Anthony Appiah, Abiola Irele, Jonathan Ngate, Paulin Hountondji, and Valentin Mudimbe himself. All offered perspectives on Mudimbe's work, with the author responding, but Hountondji's final critique, glossed by the question "*Que faire?*" raised the most serious challenge.

I open with this ASA conference session as an ethnography of a speech event—a professional dialogue—because it so clearly reflects the discursive conditions of African philosophical practice and debate. The participants on the Mudimbe panel were professional scholars (philosophers and critics) from different African countries, who spoke different national languages (English and French), possessed specific ethnic identities, were fluent in their local "ethnic" languages and dialects, trained largely "abroad" (Britain and France), and, as the theme of the session demanded, reflected on the "invention" of Africa by the West. And most were worried about the status of their own philosophical practice. At issue was the character of African philosophy itself in its professional, colloquial, and transnational dimensions. Can the professional language of Western academic philosophy translate African philosophical concepts that are grounded in local languages and epistemologies, as in

1. Mudimbe 1988, xi. See also Mudimbe 1994; Diawara 1990; Desai 2001.

Marcel Griaule's *Conversations with Ogotemmêli?* Or, as Mudimbe (1988, 69) claims, are such attempts destined to remain "philosophies of conquest," imposing categories of knowledge that disguise relations of domination? Is there such a thing as an authentically African philosophy (i.e., an ethnophilosophy), or is the concept itself invented by a patronizing Western imagination? And as was once openly articulated but now is always lurking beneath the surface, what really happens to Africans who become professional philosophers (and, in particular, have settled in Western universities)? Is their very dialogue a key to decolonizing the mind or a betrayal of their people? These and other questions inspired complex debates about missionary rhetoric and colonial histories, ethnophilosophies and anthropological paradigms, nationalist ideologies and African states, and the problematic politico-economic relations between the West and black Africa.

At the risk of grave oversimplification, we can summarize Mudimbe's position as basically a rigorous negative critique. He is, after all, interested in Africanist discourse—the Western texts and imaginations that have configured African thought and are planted as templates in African universities. The book seriously challenges the possibility of adequate translations and places the secret wisdom, or gnosis, of African thought beyond Western intellectual grasp (and beyond representation, perhaps even existence). Hence Hountondji's loaded question, "*Que faire?*" Indeed, what is to be done? The negative critique pushed to a magnificent conclusion: where does African philosophy (and philosophical practice—Hountondji's telos) go from here?

The very question invokes the complex political dimensions that are built into African philosophical debates. "*Que faire?*" Hountondji asked, and apologized for not speaking in his poor English, preferring instead the national language of the Republic of Benin, where he teaches, and of its former colonial headquarters, where he received his *agrégation de philosophie.* His dissertation adviser was Louis Althusser, from whom he gained a solid grounding in Continental philosophy and a normative philosophical orientation. Hence, the question "*Que faire?*" invokes Lenin's practical commitment to realize the revolutionary goals of Marxism. Spoken in French, echoing Lenin, challenging oppression, and framed within a discourse of French academic culture (curiously professional and colloquial in its own refined way), the question thus posed embodies the very contradictions that it seeks to resolve. For Hountondji, as we shall see, this is not a problem, since *his* answer involves critical reflection and transcendence. It is precisely with the power of philosophical dialogue to reflect on its history, conditions, and epistemological claims that "revolutions" in Africa and elsewhere can be made. African philosophy, for Hountondji, is critical philosophy practiced by African philosophers. This view, he will argue, is not racialist but realist. Philosophy developed in Europe for reasons that historical materialism explains. For related reasons, philosophy did not develop in Africa, and to claim that it did, in the form of cosmologies and ethnophilosophies, distorts the meaning of "philosophy" and establishes a double (i.e., lower) philosophical standard for what are misrepresented African "worldviews."

The aim of this chapter is to take Hountondji's challenge seriously and propose a new approach to African philosophical history and practice. My argument will develop as a "double dialectic": on the one hand, between Mudimbe and Hountondji and, on the other, between Africa and the West. Both Mudimbe and Hountondji are critical of ethnophilosophy as developed by the Belgian missionary Father Placide Tempels and the French anthropologist Marcel Griaule. Their critiques are worth reviewing because they specify the hidden knowledge/power relations of the ethnophilosophical project. In this respect their positions are similar; both agree that ethnophilosophies are Western ideological constructions that bear little relation to African realities. But what lies on the other side of the ideological fence? Here is where Mudimbe and Hountondji part ways. For Mudimbe, African philosophy is gnosis, the secret wisdom of cult initiates and elders that defies authentic disclosure.[2] For Hountondji (1983, 53), African philosophy is still "yet to come." So-called traditional African thought with its oral forms of expression and transmission may constitute a wisdom, but it lacks the power of sustained critical reflection that real philosophy demands.

My own position seeks to synthesize these views by drawing briefly on Yoruba interpretive practices in southwestern Nigeria. From what I have learned about Yoruba cosmology—its categories of power and levels of knowledge—I will argue, *mutatis mutandis* (thereby risking the error of a totalizing projection and reduction), that African philosophy is gnostic (Mudimbe's position) just because it is critical (Hountondji's demand of philosophy); what is hidden is philosophical. This critical power makes ritual revolutionary in its symbolic and material dimensions, both in (deeper) consciousness and in practice, in its power to actualize potentialities and to revise authority structures.[3] It also speaks to, and against, the West, in local responses to

2. Mudimbe credits Fabian (1980) for introducing the concept of gnosis into African philosophical debates. Turner (1967, 102, 105) describes the initiation of Ndembu neophytes into "arcane knowledge or '*gnosis*'" and the opportunity that this initiation affords for thinking critically "about their society, their cosmos, and the powers that generate and sustain them."

3. The subversive, rebellious, and "revolutionary" characteristics of many African rituals is a well-worked theme in anthropological studies, of which the Swazi Ncwala ceremony has become paradigmatic. See Kuper 1947; Gluckman 1954, 1963; Beidelman 1966; Lincoln 1987.

Christianity, colonialism, national politics, and global capital. And, I will argue, to philosophy. To break the hermeneutic circle of Africanist discourse as a history of Western illusions, African philosophy still has recourse to critical traditions that are neither borrowed nor imposed. Could this be the condition of a genuine dialogue between Africa and the West?

To argue my case, since anthropology as well as African philosophy is on trial, I will review the positions of Mudimbe and Hountondji in greater depth, focusing on their critiques of ethnophilosophy before proposing a "vernacular" solution.

Ethnophilosophy and Its Critics

To begin, it is important to consider why the critique of ethnophilosophy, invented "independently" by Tempels and Griaule in the 1940s, remains central to African philosophical debates. Their work, which involved systematic investigations into Bantu philosophy and Dogon ontology, is easily dismissed as dated, not worth attacking, since it represents an obsolete and naive mode of philosophical and anthropological inquiry.[4] I have heard critics of Mudimbe and Hountondji complain that the texts they engage are no longer relevant—that both scholars should focus their attention on contemporary research in African systems of thought. The anthropology they attack is not today's anthropology; the philosophy and theology of Tempels and Griaule were constructed under colonialism and have been transcended, so the argument goes. But, as Mudimbe and Hountondji maintain, it is precisely because ethnophilosophy has not been transcended but continues to orient so much African philosophical inquiry that its presuppositions, paradigms, and fictions warrant closer scrutiny.

To understand the politics of ethnophilosophy, and the power it still exerts over so many academic minds, Mudimbe begins with the conditions of its genesis. *La philosophie bantoue* was written (originally in Dutch) by a Belgian missionary in 1945 after twelve years in the (then) Belgian Congo, within "the arrogant framework of a Belgian colonial conquest" (Mudimbe 1988, 136). The text was thus motivated by two related interests—the explicit task of Christian conversion and the implicit goals of colonial policy—that shaped

---

4. See Tempels 1969; Griaule 1965. For a cogent argument why *Bantu Philosophy* should not be isolated for ideological critique but must be philologically and politically historicized in relation to Tempels's departures from colonial policy, see Fabian 1970. For detailed philological reconstruction and debate, see Smet 1976; Tempels 1982, 1985.

Tempels's discourse in various ways. But the work was immediately controversial. Presented in the spirit of a sympathetic revelation and philosophical
communion with the Luba Katanga, Tempels climbed into the "Bantu mind"
to disclose a systematic and living philosophy. If motivated by dominant ideological interests, the work suspended certain assumptions of the civilizing
mission, such as the natural, as well as divinely ordained, superiority of Western thought. As Mudimbe (1988, 141) acknowledges, "While attempting to
'civilize,' Tempels found his moment of truth in an encounter with people of
whom he thought himself the master. He thus became a student of those he was
supposed to teach and sought to comprehend their version of the truth." This
significant inversion of the teacher-student relation, with the West "learning"
from Africa, the Christians from the "pagans," the colonizers from the colonized, the whites from the blacks, had revolutionary implications not purely
academic. Indeed, in the context of Belgian colonialism—which was, at least
in the early days, the most ruthless and brutal in Africa (remember Roger
Casement's Congo report)—to cast this moment as a master-slave dialectic, a
moment of "sublation" in the progress of philosophy, seems historically and
politically as well as philosophically appropriate.

The theological and political implications of Tempels's study inspired Belgian Congo's bishop Jean-Félix de Hemptinne to check its circulation, advise
Rome to condemn the book as heretical, and expel its author from the country.
And the same implications inspired Alioune Diop, negritude's most eloquent
scholar and spokesman, to "pledge his faith on this little work, appending a
foreword to the French version and describing it as the most decisive work he
had ever read" (Mudimbe 1988, 137).[5] But according to Mudimbe, the Afrocentric and protonationalist implications of Tempels's work were superficial.
In the main, *Bantu Philosophy* "proposes more efficient means to . . . the task
of civilizing and evangelizing Bantu peoples" (138). The study served as an extended argument that "Christianity is the only possible consummation of the
Bantu ideal" (54) and a philosophical blueprint to fulfill the civilizing mission.

Mudimbe (1988, 138–40) summarizes *Bantu Philosophy* as expressing five
essential propositions:

1   The Bantu, qua human beings, have an implicit, lived philosophy built into
    their beliefs and customs.
2   This philosophy is an ontology of "force."
3   From the ontology of force, a spiritual and "dynamic dialectic of energy,"
    stem general laws of vital causality.

5. See A. Diop 1965.

4   Bantu ontology can be made explicit only within the frame of Western
    philosophy.
5   Bantu ontology may serve as a guide to primitive philosophy in general.

If the first three propositions attest to "independent" thought, a distinc-
tively "Bantu" mode of being and understanding, the last two subjugate this
philosophical system to Western forms and tropes of illumination and representation—as articulated by enlightened minds and extended to all primitive
peoples. And if *Bantu Philosophy* suggests African principles of knowledge and
agency, these are cast within an Africanist discourse that vitiates their political import by its conventions of constructed alterity.

I am not so sure that Tempels's text is so easily dismissed, and Mudimbe
himself notes its unresolved possibilities vis-à-vis colonial ideology (1988, 141)
and the Jamaa Christian community that it precipitated (see Fabian 1971).
Mudimbe's point, however, is one of material implication (if I may pun on
an ideo-logical formula), that is, if constructed within colonial-theological
discourse, then implicated by colonial practice. Despite the "progressive" elements of *Bantu Philosophy*, Mudimbe implies that it has held African philosophy back, and he means to implicate many of Tempels's critics and revisionists
as well as his disciples among African philosophers and theologians.[6] Their
work remains grounded within a colonial epistemology by taking Tempels's
text on its basic terms, "obstruct[ing] more useful developments" (Mudimbe
1988, 141). In his stimulating review of African philosophical studies, Mudimbe
concludes, "Though we are now beyond Tempels's revolution, his ghost is still
present. Implicitly or explicitly, the most inspiring trends in the field still define
themselves with respect to Tempels" (153).

The same argument applies to Africanist anthropology, with respect to
Griaule's "conversations" with Ogotemmêli. Beginning in earnest with the Mission Dakar-Djibouti, a twenty-one-month expedition of ethnographic research and plunder (1931–33) for the Trocadero Ethnographic Museum, followed by intensive investigations among the Dogon and Bambara of the French
Sudan (Mali), Griaule and his research team—which included Germaine Dieterlen, S. De Ganay, Michel Leiris, Denise Paulme, Jean Rouch, Dominique
Zahen, and (subsequently) Griaule's daughter, Geneviève Calame-Griaule,
among the most important members—recorded indigenous cosmologies,
ritual languages, and graphic signs and codes.[7]

6. See Kagame 1956, 1976; Lufuluabo 1964; Makarakiza 1959; Mbiti 1969; Mujynya 1972;
Mulago 1973; N'Daw 1983.

7. Landmarks of the Griaule school include Griaule 1983, 1965; Griaule and Dieterlen 1951,
1991; Dieterlen 1942, 1951; de Ganay 1942; Leiris 1992; Paulme 1940; Rouch 1960; Calame-Griaule

Characteristic of the Griaule school was an intellectual respect for African knowledge and a willing, if sometimes staged, humility to learn from the local elders. Griaule's *Conversations with Ogotemmêli* represents the ideal culmination of initiatory ethnography in a series of cosmological disclosures by a blind African sage, which not only attested to the profundity of Dogon thought but also to the writer's seniority among the people. The critical distinction that operates throughout this general corpus is between the public, exoteric, "superficial knowledge" of *la parole de face*, and the restricted, esoteric, "initiatory knowledge" of *la parole claire*.[8] The Griaule school established its ethnographic authority from privileged access—declared if not always demonstrated—to the esoteric insights of African cosmologies. What it discovered, together with specialized writing systems and precise astronomical observations, was "a logical scheme of symbols expressing a system of thought which ... when studied, reveals an internal coherence, a secret wisdom, and an apprehension of ultimate realities equal to that which we Europeans conceive ourselves to have attained" (Griaule and Dieterlen 1954, 83). This "secret wisdom," or what Mudimbe calls gnosis, constitutes the proper object of Griaule's Africanist ethnography. It is not a "lower" but an "equal" form of knowledge. It is not "explained" by the social order but instead, like anthropology, serves to explain it.

Like Tempels, Griaule suspended the colonial hierarchy of intellectual domination, switching his role from master to student and placing Dogon philosophy on an intellectual pedestal that was "separate but equal" vis-à-vis the West. He presented Dogon philosophy as original, authentic, and complex—the key, in fact, to understanding Dogon society. But unlike Tempels, Griaule had no explicit missionary agenda. His interest was "ethnological," as the new science in France was described, and influenced not only Africanist social anthropology in Britain, with its turn to the social values and cosmological ideas of African systems of thought, as Mudimbe notes, but Robert Redfield's social anthropology of civilizations as well.[9] For Mudimbe, however, Griaule's strength was also his weakness. Predicated on a cultivated sympathy (or *Einfühlung*, as Mudimbe prefers) with the African Other, achieving a kind of "mystical participation" in Dogon ontology that transcended cultural, political, and "racial" differences between the observer and the observed, Griaule's very language remains one of a priori mystification. Of the African world

---

1965. Michel Leiris and Denise Paulme distanced themselves from Griaule and renounced any association with his "school" because of his relationship with the Vichy regime (Denise Paulme, personal communication, October 1994).

8. See Griaule 1952 for the most systematic formulation of this distinction.

9. See Forde 1954; Fortes 1959; Middleton 1960; Turner 1969, 1975; Singer 1976.

that Griaule disclosed, Mudimbe (1988, 186) would ask, "Is not this reality distorted in the expression of African modalities in non-African languages? Is it not inverted, modified by anthropological and philosophical categories used by specialists of dominant discourses?" For Mudimbe, in the last instance, there is no way to separate the political and intellectual dimensions of a Western dialogue with a "vernacular" African sage. The politico-conceptual domination of Africanist discourse obscures any real understanding of African gnosis.

My own position is that such categorical pronouncements should not blind us to the empirical fact that even if perfect translation is impossible, some translations are better (more culturally nuanced, less ideologically loaded) than others.[10] But Mudimbe is arguing from foundations, not facts. For him, ethnophilosophy is overdetermined by the discursive conditions of its sympathetic claims.

The Beninois philosopher Paulin Hountondji has developed a more militant crusade against Tempels and Griaule in what Mudimbe (1988, 158) calls "the bible of anti-ethnophilosophers." *African Philosophy: Myth and Reality* is a collection of erudite and polemical philosophical essays, animated by the disciplined rage of an offended critical intelligence. Of Tempels's *Bantu Philosophy*, Hountondji (1983, 34) notes how "at first sight . . . Tempels' object appeared to be to rehabilitate the black man and his culture and to redeem them from the contempt from which they had suffered until then." But, Hountondji continues, we should not be so easily fooled:

> It is clear that it is not addressed to Africans but to Europeans, and particularly to two categories of Europeans: colonials and missionaries. In this respect the seventh and last chapter bears an eloquent title: "Bantu philosophy and our mission to civilize." In effect, we are back to square one: Africans are, as usual, excluded from the discussion, and Bantu philosophy is a mere pretext for learned disquisitions among Europeans. The black man continues to be the very opposite of an interlocutor; he remains a topic, a voiceless face under private investigation, an object to be defined and not the subject of a possible discourse. (34)

Like Mudimbe, Hountondji assails the hidden politics of Tempels's discourse, but his critique is more pragmatic. However flawed its epistemology, conventions, and tropes, Tempels's text is ultimately exposed by its communicative strategy. Speaking of Africans, Tempels wrote *for* Europeans—not a philosophical dialogue with blacks but a mystifying monologue for whites. By

---

10. For a logical argument against perfect translation, see Quine 1960, 26–79. The deconstructive challenge is of course implicit in Mudimbe's critique.

appropriating the Bantu voice, the Belgian missionary effectively silenced it. Thus, what masquerades as a Bantu philosophy remains Tempels's philosophy of the Bantu mind. It is "a science without an object, a 'crazed language' accountable to nothing, a discourse that has no referent, so that its falsity can never be demonstrated" (62). When African scholars like Alexis Kagame challenge his exposition, they will always remain trapped within a philosophical illusion if they do not possess a rigorous critique of the very concept of a Bantu (or any other culturally vague or specific) philosophy.[11]

Hountondji's mission is to provide such a critique and thereby wipe the slate clean for a genuine African philosophy to emerge. Needed are explicit criteria of what philosophy is and is not. First, philosophy is a history, not a "system," in that it moves onward within a specialized dialogue. By questioning assumptions, arguments, and conditions of knowledge—as well as the conditions of its own possibility—it changes, building on a cumulative discourse that requires open debate. Second, its development is not continuous but, we might say, catastrophic, in that it moves in revolutions. Hountondji's examples include Kant's "Copernican revolution" against Hume, Hegel's emancipation from static Kantian categories, and Marx's materialist inversion of Hegel, among many others. Hountondji valorizes Western philosophy not because it is Western, as his critics who charge him with elitism maintain, but because it is critical, and this is what matters the most.[12] Ethnophilosophies that are derived from specific African cultures and construed as spontaneous, unreflective, collective worldviews are not, by the above criteria, philosophical. To call the Bantu, Dogon, or any other African culture's worldview a philosophy is an insult cast within an apparent praise. It serves only to reconfigure Lucien Lévy-Bruhl's essentialist thesis of a prelogical mentality, in that African philosophies now appear "precritical." For Hountondji, African traditional wisdom is wisdom, but it is not philosophy. It may have transient critical moments, but it lacks a critical tradition. To call it philosophy is paternalistic and wrong.

Hountondji's general argument is refreshing because it exposes the conceits of the Western liberal imagination. For him, African philosophy is not a traditional object of anthropological inquiry but a goal to be achieved by African intellectuals. It presupposes literacy, freedom from dogmatism, and a material infrastructure affording scientific practice. In other words, a genuine

---

11. More recently, Hountondji (2002), as discussed by Masolo (2003, 79n4), has developed the postcolonial implications of this argument, criticizing how ethnophilosophy "provided legitimation of the dictator's claim to speak for the people," with specific reference to "the extremely murderous regime of Sekou Touré of Guinea." One can see parallels with "Papa Doc" Duvalier's appropriation of vodou as the "soul" of the Haitian people in his *noiriste* rhetoric.

12. See Oruka 1983. See also Yai 1978. For a response to his critics, see Hountondji 1990.

African philosophy presupposes accountable self-government and a healthy independence from nationalist ideologies and "pseudo-revolutionary lies" (Hountondji 1983, 107). Hountondji's call for African philosophy is ultimately a call for African self-determination. I do not have space to discuss the controversial implications that he develops, particularly his ideas about writing, since my aim is more general. I wish simply to challenge him on a profound ethnographic oversight. Granted that uncritical worldviews should not be called philosophies, qualified by "primitive," "ethno-," or any other prefix, vernacular evidence drawn from Yoruba "traditions" suggests that the critical power of indigenous cosmologies should not be so easily dismissed.

Ritual and Its Revolutions

To grasp the rudiments of Yoruba ritual and cosmology, we must begin, not with the usual cast of deities (òrìṣà) and categories of space, time, agency, and gender—although these are of course important—but with the form of knowledge that makes ritual powerful. We can start, not with a series of symbolic oppositions, but with Yoruba characterizations of profundity itself.

The most basic opposition in Yoruba cosmology is between official, public discourse about the world and "deep knowledge" (imọjinlẹ̀), that which is hidden, powerful, and protected. It is more a pragmatic than a semantic opposition, since it marks restricted access to powerful truths while stipulating nothing about their content. Those who have deep knowledge—priests (àwòrò) and priestesses (olórìṣà), diviners (babalawo) and herbalists (oníṣegùn)—are initiated into the secrets (awo) of their work and are trained for years in esoteric techniques. They can detect witches, cure infertility, recall the past, influence the future, and empower chiefs and kings. They have protected the community from imminent disasters by converting into concrete community gains the dangerous potentials of missionaries and colonial administrators; in recent times, the threats from party politicians and military regimes are just as real, and communities look to those with deep knowledge for the same kind of protection. Key to the practice of ritual power is the reproduction—indeed cosmological and ritual renewal—of historical kingdoms as they "disseminated" from Ile-Ife (the locus of Yoruba creation and kingship) and have responded to the interventions of Islam, Christianity, colonialism, nationalism, the World Bank, and even Nigeria's Structural Adjustment Program (SAP), which simultaneously sapped the country of its middle class *and* labor power. Nor is such reproduction mechanical or automatic; rather, it contests, reconfigures, and revises authority structures (such as rules of dynastic succession, historical charters, the ranking of civil chiefs, the boundaries of a kingdom, official gender relations, or rigged election results) to incorporate or even precipitate dramatic change within the guise of enshrined traditions.

Demonstrating this revision of internal and external power relations involves a phenomenological sketch of òrìṣà worship that traces not only the dialectics of its ritual transformations (between hot and cool valences as well as "times" and conditions of collective experience) but also the interpretive levels that render it intelligible and powerful. On the surface, at the level of public ideology (Griaule's *parole de face*), festivals of deities such as Yemoja, Oshun, Shango, and Obatala (the list is indeterminate for reasons that will become clear) apply a technology of collective renewal and empowerment. Bodies personal and social receive the powers of the òrìṣà to cure infertility, thwart witchcraft, guarantee abundant harvests and commercial success, and reinvest the king with àṣẹ—the power to rule effectively and issue commands over others.[13] Modeled on the logic of social exchange (Barber 1981), the òrìṣà are fed with sacrifices, glorified with praise (oríkì), and invoked in the bush, where their dangerous powers are enlisted and embodied by priestesses and are contained in calabashes and bottles that are balanced on the heads of the priestesses and carried through the town to the palace and central shrines, where the powers are "cooled" and "delivered" on behalf of the king and his subjects. Time is marked by the closing of the old year and the opening of the new year, a cosmological rebirth and replenishment of the polity.

It is beneath the surface of these vibrant events that a deeper drama— indeed a *critical practice*—unfolds. The work of ritual is one of passage: from the bush into the town, from the old year to the new, from a polluted to a purified condition. In the liminal moments of this passage—crossing thresholds, bringing the deities into the town, and investing the king's body with the òrìṣà's power—the authoritative taxonomies of the natural and social world are erased and reconfigured.[14] It is here, in the forbidden discourses of deep cosmological knowledge (which allow a free play of signifiers and celebrate the arbitrariness of the sign) that priestesses become kings (wearing royal icons and being addressed as "Kabiyesi," "Your Highness"), unleash their witchcraft, and negate the king with rival historical memories that dismember his sovereignty into multiple dynastic claims. Only after such contact with the òrìṣà is the king, thus empowered, "re-membered" with official history. In brief, the king—indeed the whole body politic—is ritually deconstructed and selectively

---

13. For a rhetorical definition of àṣẹ, see Gates 1988, 7–8.

14. For example, the Yoruba king becomes simultaneously male and female, immortal and mortal, dead and alive, singular and plural, polluted and pure, in a moment of pure empowerment by the òrìṣà. See Apter 1992, 97–116.

reconstructed; hegemony is thereby unmade and remade. The point I wish to emphasize is that the status quo is revised and, when conditions are right, even radically transformed.

One need only consult the rich historiography of the Yoruba to recognize the shifting centers and peripheries of power that mark its major epochs: the rise of the Old Oyo empire and its incorporation of subject and tributary kingdoms; its collapse circa 1830 (through internal political competition and Fulani jihad) and the subsequent rise of its warring successor states; the expansion of the Ibadan empire and the consolidation of the Ekitiparapo military alliance; and the intervention of missionaries, capital markets, British overrule, and the subsequent civil and military regimes that have transformed the topography of Yorubaland.[15] Less obvious—because it is hidden and deep—is the role of Yoruba ritual and cosmology in configuring and, at critical moments, precipitating such changes by appropriating official discourse and revaluing its categories and claims. The pantheon of Yoruba òrìṣà, for example, is flexible and indeterminate precisely because it establishes the interpretive ground of shifting power relations. Spiritual hierarchies vary and change to consecrate new dynasties and emerging lines of sectional competition, political alliance, segmentation, fission, stratification, and so on—not as reflections of political transformations but, more critically, as conditions of their possibility. Deep knowledge thus safeguards a space for revaluing official categories, for negating the given order of things, and for making a political difference.

In what sense, then, is Yoruba ritual a genuinely critical practice? First, it is critical in the ordinary (nonphilosophical) sense of being crucial and "essential" to its officiants and celebrants. Ritual is always risky and dangerous because it constitutes a "critical" condition between life and death, purity and pollution, from which the social body may or may not recover. The specialists invested with the power of ritual renewal possess "deep knowledge" (ìmọ̀ jìnlẹ̀), "secret mysteries" (awo), as well as "history" (ìtàn) and "tradition" (àṣà), which gloss the sacred foundations of Yoruba social life into divisions of a gnostic archive. Second, Yoruba ritual is critical in the transcendental sense that it renders Yoruba politics and social experience possible, according to an official set of cosmological categories that objectify dominant power relations—chiefs of quarters in relation to their king, lineage elders in relation to their chief, market women in relation to farmers and hunters, and the complementary powers of witchcraft and fertility that mediate bodies personal and social. In this respect, ritual provides the conceptual lens through

15. See, e.g., Ajayi 1965, 1974; Akinjogbin 1967; Akintoye 1971; Asiwaju 1976; Atanda 1973; Ayandele 1966; Biobaku 1957; Johnson 1921; Law 1977; R. S. Smith 1969.

which a community, however inclusively or exclusively defined, knows itself. Third, such ritual is critical in the evaluative and deconstructive sense that the deeper meanings of its signs and discourses contradict, destabilize, and subvert official orthodoxies. Deep knowledge is by definition heterodox and powerful because it opposes official charters of kingship and authority and reconfigures public taxonomies of the natural and spiritual world. And fourth, at the deepest and most hidden hermeneutical level, ritual is critical in the self-reflexive sense; that is, it sanctions self-conscious awareness of the role of human agency in rewriting official illusions of legitimacy, of the practical role which ritual fulfills in the unmaking and remaking of hegemony. Yoruba priests and priestesses are marked with insignia of kingship because as "kings of the bush," they are, like Plato's philosopher-kings, endowed with the authority to propagate noble lies and the power to revise them. The "levels" of knowledge in Yoruba ritual are in fact infinitely deep and polyvocal, grounded in the hermeneutical axiom "Secret surpasses secret; secret can swallow secret completely" (*Awó j'awo lọ; awó lè gb'áwo mí torí torí*).

If the critical dimensions of Yoruba ritual safeguard a space for hidden histories and subversive agency, they do so under the cloak of enshrined traditions (*àṣà*) that only exceptionally restructure the sociopolitical order in radical ways. These exceptions prove the interpretive "rules," demonstrating that the power invoked by ritual-knowledge claims is real and must be taken seriously. The founding of the kingdom of Ayede, where I lived and worked, represents such a rupture because it was during a Yemoja festival (c. 1845) that an infamous warlord, the Balógun Eshubiyi, displaced the former Iye ruling dynasty and crowned himself king, inaugurating a centralized military autocracy quite unprecedented among the decentralized polities of the Ekiti region.[16] The Eshubiyi dynasty rules to this day, although not unchallenged by the Iye chiefs, whose rival claims are ritually invoked during the worship of their *òrìṣà*, and who may someday succeed in reappropriating the kingship.

In the context of Christianity and colonial rule, the totalizing transpositions of *òrìṣà* worship appropriated church and state, together with more familiar forms of uncultivated chaos, within the metaphysical horizons of the cults. White missionaries, district officers, and their African employees, clients, and followers may have entered the Yoruba universe of power relations, but they certainly did not displace it. Because they opposed and oppressed the "pagans" from "above," with administrative structures that reached back to London, *òrìṣà* worship turned "upward" and "outward," projecting ritual idioms of the local community upon the surrounding and impending

16. For details, see Apter 1992, 35–69.

national frame. Within this indigenous interpretation of the state, the work of the cults became more vital, not less. If the missionaries and colonial administrators were dangerous forces to reckon with, all the more reason to regulate their powers by traditional, time-honored, ritual means to work for, not against, the local community. Statuettes of colonial officers carved by local artists (currently the rage among Western collectors as authentically hybrid and "neotraditional") perform a critical ritual function in this respect.[17] Placed in shrines, these figures of colonial power were ritually incorporated into local fields and technologies of cosmological command.

During the Second Republic, the transformative power of ritual was illustrated by popular protest against rigged gubernatorial elections in Ondo State, when the notoriously unpopular National Party of Nigeria (NPN) candidate (Omoboriowo) "unseated" the Unity Party of Nigeria (UPN) incumbent, Governor M. A. Ajasin, in 1983. When the results were announced on radio, hunters throughout the state sealed off towns with roadblocks and organized sacrifices at market shrines, while priestesses and market women mobilized the powers of their òrìṣà and witchcraft to rout political traitors, curse the opposition, and purify the state of NPN corruption through ritual. In this context, the town of Ayede—like other Ondo towns—became a ritual microcosm of the state, appropriating its powers to reverse the official vote. And in this respect, the people succeeded, for the judicial system reinstated Governor Ajasin after reviewing the potential for further violence. My point is not that ritual as such reversed the state's elections but that it provided a sanctified idiom—indeed a "critical" hermeneutic—for waging *effective* popular resistance against a corrupt civilian regime. The mobilization of collective action through ritual purification, the extension of local cosmological horizons to embrace the state, and the effective revision of official propaganda (in this case the election results) were built into the logic of òrìṣà worship itself and brought Christians, Muslims, and "pagans" together in opposition to the NPN.[18]

Hountondji and Mudimbe are thus correct in smashing the ethnophilosophical illusion of a communally held cosmology that governs "primitives" like clockwork. They are correct to challenge its fixation on coherence, consensus, and consistency. But in challenging this illusion, they fail to contrast it,

17. For a spirited critique of the neotraditional category in the Rockefeller taxonomy of African art, see Appiah 1991. It is appropriate that this article was presented as a paper at the same ASA panel session with which this chapter opens, and that Appiah focuses on a Yoruba sculpture, "Man with a Bicycle" (illustrated on p. 340 of Appiah's article), to drive his point home. For the record, the sculpture clearly served as a verandah post.

18. For details, see Apter 1992, 179–92.

ethnographically, to the critical function of gnosis as deep knowledge, as the negative and revisionary dialectic that renders cosmology dialogical and contestable. I would argue that the ethnophilosophical illusion does indeed bear a relation to indigenous expressions of official ideology, since such orthodoxies are the only discourses that can be freely volunteered. Deep knowledge is powerful, however, because it subverts and revises such authoritative consensus. Nor is its logic limited to the circumscribed sites of "traditional" cosmology and ritual; rather, it appropriates the discourses of the church, the colonizer, the nation, and the state. The early missionized Yoruba—like Bishop Samuel Ajayi Crowther—may have espoused Christian rhetoric and the civilizing mission that it served, but they also appropriated its conventions and reconfigured its signs to promote the role of Africans in governing their religious and politico-economic affairs. Deeper readings of Crowther's texts reveal a hidden allegory of African autonomy that erupted in the Niger Mission crisis of the late 1880s and precipitated the founding of the United Native African Church in 1891.[19] And today, Independent Nigerian churches (e.g., Aladura, Cherubim and Seraphim, and the Celestial Church of Christ) combine the uniforms and iconographies of òrìṣà worship and state bureaucracy with the ambivalent and heterodox teachings of their prophets.

By extending this critical hermeneutic to the discourse of ethnophilosophy itself, we can see that the professional African philosophers and theologians who have appropriated it are not passive heirs to a colonial mentality but are actively engaged in revising and changing it. There is indeed a political consequence to this appropriation, perhaps underestimated by Mudimbe and Hountondji, whereby the objects of this discourse become its subjects. If gnosis is more than an Occidental illusion, if it—as I have argued from the Yoruba case—sanctifies a space for configuring difference, it is from here that the critical power of a genuine philosophical practice emerges. To investigate deep knowledge, and what makes it powerful, is to recognize its revolutionary potential—the conditions not only of its possibility, as Mudimbe seeks, but also of its praxis, as Hountondji demands.

Que Faire?

To respond to the question "*Que faire?*" I have proposed, not resurrecting ethnophilosophy, but rewriting its critique within an emerging dialogue that

---

19. For Bishop Crowther's (in some ways unwitting) role in mobilizing Nigerian nationalist sentiments, see Ajayi 1961; Ayandele 1970. See also Apter 1992, 193–212.

recognizes the formal integrity of African vernacular strategies and their rhetorical appropriations of dominant discourses. If this theme is now familiar
throughout the growing literature in black critical theory and cultural studies,
it achieved its most explicit theoretical exposition in Henry Louis Gates's *The
Signifying Monkey*. It is of course convenient for my own argument that Gates
identifies Yoruba interpretive traditions—focusing on the trickster Eshu as an
agentive figure of difference—as paradigmatic of black vernacular textuality,
with disseminated analogues in the black Americas. But as Gates makes abun-
dantly clear, his is not a historical argument of a Yoruba diaspora throughout
the New World but a critical template, "a myth of origins," that outlines the
principles of black signification as it revises, refigures, and appropriates texts
and master codes.[20]

My rereading of gnosis supplements Gates's theory by focusing on the restricted archive of Yoruba knowledge—not as a hidden transcript of secret
wisdom but as an indeterminate space for configuring difference—and on the
ritual practices that put its insights to work. That our different points of entry
reach similar conclusions reinforces the argument that African hermeneutical
traditions exist, not only in philosophies of conquest but also in strategies of
resistance and self-determination. The problem lies less in establishing their
foundations (i.e., the conditions of their academic representability) than in
making the effort to learn and understand them.

The debate is hardly over, since the "vernacularist" position can be rebutted
as simply sidestepping the fundamental issue: the foundations of Africanist
discourse, its invented alterity, and, to return to Gayatri Spivak's opening
quotation, the impossibility of the subaltern voice. Indeed, the argument for
indigenous critical traditions can be attacked as the newest species of liberal
pluralism and can be deftly neutralized by the charge of "catechresis at the
origin," of "appropriating the other by assimilation," of reading critical theory
into gnosis itself, or, as Jacques Derrida has put it, of "rendering delirious that
interior voice that is the voice of the other in us."[21] Here I can only call
into question the foundations of *this* discourse, which effectively silences the
very people—their voices—whose condition it purports to demystify. Does
not this most "radical" of critical positions in fact recapitulate the logic of
colonial conquest—the negation of the Other by a magisterial discourse that
masquerades as its antithesis?

20. See Gates 1988, 3–43.
21. Spivak 1988, 308.

In the chapters that follow, I attempt to "excavate" those African voices that would otherwise remain trapped within the colonial library by locating them in dynamic arenas of negotiation and contestation. By relating texts to their interactive contexts (Duranti and Goodwin 1992), mediated as they are by colonial histories and languages, we can resurrect situated discourse genres in Africa and explore their forms of critical agency.

2

The Politics of Panegyric

The aim of this chapter is to analyze Southern Bantu praises of high office as a form of critical agency. This important dimension of Southern Bantu praises is often overshadowed by what Western scholars consider to be higher virtues of literary art: stylistic and poetic devices of dynamic stress, elision, parallelism, chiasmus, and of course metaphor and simile. These devices do abound in what Finnegan (1970, 121) calls "the most specialised and complex forms of poetry to be found in Africa," but fine-grained stylistic analysis of these works should not blind us to some of the more basic and obvious statements that they make; in particular, statements that criticize the very objects of praise. I argue that the criticism voiced through praise is of fundamental importance to their production—not as works of art abstracted onto a printed page but as communicative acts mediating between a chief and his public. This argument is not entirely original—other writers have mentioned the critical component of Southern Bantu praises—but it remains to be developed into a general model of critical agency, the basic contours and implications of which I will explore by relating particular praise-texts to their institutional contexts.

The general model that accounts for the work performed by these praises comes from John Comaroff (1975), who shows how the effective power and legitimate authority of Tswana chiefs are negotiated through a form of oratory composed of two parts. The first part, or "formal code," expresses the shared values and ideals of chiefly office, against which the more flexible, second part, the "evaluative code," assesses the chief's actual power and political performance. If a chief rules well, the formal and evaluative codes converge; if he violates the norms of his office, the two codes diverge. The Tshidi case that Comaroff examines is complicated by political competition between rival chiefs and candidates for high office exercised through their spokesmen, whose orations emphasize the code convergence of their own leader and the code divergence of his rivals. But the central idea that I derive from this case and apply to Southern Bantu praises of high office (including Tswana) is what Comaroff (1975, 144–49) calls "the indigenous model of incumbency": standards of exemplary conduct that attach to high office and to which the incumbent is expected to conform and against which his performance is evaluated. The potential for criticism expressed through praise is thus generated by way of a contrast, openly stated or merely implied, to the public values upheld and specified by the praise.

Finnegan anticipates this incumbency model as a diffuse political resource in the hands of the public when, in her general survey of African royal "panegyric," she mentions an important consequence of status validation—the obligation of a status holder to conform to its demands:

> In societies where status and birth were so important, the praise-poems served to consolidate these values. As so often with panegyric, the recitation of the praises of the chief and his ancestors served to point out to the listeners the chief's right to the position he held both through his descent from those predecessors . . . and through his own qualities so glowingly and solemnly depicted in the poetry. As elsewhere, however, praises could contain criticism as well as eulogy, a pressure to conform to expectations as well as praise for actual behaviour. In this way praise could also have the implicit result of exerting control on a ruler as well as the obvious one of upholding his position. (1970, 142)

In effect, two sets of overlapping values can be analytically distinguished in this rudimentary incumbency model: *rights* of ascription and entitlement to high office, which the king or chief possesses by virtue of his membership in a royal descent group (hence the emphasis on birth and genealogy), and norms of good leadership, that is, *duties* of incumbency. The blurred quality of this distinction is important because it allows the praise-singer to confirm the legitimate authority of the chief, by invoking his rights to office, while simultaneously voicing the public concern that he fulfill the duties associated with it. It is therefore apparent that this "tug-of-war" occurs in the idiom of the same set of values, expressed in a veiled language of indirect allusions and substitutions that can, but need not always, keep this confrontation between a chief and his public "beneath the surface" of the praise. An examination of praise-poems (-songs) of three Southern Bantu societies—the Tswana, Zulu, and Xhosa—outlines some of the contours of this incumbency model and the directions in which these contours can be pushed and pulled. Although praises are composed and sung for a wide variety of status holders and groups,

I will focus on praises of high office because they carry the greatest political weight.

Tswana Praises

Praise-poems among the Tswana (of Botswana) are called *mabôkô* (sing. *lebbkô*), a term derived from the verb *-bôka*, which Schapera (1965, 1) translates as "to honour by giving title to a person in poems; to sing the praises of." This definition applies to all praises, which are composed not just for chiefs but for headmen, distinguished warriors, and ordinary commoners, including women. The praises of chiefs, however, are of two unique types—those composed by professional praise-poets/reciters (*mmôki*) and those composed by the incumbent himself—and the difference is crucial. Self-composed praises are of course one-sided and egocentric, stressing the chiefly virtues of the incumbent himself as a legitimate leader. A praise self-composed by Chief Lentswe of Kgatla (1875–1924) glorifies his own bravery in battle, a prized chiefly quality where cattle-raiding was a significant source of tribal revenue. In an opening stanza he combines this ferocity with his recognition of moral obligation to a privileged kinsman, demonstrating both his aggression and his responsibility as a leader:

> An elephant once screamed in a pass;
> it screamed only once, then was silent,
> it was busy trampling on someone.
> I am an ape, and I conquer elephants.
> One elephant only I cannot conquer;
> he is my mother's kinsman Mothulwe,
> son of Ramoletsana of the Elephants.
>   (Schapera 1965, 84)

The elephant refers to the "totem" of the ruling family of his enemies (the Kwena clan). The ape is Lentswe's own totem. He conquers all his enemies but one—his kinsman Mothulwe—who from Schapera's footnote (Schapera 1965, 84) is seen to be his mother's brother: "Lentswe's mother, Dikolo, was a daughter of the Tlhako chief Ramoletsana, and Mothulwe was her brother." In another stanza Lentswe exhorts his people to provide him with greater allegiance, at the same time demonstrating his legitimate right to the chieftaincy as son and grandson of the former chiefs Kgamanyane and Pilane (son of) Pheto:

> When you try to praise a brave man,
> you praise a butterfly (i.e. as if he were of no consequence)
> you keep on just prating about him,

> you do not praise him with due regard;
> you likened him to other chiefs
> though in fact he surpasses those chiefs, he is startling in his bravery;
> he is like his father Kgamanyane,
> he is like the master, Pilane Pheto.
>
> (Schapera 1965, 85)

Tswana praises composed by the *mmôki* themselves stress the duties of a chief to his people as well as his legitimate rights to high office. A praise to Chief Molefi (son of) Kgafela sung at his installation ceremony establishes his royal pedigree in the first stanza, only to urge him to perform some remarkably mundane tasks for the town in the second stanza:

> Molefi, sweep the town free of refuse,
> that old men may go where it is clean.
> Fill up the holes and choke them;
> also smash the stones, they trip us,
> and always make us turn up our toes
> when we go across to the chief's palace.
>
> (Schapera 1965, 115)

The third stanza praises his generosity and kindness, based more on future expectation (he was just installed) than past performance, to combine legitimate authority and duties/obligations of office in the same idiom of praise.

The narrative content of Tswana praises is largely biographical. History, like genealogy, is a charter for legitimate authority, but it is personal history, not family history alone, that distinguishes the incumbent and demonstrates his social worth. For unlike genealogy, personal biography illustrates greatness that is achieved rather than ascribed; a chief is judged by his deeds, not by his blood. Praises thus provide a public record of the incumbent's deeds and character. In the words of G. P. Lestrade, "they narrate deeds for which the subject has acquired fame, enumerating, in hyperbolic apostrophe, those qualities for which he is renowned" (quoted in Schapera 1937, 296). But this record works to his advantage only if deemed worthy by his supporters. The chief's incentive to achieve a good record, however, extends beyond the establishment of legitimacy in "this world" to the reception of great praise as an ancestor. I mention this eschatological point—the "judgment" of a chief after his death—because it underlies the power of the public to negotiate the legitimacy of the incumbent.

The praise to Molefi reveals how this negotiation between legitimacy and obligation is somewhat crudely expressed. A praise of Chief Tshekedi (son of) Khama (Ngwato tribe) illustrates how the praiseworthy qualities of belligerence and ferocity merge with the disreputable qualities of cruelty and excess within a single loaded image. Tshekedi is lionized, literally and figuratively, as a "man-eater" who consumes his enemies, and this image is earned by his achievements in battle: while other chiefs are lions without manes, Tshekedi has a mane because "an all-powerful one can never be shaved" (Schapera 1965, 222, line 69). This image also proclaims his successes as a cattle-raider: "The lion attacks many cattleposts / it attacks the cattleposts of the contentious" (line 155). But this same lion who is praised for his severity with enemies is criticized for treating his own subjects the same way; "Here, at his home, Tshekedi is a man-eater / here at his home he swallows people" (lines 142–43), behavior that actually led to an assassination attempt by the brothers of a rival whom he had publicly thrashed. The image of the lion is thus contradictory, praiseworthy or blameworthy depending upon whom it "eats." It can represent power violating the limits of authority.

Through such loading of imagery and indirect allusions to actual events, Tswana praises (and praises of high office generally) become heavily encoded. Many passages of older praises are, according to Schapera, incomprehensible to living Tswana specialists themselves. This is to be expected if praises sustain confrontations beneath their "surface," but it makes the analysis of submerged conflict very difficult for someone unfamiliar with the events alluded to and the personal histories of the incumbents. The examples of criticism that I do cite are by necessity the most explicit because I cannot even identify the subtler forms that I suspect are there—for praises of high office pertain to insiders. They are in Bernstein's (1974) sense restricted codes, highly gestural, intoned, and rich in metaphor, as can be seen from a nineteenth-century description of their performance. Casalis wrote about the Southern Sotho, of the same linguistic cluster as the Tswana (Greenberg 1955): "During the early part of our sojourn among them we often heard them recite, with very dramatic gestures, certain pieces, which were not easy of comprehension, and which appeared to be distinguished from the ordinary discourse by the elevation of sentiment, powerful ellipses, daring metaphors, and very accentuated rhythm. The natives called these recitations *praises*" (Casalis 1861, 345–46). Not all criticism, however, is heavily veiled, and an important question that I will consider is why some praises are more overtly critical than others. The praise of Chief Sekgoma, for example, refers to the specific violation of his obligation to his affines, whose cattle he unjustly confiscated. A passage contrasts this impropriety to the norms of prescriptive altruism:

> Sekgoma, you are a thief,
> what were you doing with goats of the Phaleng?

And the cattle of your wife's people,
what were you going to take from them?
In-laws are not deprived of their cattle;
we'll eat them when we've gone there to visit,
eat them when we've gone to make a feast,
eat them when they've been stewed for us.
(Schapera 1965, 194, lines 22–29)

The passage concludes with the injunction "great initiate, you are going astray."
The confrontation between community and chief, explicit in any case, is heightened by the inclusive "we" as indexical ground of the figured "you" directed at the chief.

The impact of public criticism through praise derives from principles of Tswana chieftaincy and succession. The rightful heir to the throne is the eldest son of the chief's "great wife" (usually but not always his senior wife); the privilege of this filiation is illustrated by the proverb "A chief is a chief because he is born to it" (Schapera 1937, 175). This prescriptive principle, however, is counterpoised by the requirement that a chief sustain the support of his people—hence the complementary proverb "A chief is a chief by grace of his tribe" (1937, 184). The institutional mechanisms of mediation between the chief and his people consist of several councils, ranging from (1) royal advisers (*bagôkôlôdi*) selected by the chief from among his senior agnates and matrilateral kinsmen, (2) a representative forum of ward headmen (*lekgôtla*), to (3) public assemblies attended by age-sets (*pitsô*), with whom general policy proposals, such as taxation and levies, the undertaking of new public works, the formation of new regiments, and public disputes, are successively discussed (Schapera 1937, 183 ff.; 1938, 82; 1965, 32). These arenas constitute the institutional contexts of praise-singing, especially the *pitsô* assembly, where the largest public aggregate is organized into age-grades, for it is here that the chief's constitutionally unlimited power to execute policy decisions could be informally checked by the withdrawal of public support: "In theory, a chief is permitted to take any decision he chooses at the end of a meeting. But decisions which do not reflect majority opinion are dangerous. Not only do they stand little chance of being implemented, but they may also be used subsequently as the basis of negative evaluation of the incumbent and hence affect his general standing" (Comaroff 1975, 149).

Now it is true that the expression of negative evaluation is by no means limited to praise-singing. Schapera writes of the *pitsô* assemblies: "Here much freedom of speech was allowed, and, if it seemed necessary, people could even criticize the chief or his advisors, without fear of reprisals" (1965, 33), and I suspect that this refers to the evaluative code in Comaroff's analysis of

Tswana (Tshidi) oratory within the same assembly. But this oratory is very different from praise-singing. Where the speeches are impromptu, praises are composed and relatively fixed. Where the performative contexts of the evaluative speeches are restricted to the *lekgôtla* and *pitsô* assemblies, praise-singing occurs in these contexts and others as well—royal weddings, funerals, age-set initiations, installations, and occasions of general public festivity (1965, 32), where I suspect that greater constraints against explicit criticism obtain. Furthermore, critical speeches are voiced by individuals, while praises voice the opinion of the public. Whatever the mode of expressing public disaffection, the effect is to activate rival claims to the chieftaincy. When the Tswana principle of primogeniture-type succession (by the senior son of the "great wife") clashes with the principle of consensual support, the eldest son of the wife next in rank can "claim" seniority and, if deemed more capable by the people and backed by a sufficient faction, assume power. Thus, a praise to Chief Gaseitsiwe opens with a warning which refers to his conflict with a rival:

> Don't sit at ease, be alert;
> a man seeking a village must be alert
> when fighting his half-brothers for the village;
> the junior wife's people have taken the breast,
> and I feared when they gave me a hind leg.
>   (Schapera 1965, 158)

The breast taken by the rival group is the tribute due to the chief, whereas the hind leg is the joint given to a younger brother (1965, 158n3). The praise thus validates the chief's senior status, hence his legitimate succession, while emphasizing the vulnerability of his position. This vulnerability to rival claims to the chiefship has important implications for the distribution of legitimate authority "outward," an aspect of praise-singing which is just as actively political as the channeling of public opinion "inward" to bear upon the incumbent. The incumbency of the Tswana chief relies upon public support, and this support must be maintained in the face of rival claims to office. An effective praise must therefore appeal to as wide a following as possible, and it is this function of maximizing public support as a scarce political resource which accounts for another characteristic feature of these praises— the identification of the incumbent by a variety of different names. These names identify his affiliation with different groups with which he shares special interests and from which he can therefore expect support. In addition to the two proper names (one from his father's line, one from his mother's) that every Tswana citizen possesses, a chief's praise may include the name of his totem (e.g., Kwena, "Crocodile"; Kgabo, "Ape"), the name of his age-set (e.g., Leisentwa), and a variety of appellations, often ad hoc, that appeal to a potentially hostile and competitive web of kinsmen and affines through bonds of solidarity. Thus, praise of a chief by his clan totem generates clan solidarity, praise by his age-set name appeals to the loyalty of his age-mates, a support base that is particularly important at the *pitsô* meetings, where attendance is grouped according to age-sets (*mophatô*) for discussing collective affairs. Identification of collateral and affinal ties in praises bonds potential cleavages between rival brothers or affines supporting their own kinsmen's claims to high office. Thus, we find in Senwelo's praise of only forty-two lines the appellations "radiant son of Molefe," "brother of Nyetsane," "brother of Babopi," "brother of RaMmopyane," "husband of Nketso," and "husband of Setholatlung" (Schapera 1965, 52–53).

Zulu Praises

As is the case throughout most of Africa, Zulu praises are not limited to high office but perform an important function of status validation in many spheres of social action. Parents praise their children as a reward for good conduct, and Cope (1968, 21) describes how this constitutes an important part of their socialization: "Praises are an important instrument in the educational system. Not only do they act as an incentive to and reward for socially approved actions, but their recital is a reminder to all present what qualities and conduct are considered praiseworthy." These praises establish a means of bringing about conformity to ideals of social behavior that obtain among children of the same age-group (*intanga*), young men of a more senior age-set (*ibutho*), and members of the same age-graded warrior regiments (*impi*), who praise each other according to the code of conduct expected of a warrior (1968, 21). But these praises also constitute a form of social control, for if they promulgate norms of ideal behavior, they also set the standards of appraisal, that is, the evaluation of actual behavior. Cope identifies this critical component of Zulu praises as a function of their public recitation: "Praises are usually flattering, but not always so. These praises are the expression of public opinion and provide an effective means of social control, for on occasions they are shouted for all to hear" (1968, 21). Unfortunately, Cope never identifies these criticisms or the occasions of their recitation, nor do we learn who makes up the omnipresent "public." But the general principle is clear that praise has a critical or regulatory function at all levels of status validation, even if this function is most clearly political when directed against incumbents of high office.

The Zulu praises of high office provide an interesting record of the politics of incumbency, for they echo the rise of the Shaka and his consolidation of the Zulu chieftaincy into a powerful military state. During the seventeenth and eighteenth centuries the Zulu was one of a large number of Nguni-Bantu "tribes" that had migrated (sometime during the thirteenth through fifteenth centuries) into present-day Zululand and Natal to form scattered, small-scale, clan-based chiefdoms supported by pastoralism and shifting cultivation. As reconstructed by Gluckman (1940, 25), these early Nguni-Bantu "lived in scattered homesteads occupied by male agnates and their families; a number of these homesteads were united under a chief, the heir of their senior line, into a tribe. Exogamous patrilineal clans tended to be local units and the cores of a tribe. A tribe was divided into sections under brothers of the chief and as a result of a quarrel a section might migrate and establish itself as an independent clan or tribe."

I include this gloss on the political structure of the early Zulu because it informs the values of incumbency found in early Zulu praises. Based on a tenuous balancing of sections which would divide and separate under poor leadership, the political structure fostered values of reciprocity, shrewdness, and diplomacy as the praiseworthy attributes of incumbency. These values changed, however, along with the office of the chieftaincy itself, when the Zulu organized into a powerful military state, which devastated and incorporated its neighbors. This transformation began during the reign of Dingiswayo (1808–18) and reached the height of its power and terrorism during the reigns of Shaka (1818–28) and Dingane (1828–40). The praises of these latter two kings depict changes in high office—values of good leadership have shifted from shrewdness through diplomacy to prowess and ruthlessness in war, while the images for the incumbents themselves used in praises have shifted from small animals of beauty, brightness, quickness, craftiness, and ingenuity in the early praises (e.g., for Jama and Senzangakhona) to large animals such as elephants, lions, and leopards, depicting force and brute strength (e.g., for Shaka and Dingiswayo).

Within this shift, however, general "core" values of incumbency remain constant. These are basic generosity and responsibility for the well-being of the people, built into a set of duties or expectations: "A chief is expected to be generous in his disposal of cattle and land to deserving subjects, and in his provision of food, especially meat and beer, to visitors and to tribesmen when in council or on ceremony. He is expected to protect the interests of the tribe and to govern it in accordance with the advice of his counsellors. The praiser expresses the opinion of the people and so presses conformity to the approved pattern upon the chief" (Cope 1968, 31). It was against these duties that the incumbent's performance was evaluated. The praise to Jama (great-grandfather of Shaka) portrays his streak of stinginess by referring to him as "He

who chewed with his mouth when he had nothing to chew / As if he were
the son of Chewer of the Scrapers Clean," an embedded epithet which refers
to a man whose snuffbox was always scraped clean when he was asked for a
pinch of snuff (1968, 74). Senzangakhona's praise contains a subtle criticism
of his unpredictability: "... son of Ndaba / Gurgling water of the Mpembeni
Stream / I don't even know where it is going to / Some runs downhill and
some runs uphill" (78, lines 50–53). And his general lack of political ability
is implied by the epithet "the gate-post... on which owls perched" (lines
54–55), the owls being neighboring chiefs listed in the following lines (Chiefs
Phungashe, Macingwane, and Dladlama). The concluding stanza contains a
veiled implication that Senzangakhona was headstrong and obstinate, that he
did not accept advice from his counselors: "Shaker of the head until the neck
dislikes it / Perhaps in another year the trunk will protest" (80, lines 86–87),
the "trunk" signifying the public, which supports its "head" or, if threatened,
withdraws its support.

The analysis of public criticism embedded in Shaka's praise should be
prefaced by a sketch of his political deeds and misdeeds to illustrate what
Walter (1969) calls the "terrorism" that his people were up against. The Shaka
rose to power during his brother's (Dingiswayo) rule by reorganizing the
military into disciplined regiments and training his warriors in a new method
of fighting—modifying the traditional *assegai*, a long throwing spear, into
a short, thrusting weapon (hence his praise epithet "Spear that is red even
on the handle"). When Dingiswayo died in battle against the Ndwande of
the north, the Shaka had his legitimate heir (a half brother) murdered and
placed himself in control. At first the strongest chiefs did not accept the Shaka
as the legitimate successor. He was opposed by the Ndwande to the north,
the Quabe to the south, and the Thembu to the west and responded with
a campaign of vicious conquests: "In less than three years, thirty chiefs and
their people were gathered into a single political system, and the former enemy
troops incorporated into the Zulu military forces.... Throughout the decade,
military activity continued with little respite" (Walter 1969, 128).

This expansion of the Zulu state followed a pattern, not of conquest and
conciliation, but of conquest and devastation that Walter (1969) calls military,
or external, terrorism. After conquering a chiefdom, the Shaka would plunder
what he needed for his state and destroy the rest: "Admitting the young
warriors into his regiments, he usually destroyed women, infants and old
people. Sometimes he spared the girls, who, presumably, entered the royal
seraglios, and the stout lads, who became herd boys, baggage carriers, and
ultimately, Zulu warriors. All who were admitted into Zulu society in this
way were absorbed as individuals, giving up their former tribal loyalties and

assuming a Zulu identity" (1969, 138). Such external terrorism, however, was
motivated by internal terrorism. One direction this took was against the
warriors themselves. After a battle, each regiment was expected to "bring forth
the cowards," who were then executed. If one of the regiments suffered actual
defeat or was forced to retreat, the entire organization would be massacred
together with the families of the warriors.

Civil terrorism was no less spectacular and was directed against any potential opposition, no matter how slight, to the Shaka's power and authority.
Witch doctors (*izanusi*), who were capable of "smelling out" witches and
accusing them of foul deeds, were persecuted because their sacred authority as spirit-mediums (linking the ancestors with the living) threatened the
Shaka, not directly, for he was immune from their accusations, but indirectly,
because his circle of lieutenants, generals, and counselors were vulnerable.
The Shaka reduced the power of the *izanusi* by immunizing his entire army
against their pronouncements and by taking the title of "Dream Doctor,"
making himself the only legitimate rainmaker and witch doctor. This erosion
of ancestral authority as embodied by the *izanusi* went hand in hand with the
dissolution of the primary bonds of kinship and marriage. Men were forced
to kill their sons as public examples of loyalty and were themselves killed if
they hesitated to deliver the blow, such was the Shaka's concern that paternal authority could compete with his own. He further reduced the authority
of kin groups by regulating marriage between men sectioned off from their
families in army barracks and women in age-grade seraglios commanded by
adopted royal mothers and queens. Final destruction of kinship authority
was directed against lineage elders, who represented customary wisdom and
exerted a moral influence on the chief. Because this constituted a potential
challenge to the Shaka's authority, he redefined the status of old men as "old
women" and had them butchered in the thousands.

This brief, if somewhat overdrawn, sketch of external and internal "terrorism" under the Shaka—of power unregulated by the constraints of authority—
introduces some of the political dynamics mediated and articulated by his
praise. As the Zulu chief became the king of a nation formed from the living
remains of different tribes, the function of the praise as a unifying force—
distributing legitimate authority—became more important. According to
Cope (1968, 32), during the rise of the Shaka it became "necessary to build
up national loyalty towards the king as the embodiment of the nation, for he
was not related by blood to the great majority of his subjects." At the same
time, however, the potential channels of political opposition by a disaffected
public were blocked and undercut by his extraordinary power—by periodi-
cally purging his counselors and subchiefs, persecuting the *izanusi* and lineage

elders, and even controlling marriage alliances and the distribution of adult statuses. The single institution that appears to have retained relative autonomy was that of the *imbongi*, or specialist praiser. The political significance of praise-singing in Zululand under the Shaka is thus underlined by the fact that it constituted the sole voice of opposition, albeit a muted voice, tolerated by the leviathan.

Just why the Shaka tolerated critical praise is not clear, but judging from the criticisms that do occur in his praise, it worked as a propaganda device to enhance his total power by reputation as well as deed. Thus, when the Shaka is addressed in the opening stanza of his praise as "He who armed in the forest, who is like a madman / The madman who is in full view of the men" (Cope 1968, 88, lines 11–12), the image of a madman embodies his total and arbitrary power as a dictator. Similarly, an embedded exhortation to refrain from fighting—"Trickster, abstain from enemies, it is summer / The grass is long, it will get the better of you" (94, lines 111–12)—may constitute a criticism of his actions, but it also enhances his status as a perpetually aggressive warrior. In another stanza, the Shaka is called "He who devoured the trust cattle / Even today he is still responsible" (108, lines 321–22), an epithet with several possible interpretations. Cope explains the epithet as a reference to cattle lent on trust—according to the *sisa* custom—which the Shaka appropriated. But this reference is itself "loaded" with implications for the incumbency model. According to Krige (1936), the *sisa* (*ukuSisa*) was a practice by which a man placed some of his cattle in the care of another kraal owner as a way of reducing his risk of cattle disease and appropriation; the system was based on mutual trust and cooperation. By "devouring" the trust cattle, the Shaka violates the collective obligations of this system and, by implication, the duties of his office, which include responsibility for the well-being of his people. But this criticism at the same time is a warning against possible organized resistance to his rule, for the *sisa* created a system of alliances that, like marriage, he may have felt threatened his power until brought within his control. An alternative warning is also implied: you may be able to reduce your risk of disease, but this strategy will not work against the Shaka.

An overt criticism of the Shaka found in the middle of his praise works in much the same way. Here the *imbongi* chastises the Shaka directly: "King, you are wrong because you do not discriminate / Because even those of your maternal uncle's family you kill / Because you killed Bhebhe son of Ncumela of your maternal uncle's family" (Cope 1968, 110, lines 348–50). The historical reference is to the Shaka's massacre of the Longeni clan (of which his mother was a member), which had ostracized and banished him when he was a boy. In terms of incumbency, the criticism points to his violation of

TABLE 1
Composition of Xhosa tribal clusters

Cluster	Related chiefdoms	District	Unrelated (tributary) chiefdoms	District
Xhosa	Gcaleka	Willowvale	Gqunukhwebe	Middledrift
	Ngqika	Kentami		
	Ndlambe	East London		
	Dushane	King William's Town		
	Qhayi	King William's Town		
	Dange	King William's Town		
	Gasela	King William's Town		
	Ntinde	King William's Town		
	Hleke	King William's Town		

Source: Hammond-Tooke 1965, 146.

basic kinship values—the Shaka is wrong, not because he kills, but because he does not discriminate between kinsmen and enemies. Again, the criticism is a warning—nobody is safe from the Shaka's deathblow. In this way, the Shaka may have tolerated critical praise when it enhanced his reputation as a dictator, transforming violations of high office into virtues of total power. In this rather limiting case, praise is no longer a diffuse political resource in the hands of the public, because the Shaka's power and authority rest, not on public consensus, but on his monopoly of force. Instead, praise functions as a propaganda device to mix loyalty with fear in the hearts and minds of his growing number of subjects.

Xhosa Praises

Xhosa praises can be fruitfully compared with Zulu praises because they highlight the cultural similarities between the two societies while revealing basic institutional differences. Although the ethnolinguistic identities of Southern Bantu peoples present a complex picture, mediated by ideologies of tribalism, it is generally held that the Xhosa are among the descendants of fragments of ethnic chiefdoms (collectively called "Cape Nguni") who fled from the Shaka and settled in the present Transkei and Ciskei during the third decade of the nineteenth century (Pauw 1975, 3). The cultural affinities between the Zulu and Xhosa are reflected by the use of the same terminology for praises (*izibongi*, lit., "surname" or "clan name") and specialist praisers (*iimbongi*). But the praises themselves are very different and constitute very different forms of political action within different institutional frameworks.

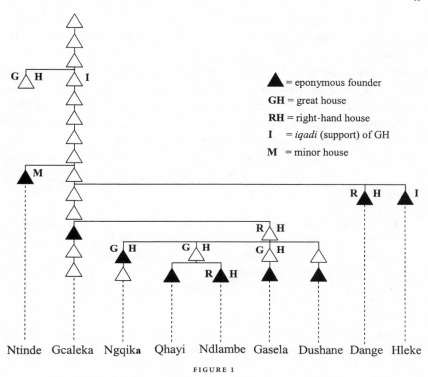

= eponymous founder
GH = great house
RH = right-hand house
I = *iqadi* (support) of GH
M = minor house

Ntinde Gcaleka Ngqika Qhayi Ndlambe Gasela Dushane Dange Hleke

FIGURE 1

Genealogical relations between Xhosa "houses" (from Hammond-Tooke 1965, 150)

In contrast to the highly centralized and regimented Zulu state (under the Shaka), expanding and incorporating neighboring chiefdoms into its jurisdiction, the Xhosa comprise a cluster of independent chiefdoms. These chiefdoms remain associated by imputed genealogical ties under a "paramount" chief (table 1 and fig. 1), but each retains independent sovereignty and jurisdiction (Hammond-Tooke 1965, 156). Each chiefdom was also subject to fission built into the very mechanism of "house succession," by which the eldest son of the senior wife (i.e., of the "right-hand" house of the head) was expected to break away and form an independent household, resulting in fission of the chiefdom. Fission, of course, would not occur in every generation, but only when disaffection with the incumbent was sufficient to mobilize a faction in support of his heir: "A common cause of fission was dissatisfaction with the incumbent of the chiefship—the chiefship itself was never questioned—but among all the Cape Nguni the dichotomizing tendency was, as it were, built into the institution. This was the preemptive right for the heir of the right-hand house of a chief to establish his own independent chiefdom separate from that of his father" (Hammond-Tooke 1965, 152).

It is in relation to this fissiparous institution of succession that the incumbency model in Xhosa praise-singing works as a form of political transaction, evaluating the performance of the incumbent clearly and forthrightly. Where the Shaka's support was imposed by internal and external "terrorism" which prevented the opposition necessary for fission to occur, the Xhosa chief depends upon the effective distribution of legitimate authority, for he is openly vulnerable to the fission that results from loss of public support. This vulnerability, I would suggest, accounts for the overt character of the evaluation or appraisal of the incumbent, voiced through praise. This delicate balance of public support and public criticism expressed by the praise is described nicely by Opland:

> The *imbongi* fulfills a complex of functions in [Xhosa] society . . . in arousing his audience to loyalty for a chief, he acts as a propagandist or cheerleader. In expressing in public the sentiments current in his society, he acts as a spokesman for the common man. He serves a chief, and his chief is the most frequent subject of his poetry. But this does not mean that his poetry mindlessly praises his chief or comprises merely a litany lauding the greatness of his deeds. While the *imbongi* is associated with a chief, he is also a *tribal* poet responsible to the community, and, above all, he is committed to telling the truth as he sees it. He has a duty to the chief to inspire in his audience feelings of loyalty for the chief, but he also has a duty to the people to decry the actions of the chief whenever he feels them to be unworthy of a chief. (1981, 7)

I argued earlier that the politics of this incumbency model—by which I mean the evaluation of the incumbent's performance against the values and duties of good leadership—can lurk beneath the surface of praise. But it can also erupt into a public threat. A praise to Chief Matanzima brings public pressure to bear on him by drawing attention, metapragmatically speaking, to the politics of the praise as a performative utterance:

> As a spokesman of the nation, I deny your claim.
> You have deviated from the views of the people.
> As a spokesman of the nation, I deny your claim.
> Turn back and you will see that you are alone, you have no following.
> (Opland 1983, 102)

But if this *imbongi* warns his chief that he is losing support, it is to prevent his natural successor from breaking away, that is, to militate against what is institutionally entailed when the Xhosa chief really does lose public support (but cf. Opland 1983, 99–105, for a richer account of the *imbongi* Mbutuma's political agenda in the context of apartheid):

My chief's son causes a problem,
he causes a problem,
he causes a problem for his people.
For they say what is the chief's son going to feed us with when he says we must
get together.

(Opland 1981, 18)

In institutional terms I interpret this passage to mean that the chief's son is
not yet powerful or wealthy enough to lead his own faction, for traditionally
a chief built up support by lending out cattle. Thus, the *imbongi* remains loyal
to his chief and, by threatening loss of public support, helps to prevent it from
actually happening.

The language of the Xhosa *imbongi* is exceptionally ribald and provo-
cative—he has license to ridicule and criticize with impunity (Opland 1983,
66–68). In terms of the incumbency model (the evaluation of performance
against the duties of office), this freedom of speech is essential for communication between chief and public to take place. In terms of local ideology, this
freedom of speech is sanctioned, even voiced, by the chief's ancestors. The
imbongi is thus a ritual specialist, a spirit-medium praising, not with his own
words, but with the words of the royal ancestors on behalf of the community.

Conclusion: Praise-Singing and the Speech Act

Throughout this chapter I have looked at particular Southern Bantu praises
in terms of an incumbency model developed by Comaroff (1975) and applied
to a wider range of data. Whereas his analysis focuses on the political oratory of a single Tswana chiefdom (Tshidi), I extended his model to analyze
Southern Bantu praises of high office. For Comaroff, the incumbency model
is *indigenous*—an ideology of norms, values, and obligations associated with
high office, against which the incumbent's actual performance is publicly
evaluated. As such, it remains an empirical concept, rooted in the specific
culture where he found it. To generalize this concept for comparative analysis,
I have worked this indigenous incumbency model into a more abstract, ana-
lytic concept of critical agency that refers to the reflexive bifunctionality of the
message communicated by praise—the distribution of legitimate authority
"outward" and the channeling of public opinion "inward" to bear upon the
incumbent.

In the Tswana, Zulu, and Xhosa praises compared, I highlighted the "contours" of this model as implied, and sometimes explicitly stated, by the praises
themselves. Through a rudimentary content analysis of particular passages

and references, I outlined some of the institutional mechanisms through which public support could be mobilized or divided. Among the Tswana, support for the chief or the rightful heir can be challenged by a political rival, while among the Xhosa the rightful heir becomes a rival by exercising his right to establish an independent chiefdom. The Zulu under the Shaka represent a special case, where public criticism was tolerated when it strengthened allegiance to the king through fear and intimidation. But in focusing on praises as texts, I paid very little attention to the speech act of praise-singing itself—the actual process by which the praise communicates its bifunctional message. Some of this important material can be found in Mafeje 1963, 1967; Opland 1983; and Vail and White 1991. Instead, I examined the praises as texts abstracted from specific events—assuming that the basic principles of the incumbency model could be held constant—and sketched the basic institutional mechanisms and structures invoked, sometimes into action, by the praises. I have proceeded in the dark, needing more sociolinguistic information and knowledge of the original languages to determine just how praise-singing exploits elements of the speech act to accomplish its political work in the first place, but a very general outline can be sketched.

A simple communicative model of sender, message, and receiver is inadequate for this demonstration because, as such, the components are too crude. The incumbency model of praise-singing exploits significant differences between addresser and speaker and between addressee and hearer in a public and political interaction. The specialist praiser (addresser) is literally the speaker, but he speaks, not as an individual for himself, but as a spokesman for others. In terms of the bifunctionality of his message, he speaks formulaically (1) to the public on behalf of his chief to distribute his legitimate authority and (2) more directly to the chief on behalf of his public, who evaluate his performance against the requirements of high office. Role distance is a dependent variable of this bifunctional communication. By distributing legitimate authority, the praiser minimizes the role distance between the incumbent and his office, bringing those qualities of his character and notable actions of his past into the general model of chiefly conduct associated with high office (Comaroff's formal code). But by bringing public opinion and evaluation to bear upon the incumbent himself, the praise-singer maximizes the role distance between incumbent and office, highlighting the divergences between individual character/performance and the normative attributes of the office (Comaroff's evaluative code).

An additional variable in the interaction between public and incumbent is the "political distance" between them, by which I mean the degree to which the powers of an incumbent overrule the powers of his public to depose or desert

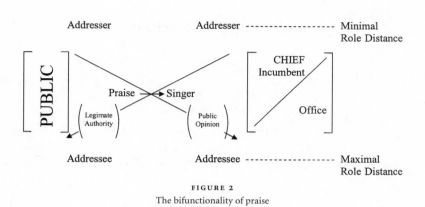

FIGURE 2
The bifunctionality of praise

him (fig. 2). If we postulate the rule that the less the political distance, the more forthright the language of evaluation, and, correspondingly, the greater the political distance, the more veiled the language of evaluation, we can account for the otherwise-surprising differences between the less explicit Tswana and more explicit Xhosa evaluations expressed through praise-singing. Although this model is crude and its implications are tenuous, it points to an extended theory of deixis that relates the wider structures of social and institutional action to the dialectics of critical agency. In the following chapter, I extend this model, focusing on "dispraise," rebellion, and the king's two bodies in the colonial ethnography of Swaziland.

3

Rituals against Rebellion

A cluster of criticisms surround Gluckman's now-classic theory of rituals of rebellion in southeastern Africa. Some stem from a basic confusion about what Gluckman means by "rebellion" and "ritual of rebellion" (M. Wilson 1959; Reay 1959), but these are definitional and semantic issues. Beidelman, however, develops a more substantial critique. His "Swazi Royal Ritual" challenges Gluckman's analysis of the Swazi Ncwala—a sort of ideal type of the ritual of rebellion—in an alternative interpretation of the same ethnographic material.[1] For Beidelman (1966, 401), "the main theme of the Incwala is not rebellion or the expression of aggression or conflict, as Gluckman maintains, but the separation of the king from the various groups within his nation so that he is free and fit to assume the heavy supernatural powers of office as king-priest of the nation."

Such rival interpretations stem from different styles of anthropology. Gluckman is concerned with the latent functions and consequences of institutionalized rebellion and its representation in ritual.[2] Beidelman is interested in what this ritual means from the indigenous point of view, as a form of symbolic action. Both theories focus on the significance of sacred *simemo* songs, which are performed and dramatized in the Ncwala and appear to insult, reject, and generally blaspheme the Swazi king. Gluckman's theory of

1. I write "the Ncwala" instead of "the Incwala" following Kuper's (1972, 593) recommendation for greater accuracy of noun-prefix use.

2. The Swazi Ncwala has had a lively postcolonial history in Swaziland and continues to animate contemporary political struggles over the legitimacy of traditional chieftaincy. I return to this earlier debate between Gluckman and Beidelman because it clarifies a localized field of ritualized oratory.

rebellious ritual rests on a "face value" reading of the *simemo* songs: literally against the king, they are functionally in support of the kingship, marking a separation between person and office that proves crucial to the logic of rebellion itself. Beidelman's distaste for latent functions and predilection for the actor perspective produce a countertheory. *Simemo* songs are symbolic: literally against the king, symbolically, in terms of Swazi concepts and categories, they indicate the king's separation from his people.

While each has something important to say about these ritual insults— what I call "dispraises," in marked opposition to "praises," of the king— neither interpretation is fully satisfactory or accommodates the other. In this chapter I argue that both theories can be revised and combined by analyzing Swazi dispraises of the king as a species of joking relationship. This does not imply that *simemo* songs are humorous. The value of Radcliffe-Brown's original theory of "permitted disrespect" lies in its specification of paired concepts—familiarity and avoidance, disjunction and conjunction, alliance and contract—that bring the politics and symbolism of the Swazi Ncwala into closer correspondence. This ritual, in turn, casts brighter light on the sociolinguistic components of the joking relationship.

The Ncwala

The interpretations of the Ncwala developed by Gluckman and Beidelman rely primarily, but not exclusively, on Kuper's classic ethnography (1947, 197–225). In this "period piece" account, the Ncwala is introduced as "the most important of all national ceremonies, and the most essential event of the year" (1947, 197). Performed in two parts, the "Little" and "Great" Ncwala, the ritual has a fixed cast of actors. These are the king, the queen mother, the king's royal and ritual wives, his sisters and daughters, the national priesthood (*bemanti*; the head priest of which ranks as a leading chief), the ritual blood brothers of the king (*tinsila*), the royal princes, the king's fighting regiments, and the "rank and file of the nation," who arrive in local contingents, each led by their chief or his representative.

The Little and Great Ncwala are separated by a fifteen-day interim. The Little Ncwala, which occurs when the moon is new, involves those in a close relationship to the king—his mother, the queens, the *tinsila*, the king's royal regiments, and the *bemanti* (Ncwala priests). The regimental praise-singer opens the ceremony with a praise to the king, after which the leader commands silence. The warriors then begin the sacred "hand song," which they dance and sing at the same time, in dispraise of the king:

Uye uye oyeha—you hate the child king
You hate the child king (repeated)
I would depart with my Father (the king),
I fear we would be recalled.
mm m u oyeha—they put him on the stone:
mm m u oyeha he—sleeps with his sister:
mm m u u u he—sleeps with Lozithupa (Princess):
uye uye oyeha—you hate the child king.
(Kuper 1947, 203)

During this song, regiments from other villages join in while the royal women enter and assemble according to their statuses. A sacred chant follows which appears to adopt the queen mother's point of view:

Shi shi ishi ishi—you hate him,
ishi ishi ishi—mother, the enemies are the people.
ishi ishi ishi—you hate him,
Mother—the people are wizards.
Admit the treason of Mabedla
ishi ishi ishi—you hate him,
you have wronged,
ishi ishi—bend great neck,
those and those they hate him,
ishi ishi—they hate the king.
(Kuper 1947, 204)

These sacred dispraises are followed by *imigubo*, solemn (but not sacred) chants full of historical allusion and moral didacticism that express public support for the king. The king is meanwhile doctored with sacred medicines in the royal cattle byre, where he is surrounded by his closest subjects and the royal regiments. The *indvuna*, the highest councilor of the capital and the people's representative, starts the sacred *simemo* song, which contains the following refrain:

Jjiya oh o o King, alas for your fate
Jjiya oh o o King, they reject they reject thee
Jjiya oh o o King, they hate thee.
(Kuper 1947, 205)[3]

3. Vail and White (1991, 46–48, 155–97) provide a brilliant corrective to the idea that these dispraises are timeless texts by historicizing their invention, circulation, and elevation during the reconsolidation of the Swazi monarchy in the 1940s. For a historical interpretation of the *simemo* songs as an expression of resistance against British colonialism, see Lincoln 1987. See also Apter 1988. As I argue in chapter 4, the historicizing of poetic license is crucial to our understanding of

The song ends abruptly when one of the *bemanti* priests shouts, "Out, foreigners!" referring to anyone present who does not owe allegiance to the king.
Kuper adds that at this moment the king, at the height of his ritual power, must
be surrounded by his loyal but *unrelated* supporters. He then spits medicines
to break the old year and prepare for the new, and is thereafter praised as "Our
Bull," "Lion," "Being of Heaven," "Unconquerable," and "Great Mountain."
This whole cycle of praise–dispraise–praise is performed again before dawn.

In fifteen days, when the moon is full, the Great Ncwala reproduces a
similar cycle of activities but with elaboration and on a larger scale. The warriors and the public praise the king and bring medicines to his sacred enclosure
within the cattle byre. At noon, the warriors undress and pummel to "near
death" a pitch-black ox that is called "bull." The king, now naked, is brought
into contact with a different black ox (*cwambo*) from his sacred herd, and both
are washed in medicines. Regiments surround the king and sing *simemo* songs.
The next day the king emerges naked save for an ivory penis-cap and walks
through the crowd to a sacred enclosure. Inside, he "stabs" and "bites" the
new year in what is elsewhere called a *luma* rite (e.g., Junod 1927); afterward,
people gather to dance about him. His royal kinsmen sing that they plan to
depart with him while trying to force him back inside the sacred enclosure.
The commoners lament and try to entice him back out. He emerges as Silo, a
powerfully doctored monster dancing wildly and reluctant to join the people.
Silo disappears into the sacred enclosure, the royal kin and aliens leave the
vicinity ("Out, foreigners!"), and the king reappears without demonic garb
and hurls a green calabash at his warriors, who catch it on a black shield. The
"dirt" of the king and the nation, in the form of used medicinal substances, is
burned on a pyre, and this cleansing concludes with final praises, feasts, and
dancing.

Two Theories

There is more to the Ncwala than the singing of praise and dispraise of
the king by specific status holders, social groups, and categories. The royal
ritual has also been labeled a "First Fruits" ceremony (Cook 1930, 205), performed before eating the new harvest and identifying the ritual powers of
the king with the fertility of the land. The rival theories of Gluckman and

---

ritualized insults, but in this chapter I would emphasize the corollary principle that, underlying
their historical conditions and mediations, the "structural" dimensions of *simemo* songs as a
type of "joking" can still be discerned and thereby illuminate significant dynamics of power and
authority in Swazi kingship.

Beidelman, however, focus on the singing of dispraise as the critical feature
of the Ncwala.

According to Gluckman (1956, 1963), the Swazi Ncwala, with its ritualized
rejection of the king, represents the ritual of rebellion par excellence. Just what
rituals of rebellion are has given rise to some debate, attributable, in part, to
Gluckman's inconsistent use of the term "rebellion." His initial definition
comes from Aristotle (Gluckman 1956, 46): "rebellions attack the personnel
of office and not the offices themselves." That is, they attack and, if successful,
remove, individuals within the political system but leave the system intact.
Later, in a reply to Monica Wilson, Gluckman (1963, 26) widens the concept
of rebellion "to refer to the whole relation between ritual and the structure of
the political system." But here Gluckman is talking about the political *ritual*
of rebellion, not the political act. The rebellion performed in sacred ritual,
however, is not identical with secular political rebellion—the king remains
king in the former but not in the latter. It is essential that this distinction
between ritual rebellion and actual rebellion be clarified, for it is their relationship that Gluckman's theory addresses.

Actual rebellion, Gluckman argues, is built into the very structure of traditional southeastern Bantu kingdoms in order to maintain their long-term
integration and stability. First, "rebellions represent the values of kingship
and restore its power" (Gluckman 1956, 45); that is, they are led by rivals with
legitimate claims to high office who aspire to conform to its publicly maintained rights and duties. Second, "the rebellion is in fact waged to protect the
kingship from the king" (Gluckman 1963, 129); that is, rebellions are publicly
supported only when the ruling incumbent fails to rule well, according to the
duties of his office. And third, rebellions prevent fission of the kingdom: "All
sections struggle for the kingship, and this unifies them. They seek to place
their own prince on the throne; they do not try to become independent of the
kingship" (Gluckman 1956, 45).

The Swazi Ncwala, according to Gluckman (1963, 119), is a national ritual
"in which the theme of rebellion is made manifest." This theme is expressed
through the sacred *simemo* songs performed by various categories of actors
to criticize, revile, and "reject" the king but at the same time strengthen the
Swazi state: "This ceremony is not a simple mass assertion of unity, but a
stressing of conflict, a statement of rebellion and rivalry against the king,
with periodic affirmation of unity with the king.... the dramatic, symbolic
acting of social relations in their ambivalence is believed to achieve unity and
prosperity" (125–26). Gluckman's theory tries to explain how this dramatic
and symbolic acting of rebellion achieves unity and prosperity in terms that are
"first" comprehensible to the Swazi and "second" comprehensible to the social

anthropologist. From the Swazi point of view, the performance of the Ncwala purifies the king and his nation, bringing strength, fertility, and prosperity to the people and land. For the social anthropologist (i.e., Gluckman), the content of these beliefs is not too important. More important is that the Swazi have some set of beliefs which imputes a causal or instrumental relationship between the performance of the rebellious ritual and an improved state of affairs. The anthropologist accounts for these beliefs about the ritual, whatever they may be, in terms of the social value of its performance.

Here lies the crux of Gluckman's argument, which can be summarized in syllogistic form. Rebellions in southeastern Bantu societies have a political function: they uphold the office of kingship in perpetuity and unify the kingdom. Rituals of rebellion are (somehow) related to actual rebellions; hence, their political function is (somehow) related to the political function of real rebellions. The gray area in this formulation is explaining just how rituals of rebellion are related to actual rebellions and how their respective functions are linked.

Rituals of rebellion are, for Gluckman, an "acting of conflict" in a sacred context that allows "unbridled excess." In these ritual acts, the implicit tensions surrounding the kingship—the threat of rival heirs or a disaffected public—are made explicit. To a certain extent this public expression and acknowledgment of conflict surrounding the king serves as a collective psychological release, what Van den Berghe (1963, 414) glosses as the "blowing-off-steam" hypothesis and what Gluckman (1963, 126) himself recognizes as "the general problem of catharsis . . . the purging of emotion through 'pity, fear and inspiration.'" Gluckman, however, is interested, not in psychological explanation, but in "the sociological setting of the process" (126). This sociological setting is none other than the rival claims of princes, bolstered by sectional bases of public support, to achieve the kingship for themselves:

> The ceremony states that in virtue of their social position princes and people hate the king. . . . The critically important point is that even if Swazi princes do not actually hate the king, their social position may rally malcontents to them. Indeed, in a comparatively small-scale society princes by their very existence have power which threatens the king. Hence in their prescribed, compelled, ritual behaviour they exhibit opposition as well as support for the king, but mainly support for the kingship. This is the social setting for rituals of rebellion. (128)

In other words, rituals of rebellion emphasize "potential rebellion," which, like active rebellion, strengthens the values of kingship and the unity of the kingdom. They exhibit "mainly support for the kingship" by consecrating the perpetual office of authority over and above the holder: "it is the kingship and not the king who is divine" (129). The king himself is frail: "His personal inadequacy and his liability to desecrate the values of kingship are exhibited in the insults he suffers" (135).

Beidelman (1966) offers an alternative analysis. In Gluckman's approach, the content of Swazi beliefs about the ritual is not too important, as long as there is some set of beliefs which motivates and rationalizes its performance. Gluckman is interested in the function, or social value, of the ritual, rather than its meaning for the Swazi. This neglect of belief and symbolism has, according to Beidelman (1966: 375), flawed Gluckman's interpretation, "in that he has sometimes found conflict, aggression and rebellion as dominant themes where this does not seem to be so." Where Gluckman assumes rebellion from the beginning, and perceives it where it may not actually be, Beidelman (387–88) begins by considering ritual symbolism, which derives from cosmology: "Cosmology is a system of categories, and ritual involves manipulation of symbolic objects from these various categories. This takes two basic, antithetical forms: (1) a mixing or confounding of categories which is both dangerous and potent . . . or (2) a separation out, a reordering or check upon the existing ordering of categories, which should be kept apart." Beidelman associates these expressive forms of ritual action—the symbolic conjunction or "confounding" of categories and the symbolic disjunction or "separation" of categories—with different aspects of the ritual process. Symbolic mixing of categories creates a "potent and dangerous" condition, a releasing of mystical power (such as lightning, trembling, uncontrolled dancing, possession) believed to be violent and polluting. Symbolic separation of categories is associated with controlled ordering, avoidance and respect, purgation and purification. Both forms guide Beidelman's interpretation of the Ncwala. The first half of the ritual "gradually increases all the powerful supernatural attributes of the king" and reaches its climax in the appearance of Silo, the king as "a monster, cut off from men and society owing to the very strength and disorder of varied opposing attributes condensed within him" (377). The second half of the Ncwala represents a defusing and purging of this dangerous admixture of attributes, so that "basic categories are again clearly defined and may then be readily separated into those aspects to be retained and those whose embodying objects are burned" (378).

To heighten the king's ritual potency in the first half of the Ncwala, a large black ox is pummeled nearly to death by undressed warriors and then slain by rain priests in the king's sacred enclosure. Beidelman explains that the pummeling is supposed to loosen the beast's potent attributes and that certain of its organs—especially its lower lip and gall bladder—give power to the king.

The ox itself is anomalous: black, it possesses the heavy, "dark" potency of the male beast, but castrated, its distinctive sexual attribute is removed. By nightfall, when the king is highly doctored, the surrounding regiments sing *simemo* songs and then wash in the river. The "songs of hate" are repeated at dawn, when the king emerges naked from his sacred enclosure, indicating, according to Beidelman (1966, 397), "a unique, lonely, denuded status outside any single social category," the consequence of his "terrible asocial powers." These songs do not "reject" the king but express the "burden" of his power, the isolation of a superhuman from humans. In this potent state, as the *simemo* songs are sung, the king "bites" medicines to separate the new year from the old.

After further doctoring within his sacred enclosure, the king emerges and is surrounded by his royal kinsmen, "who sing songs about forsaking the nation and taking off with him" (Beidelman 1966, 398), but then force him back inside his enclosure. He reemerges, this time as Silo, a monstrous figure wearing animal fat from the royal herd (thought to produce madness in others), potent medicines, a fat-smeared shield in his left hand, the hand of disorder and pollution, and nothing in his right, the hand of order. Reluctant to join his people, the monstrous king again retreats, royal kin and foreigners are sent away, and only then he reemerges to join his people by throwing a green calabash to his warriors. The Ncwala has now reached its turning point. The second half of the ritual purges dangerous medicines and cleanses the nation. The king's monstrous costume, his worn-out utensils and garments, and the remains of the sacrificial ox-bull are all burned on a pyre, turned to ash, and washed away by rains, separating the impure from the pure. Only after all such objects of power and pollution are destroyed can order again prevail in the capital (1966, 400).

Beidelman's exegesis is much fuller and richer than this brief summary suggests, for he traces the meanings of symbols in other Swazi contexts and in relation to broader cosmological concepts. His basic critique of Gluckman, however, is that the ritual action of the Ncwala, when analyzed from the Swazi point of view, says little, if anything, of conflict or rebellion. "Much of Gluckman's and Kuper's accounts of the themes of hatred and aggression towards the king depend upon their interpretation of the *simemo* songs at these rites. These are sung when the king, or objects associated with him, are being isolated so that they can take on increased supernatural powers. Far from being periods when the king is symbolically weak, they mark his assumption of great power. If there is an aspect of strain, it involves the 'heaviness' and isolation of the king's task" (1966, 401). Beidelman does not deny that the main Ncwala theme has political, as well as symbolic, significance, for the separation of the king from various groups within his nation is a unifying political act: "the king must transcend loyalties towards any particular groups if he is to unify all his people" (394).[4] But he neglects to analyze fully these political principles of faction and unity, addressing native conceptions of power and purity on their own terms instead. The king is separated from (and reunited with) his nation to assume the supernatural powers of his position because it "makes sense" to the Swazi. Beidelman follows this line of reasoning to its logical conclusion—a plea for a greater psychological understanding of ritual action and the efficacy of its symbols (401–4).

To compare Gluckman's and Beidelman's interpretations of the Ncwala is thus to compare two types of theory: one sociological, the other more cultural and psychological; one concerned with (latent) function, the other with (implicit) meaning. Both interpretations, however, are flawed. Gluckman's "rebellious ritual" interpretation is based on an assumed, but by no means demonstrated, correspondence between actual rebellions and their political function, on the one hand, and ritual "rebellions" and their political function, on the other. Pushing this parallel too far, Gluckman interprets the Ncwala in general, and the *simemo* songs in particular, as against the king but in support of the kingship, because actual rebellions work this way. What this theory cannot account for is how the Ncwala and its *simemo* songs support not just the kingship but, more importantly, the king himself. Beidelman's interpretation is more successful in this respect, for it demonstrates how the king's separation from his people reflects and enhances his supernatural power. But Beidelman fails to explain why *simemo* songs in particular should mark the king's separation from his people—songs praising his extrahuman powers could do the job equally well.[5]

The Joking Relationship

When ritualized dispraises of the king are analyzed as a species of joking, the shortcomings in Gluckman's and Beidelman's interpretations of the ritual can be avoided and their insights combined in a third interpretation, which transcends the limitations of what, in another context, Augé (1979) has called the meaning-function alternative.

4. This is Evans-Pritchard's argument with regard to divine kingship among the Shilluk.

5. Beidelman might argue that since the separation of categories is associated with purity and respect, the converse holds that the confounding of categories, embodied by Silo as monster-king, is associated with disrespect. This may be true, but still begs the question of why these symbolic modes and attitudes are associated in the first place.

In his original article, Radcliffe-Brown (1940) assigns a variety of cross-culturally observed patterns of behavior to a common class of social relationship which he calls "joking relationships" or relationships of "permitted disrespect." These are of two general types, symmetrical and asymmetrical, depending on whether joking between both parties is reciprocal or one-sided. The joking itself takes several forms: it involves verbal and sometimes physical horseplay, teasing and making fun of the other person, flaunting of irreverence, and often elements of obscenity. Diagnostic of this joking behavior is that it is not taken literally: "There is pretence of hostility and a real friendliness" (Radcliffe—Brown 1952a, 91). Examples of joking relationships are often cited between affines or between individuals linked by complementary filiation (and thus separated by descent) such as the classic mother's brother and sister's son in a patrilineal kinship system. But they can also obtain between clans, as Fortes (1945) notes among the Tallensi, Goody (1962) among the LoDagaba, and Rigby (1968) among the Gogo. The structural situation underlying such examples is generically the same, involving both attachment and separation, both social conjunction and social disjunction, between the joking partners. (Affines are "attached" by marriage, "separated" by descent; clans are attached by myths of common provenience, separated at lower levels of segmentary opposition.)

Structural attachment and separation are necessary but not sufficient conditions of the joking relationship. Joking partners must also be counterpoised in potential hostility and conflict (Radcliffe-Brown 1952a, 103). The function of the joking relationship is to buffer such potential conflict by expressing a sort of mock hostility that acknowledges both the possibility of conflict and the desire to avoid it. It establishes, in Radcliffe-Brown's terminology, an alliance between joking partners as opposed to a full-fledged contract, precisely because no binding set of legal norms clearly defines a nonhostile relationship between them. Another way of defusing this potential hostility is through avoidance of face-to-face interaction as an expression of extreme politeness and respect. Although diametrically opposed as styles of behavior, both avoidance and joking militate against open conflict between two persons or sets of persons.

The Swazi Ncwala exhibits many characteristics of the joking relationship. The public, and its various sections, "joke" at the king's expense, but the king does not "joke" with his public. Permitted disrespect is in this case asymmetrical, inversely related to the king's power over his people. Warriors assembled at the Little Ncwala blaspheme the king's successor with reference to incest in the hand song and dance: "you hate the child king . . . he sleeps with his sister." The royal women—the queen mother, her retainers, the co-wives of the late king and of the ruling king, and the princesses—sing out against the king himself: "Mother, the enemies are the people. You hate him." And in the final refrain, led by the people's representative (the *indvuna*)—"King, alas for your fate . . . they reject thee . . . they hate thee"—the king, standing alone, is dispraised.

Taken literally, as they are by Gluckman, these sacred songs are rebellious, expressing public disaffection. But the effrontery of a joking partner is not meant to be taken literally; rather, it is a sign of friendship. This unspoken meaning of the *simemo* songs is suggested by an informant cited by Kuper (1947, 207): "The songs show the hatred evoked by the king, but they also demonstrate the loyalty of his supporters. . . . It is a national expression of sympathy for the king." In another statement: "I think these songs are magical preventatives against harm coming to the king"; and of the dance associated with the *simemo* songs: "it strengthens the king and the earth." *Simemo* songs, then, do not mean what they say but imply something of the opposite.[6] They express sympathy and loyalty toward the king and increase his strength and power. Consequently, it is *nonparticipation* in these ritual dispraises of the king that "is regarded as an act of rebellion" (207). From the perspective of the joking relationship, which also concurs with the Swazi point of view, Gluckman's thesis, like the literal meaning of the songs on which it is based, is negated.

The structural situation of the Ncwala also fits the joking pattern. Sociopolitical conjunction and disjunction characterize the king's relationship to his public, and its units, which engage in his dispraise. The queen mother, for example, is both joined with and separated from the king in a sort of "dual monarchy." King and queen mother rule together but live in separate villages. He presides over the highest court; she presides over the second-highest court. Where he controls the army, she has regiments at the capital under princes, who are always potential contestants for the throne. Even in ritual they are united and opposed. In the Swazi rain ceremony the king and queen mother undergo ritual treatment together (Schoeman 1935), but in the Ncwala the king is treated alone. The character of this structural situation is thus potentially disruptive. The queen mother can challenge the king's authority. She can rebuke him for wasting national wealth. She can mobilize regiments to oppose him. But she "hates him" in ritual because she must love him in social life. Kuper (1947, 247) quotes the queen mother: "It is a pain to see him a king; my child goes alone through the people." It is this bond of compassion that

---

6. Krige (1968) makes the same observation of Zulu puberty songs and challenges Gluckman's claim that they too belong to a ritual of rebellion.

is implied by the logic of the joking relationship and prevents open political conflict between them.

The age-graded fighting regiments are similarly joined with and disjoined from the king. Division occurs at the highest level between regiments of the king and of the queen mother. Regiments are also divided into platoons (*emachiba*) by the locality of the royal villages where they reside. Since many of these royal villages are headed by princes, natural rivals of the king, any resident platoon led by a prince could rise against the king and his more loyal supporters. Thus, we find hostile references to the "child king," which might refer to the king's natural rival as well as successor, sung by regiments organized into platoons. In the Great Ncwala they stand united in a circle around the king, singing of his rejection but committed to his protection. Beyond this circle of regiments gather the local contingents of the Swazi nation, clusters of homesteads (*umuti*) structured into village segments, united under one king but competing against one another for their own parochial interests.

The concepts of alliance and contract in Radcliffe-Brown's theory of permitted disrespect further illuminate the political function of the Ncwala. Where contract is a recognized legal agreement between parties (as individuals or groups) according to terms protected by coercive sanctions, alliance is a less formal and binding relationship, defined by general obligations of mutual aid and loyalty subject to ritual sanction. The joking relationship itself is a form of alliance, for "instead of specific duties to be fulfilled there is privileged disrespect and freedom or even license, and the only obligation is not to take offence at the disrespect so long as it is kept within certain bounds defined by custom" (Radcliffe-Brown 1952a, 103).

Why would there be such an obligation between a king and his public, if indeed the Ncwala represents a species of joking relationship? The answer, I believe, lies precisely in the nature of the political alliance between king and public. There is no legal contract binding the Swazi in support of their king. There is nothing *illegal* about public disaffection or successful rebellion led by a rival claimant to the throne or even fission of the political community. Instead, the alliance between the king and his public is inherently unstable, based on general obligations of mutual protection and support. The Ncwala dramatizes the very links through which opposition can be mobilized—through the queen mother and the regiments of the princely rivals—and thematizes the process of successful rebellion ("the enemies are the people . . . they hate him") and fission ("I would depart with my father") in order to mobilize the opposite obligation of the joking relationship—which is to not take such threats seriously but to treat them symbolically as an expression of loyalty. This interpretation of the Ncwala concurs with Gluckman's realization that

the social setting of the ritual is rebellion, but it shifts the focus of its performance away from the kingship and onto the king. *The primary function
of the Ncwala is not to protect the kingship but to strengthen the alliance between the king and his public—that is, to protect the king himself.* Because such
protection is not positively enforced by law, it is ritually maintained by the
religious obligation to perform the Ncwala for the benefit of the nation as a
whole. The Ncwala is in this manifold sense a ritual *against* rebellion, and this
explains why *non*participation, from Swazi perspectives, is regarded as an act
of rebellion.

The strength of this interpretation is that it builds on Gluckman's insights
but avoids his major mistake. The idea that rebellion constitutes the social
setting of the ritual, and that the king is distinguished from his office by the insults he suffers, can clearly be seen in the way the joking relationship operates.
But Gluckman's argument that the positive function of the ritual of rebellion
relates to the positive function of real rebellion, by supporting the kingship
over and above the king, finds no support in Radcliffe-Brown's theory of
permitted disrespect. The "functional" explanation suggested by the joking
relationship is simpler and more direct: the sacred dispraises of the Ncwala
prevent rebellion by strengthening the loyalties between a king and his public
where they are most likely to break down.[7]

This focus on the king, rather than his office per se, also informs the
symbolism of the Ncwala as a ritual of purification. In fact, most of the symbolism revolves around the king's body, when it is naked, exposed, secluded,
or smeared with medicines, and not the office of kingship, which remains
pure. The king's body is even extended to his *tinsila*, ritual blood brothers
who sicken for the king by absorbing his dirt. Hence, the second meaning of
the term *insila* is glossed by Marwick (1940, appendix 2) as "dirt." This dirt
derives from the petty quarrels, sorcery, and witchcraft that result from the
king's crosscutting obligations. For Beidelman, the king's purification con-
sists in his separation from the nation, its subgroups and social categories, a
transcendence of particularistic loyalties that unifies the nation as a whole. We
can push this interpretation further to show how the Ncwala symbolism of
purification in general, and the *simemo* songs in particular, correspond to (1)
the separation of the king's person from his office and (2) the recombination

---

7. Dispraise prevents rebellion, and praise can actually provoke it. Praise protects the kingship against the king by voicing ideal standards of incumbency against which the incumbent
is implicitly and sometimes explicitly criticized. For an elaboration of this theme, see John
Comaroff 1975 and chapter 2 of this volume.

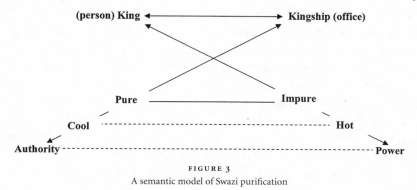

FIGURE 3
A semantic model of Swazi purification

of these identities into a purer "state." For it is the king, and not the kingship, who becomes impure during the course of the year.

The symbolism and "logic" of the Ncwala purification is heuristically summarized in figure 3: horizontal lines indicate symbolic opposition,[8] and diagonal lines indicate symbolic association. Ideally, the king and his office should be one, for the good king rules according to the values and duties of his office. This is indicated by the laudatory passages of the king's praises, which proclaim that the king is indeed *fit* to rule, exhibiting strength, courage, impartiality, generosity, and similar values of incumbency. That the king must be pure is stated openly in the praise of the late Sobhuza II: "Cleanse him of pollution" (Kuper 1947, xi). An impure king who has accumulated the "dirt" of his subjects over the year must be purified, and his person made powerful and healthy again. Purification is effected, following Beidelman, through categorical separation, but in the analysis suggested by the joking relationship, it is effected upon the king's body. The king is stripped of official dress, indeed of all clothing, and his body "darkened," made potent and dangerous with medicines. In this condition the king is anomalous: betwixt and between agricultural seasons, outside his office, set apart from his people, he emerges as Silo, a monster of liminal status, the incarnation of raw, uncontrolled power. Even his dance follows no regular form but is wild and improvised. This power is dangerous because it is *unregulated by the office of kingship*. The semantic opposition between the king's person and his office becomes loaded with associations: at the point of maximum separation, when the king is a monster, darkened, and the year is at its turning point, the king represents power, his office authority; the king is impure, his office pure; the king is "hot," his

8. The dotted lines indicate "secondary" symbolic opposition.

office "cool." Thus, after Silo's emergence, the king is systematically "cooled" (Beidelman 1966, 391). His costume and medicines are removed, burned, and washed away by the rains. The king is cleansed for his office, so that power combines with authority, and the king returns to his people, fit to rule.

The separation and recombination of the king and his office is further represented by the sequence of praise–dispraise–praise that marks the ritual's processual form. Praise validates the authority of the king by fusing, so to speak, the attributes of his person with the values of high office. Dispraise, within the symbolic scheme sketched so far, marks, by way of a contrast, the separation of the king from his office. As an illocutionary act, a behabitive (Austin 1962, 152) to be precise, it blatantly denies the formal authority of high office, addressing instead the king's person in familiar, disrespectful, even obscene terms. Since the king is momentarily outside his office and without authority, such dispraise is permissible. And at the same time, in the joking relationship, dispraise of the king reinforces personal and sectional loyalties to the king himself. Thus, in concrete terms, as well as according to cosmological categories, the king's power is revitalized. Final praises conclude the Ncwala, bringing together the king and his office with renewed respect for his power and authority.

Conclusion

The value of analyzing the Swazi Ncwala as a species of joking relationship is both ethnographic and theoretical. The importance of the king's person, brought out by the joking relationship, corresponds with the identification of the king's body with the land in what has also been called a First Fruits ceremony. This association between the king's body and the ritual explains why the Ncwala was not performed during an interregnum, nor when the king was very young, but rather grew in potency as he achieved physical and social maturity (Kuper 1947, 221). The political function of the Ncwala as a joking relationship—the mobilization of loyalties to the king where structurally they are most vulnerable—also explains why the ritual was performed before waging battle (1947, 225), for at that strategic moment the withdrawal of the king's armed support could ruin him and clear the way for his rivals.

There remains a problem of classification. In Radcliffe-Brown's original theory, the joking relationship is sanctioned at all times. The Swazi Ncwala occurs at wide intervals and is prohibited at all other times. It is just this difference between joking relationships and what Van den Berghe (1963, 413–14) calls institutionalized license that prevents him from considering them both as a common type of social behavior. But there is nothing a priori in

Radcliffe-Brown's theory that says a joking relationship must operate at all times. Just as some joking relationships are symmetrical and others asymmetrical, and some are between close kin or affines and others between distant clans, we can argue a space for joking relationships that operate during specific times only, such as the Ncwala and perhaps many other rituals of "rebellion" (Gluckman 1954, 1956, 1963), of "conflict" (Norbeck 1963), and of "institutionalized license" (Van den Berghe 1963).[9] Moreover, if we do, the concepts of "familiarity" and "avoidance" in the original theory acquire a new dimension.

For Radcliffe-Brown, familiarity, as expressed in the joking relationship proper, is functionally equivalent to avoidance, because both forms of social behavior prevent open conflict between sets of potentially antagonistic actors. Given this functional equivalence, why do some relationships fall into a joking or familiar pattern while others assume a pattern of avoidance? The Ncwala provides a clue toward an answer because it contrasts ritualized "familiarity" between the king and his public, in the form of dispraise, with what is normally "avoidance" and respect for his authority, in the form of praise. Normally, the Swazi avoid their king: the queen mother and princes live in separate royal villages, the king himself settles away from the official capital, and when he appears in public, "men sit at a distance from him, women do not raise their eyes to his, when he moves, attendants *shout his praises*" (Kuper 1947, 70; my emphasis). At the height of the Ncwala, however, the king is dispraised in exceedingly familiar terms. Praise and dispraise thus correspond consistently with avoidance and familiarity and contrast the authority of the king's office with the power of his person.

The Swazi king requires both forms of address from his public: praise to validate the authority of his office, dispraise to purify his person and revitalize his power. As speech acts, the "avoidance" of praise and the "joking" of dispraise mobilize complementary sets of obligations. By merging the king with high office, praise obliges the king to maintain the values of incumbency. By separating the king from high office, dispraise obliges the public to maintain loyal support for his person. Far from violating the attributes of a proper joking relationship, the Swazi Ncwala helps to situate them within a broader sociolinguistic theory.

9. Cohen (1982, 24) approaches this position when he likens a polyethnic London carnival to "a grand 'joking relationship.'"

4

Discourse and Its Disclosures

It is not uncommon for those who live amongst primitive peoples to come across "obscenity" in speech and action. This "obscenity" is often not an expression by an individual uttered under great stress and condemned as bad taste, but is an expression by a group of persons and is permitted and even prescribed by society. (Evans-Pritchard 1965, 76)

Thus opens an early essay by E. E. Evans-Pritchard, excerpted from his doctoral thesis and first published in 1929: "Some Collective Expressions of Obscenity in Africa." Although lacking the polish of his more mature writings, the essay represents the first systematic approach to ritually sanctioned license and "licentiousness" in Africa, bringing together scattered texts in published accounts with his own Azande material. Several important ideas were foreshadowed in this essay, anticipating Radcliffe-Brown's theory of "permitted disrespect," Gluckman's work on rituals of rebellion, and even Turner's studies of ritual liminality,[1] for central to Evans-Pritchard's argument was the insight that sanctioned obscenities made social sense by channeling repressed desire and "pent-up emotion" (1965, 95) into harmless "palliatives" (100) and collective activities that were generally (but not exclusively) sanctified by ceremonial. I am not suggesting that Evans-Pritchard was *ever* a psychological reductionist, despite his flirtation with Freud in the essay.[2] As his 1937 study of Zande witchcraft would later reveal, he might incline toward a social theory

1. For exemplary statements of these theoretical positions, see, e.g., Radcliffe-Brown 1952a; Gluckman 1954; Turner 1967. For related discussions of licentious discourse as "joking," see Junod 1927 (especially the *Annotatio quarta* 1, p. 516); Labouret 1929; Paulme 1939; Griaule 1948.

2. Evans-Pritchard (1965, 100n1), for example, states that "the explanation I have given here is largely in accord with psychoanalytical theory which would consider that the function of such obscenity is to act as a drive and palliative of labour, regarding the obscenities as a result of a

of the psychological but never toward a psychological theory of the social. Nonetheless, the problem of repression remained central to his earlier essay, a problem which has returned, in various guises, to haunt anthropological studies of ritualized license despite principled stands against psychological explanations (Reay 1959; Norbeck 1963; Van den Berghe 1963; Harris 1978; Heald 1982, 1989).

Today Evans-Pritchard's essay is history, and its relevance remains more a matter of intellectual genealogy than of contemporary research. It is now de rigueur to locate verbal art and performance within sociopolitical relations of textual production, exploring the poetic and strategic values, dynamic ambiguities, and complex historicities of what Barber and de Moraes Farias (1989) have called "discourse and its disguises." The effect has been to destabilize conventional distinctions between oral texts and social contexts precisely because oral literatures produce such instabilities—by remapping social categories, refashioning social identities, and invoking rival histories and memories to shape and reorient social action.[3] But if discourse masks and disguises, by cloaking protest and criticism in poetry and praise, it also reveals and discloses, giving active voice to hidden passions and secrets that are otherwise repressed. It is this latter aspect of ritual discourse—one first theorized by Evans-Pritchard—that this chapter will explore in songs performed during the Oroyeye festival of Ayede-Ekiti in northeastern Yorubaland. Following more dynamic approaches to the interpretation of African oral texts (Barber 1991a; Barber and de Moraes Farias 1989; Irvine 1993, 1996), I will locate these songs within a variety of shifting contexts, ranging from the specific social project of the festival itself—which is to ostracize thieves and stigmatize "evildoers"— to the sexual, sociopolitical, and historical "subtexts" which, when voiced, account for the festival's deeper meanings and ritual power.

In so doing, I hope to go beyond canonical accounts of how ritualized ostracism upholds general norms of sociability (although such norms are clearly invoked), for, as we shall see, the "canalizing" functions of sanctioned obscenity and abuse are far from harmless palliatives for those under attack and represent considerable agency on the part of those who control the discourse. Nor do they merely redress antisocial behavior, for the "grandmothers" (*yeye*)

---

clash between necessary labour (reality principle) and the desire to avoid exertion (pain-pleasure principle)," although he proceeds to distance himself from further developments of this thesis.

3. The concept of "entextualization" has been developed by Silverstein and associates to identify the discursive separation of text from context, which is in a sense the logical complement of discursive contextualization. For theoretical elaborations and applications of this perspective, see Silverstein and Urban 1996.

of the Oroyeye festival recover repressed historical memories and dynastic claims that, in times of crisis, can trigger social and political change. True by definition, Oroyeye texts not only constitute an effective form of political criticism—in one famous case rallying the public to depose an errant *ọba* (king)—but also establish a public archive of evidence for local magistrates and historians in adducing testimony, citing precedents, and recalling critical moments in Ayede's turbulent past.

Oroyeye in the Kingdom of Ayede

The cult of Oroyeye is not typical of the Yoruba ritual associations convention-ally referred to as orisha cults in that its ritual functions are much more spe-cialized. Whereas cults of the orisha—such as Shango, Ogun, Yemoja, Oshun, and Obatala, to name the most widely known—have complex priesthoods with various grades of titleholders, ritual specialists, and devotees housed in town shrines (*ipara*), the Oroyeye cult is relatively simple, consisting of a core of eight untitled women from Imela lineage in Ayede's Owaiye quarter. And unlike Ayede's dominant orisha cults (Yemoja, Orisha Ojuna, Orisha Iyagba, Olua, and Oloke), which, as I have described elsewhere (Apter 1992), invoke the power of their deities to remake and revise the body politic during elabo-rate annual festivals, the powers of Oroyeye priestesses are explicitly punitive. Their task as social critics is to expose, abuse, and, in the most serious cases, curse malefactors, mobilizing the force of public censure and condemnation to bear upon their misdeeds and reputations. The consequences of such criti-cisms vary, ranging from the immediate payment of a small fine to save face in response to mild teasing[4] to full-fledged ostracism, exile, and death resulting from the most serious abuses (*èébú*) and curses (*èpè*). As one Ayede man ex-plained to me, "If you provoke the worshippers of Oroyeye, they will mourn for you as if you are dead. If you are not careful, you will die." He went on to illustrate the cult's sweeping powers and indifference to status and office: "Nobody is too high or too low for the 'sting' of Oroyeye. Not even Kabiyesi [lit., "His Highness"; i.e., the king]. People have gone into exile after Oroyeye. In the past, if you mistreated your slaves, you got into trouble."

Although, as far as I can tell, the Oroyeye cult is regionally limited to cer-tain northeastern Yoruba towns, such as Iye and Itapaji, within Ayede's wider

---

4. After paying the fine and begging the Oroyeye cult for mercy, such a mild offender must sacrifice to his or her ancestors in a ceremony called Àawọ. The connection between Oroyeye and lineage identity is discussed below.

political kingdom (see fig. 4), similar ritual functions have been recorded in the Orepepee segment of the Oramfe festival in Ondo (Olupona 1991, 96–105) and in the Gelede festivals of Egbado, Awori, and other subcultural areas in southwestern Yorubaland (Drewal and Drewal 1983, xix–xx et passim; R. Thompson 1976, 14/1–7; Harper 1970, for the northwestern town of Ijio, near Sabe) during the nocturnal ceremony of Oro Efe.[5] Describing an Efe ritual in the town of Ajilete, Thompson (1976, 14/4–5) relates how "the priestess leads the singers to the night market where they perform criticisms of local society," adding that "the word, Efe, means 'just joking' to emphasize the license by which the singers allude to misdemeanors and other indiscretions." Drewal and Drewal (1983, 38–61) provide extended documentation and analysis of Efe songs, which invoke the power of witches in the euphemism of "the mothers" (*iyá wa*) to lampoon, chastise, and curse targeted enemies of the people.[6] Resembling Oroyeye songs in both substance and spirit, with similarly complex intertextualities and discursive functions,[7] Efe songs belong to an elaborate masquerade association totally absent among Ekiti Yoruba. But, despite their different ritual media and iconographies, both cults seem to share an underlying cultural logic,[8] for, like Oro Efe and its Gelede dancers, Oroyeye appeals to the power (*àṣẹ*) of women and witches to placate "negative" witchcraft and disclose malevolent agency.

In this respect, the term *yeye* conveys a range of related meanings. Its primary denotation of "grandmother" (in Ekiti dialect) represents the senior

5. The Edì festivals of the goddess Moremi celebrated in Ife also feature priestesses who indulge in obscene songs and target evildoers. In addition, Ogunba (1982, 37) cites interesting examples of what he calls satirical, political, and interrogatory genres of "occasional festival songs," some of which are sung by women and resemble Oroyeye songs in content if not in form. He collected them from different Ijebu "purification festivals" but neglects to tell us which ones. Moreover, he argues that the songs developed out of earlier ritual genres into more secular performances. Certainly, the political song praising Chief Obafemi Awolowo as a "sanitary inspector" (1982, 43–45) is a gem of neocolonial allegory.

6. Drewal and Drewal also cite Asiwaju 1975 and Olabimtan 1970.

7. Drewal and Drewal (1983, 40) analyze the functions of Efe songs in terms of (1) incantation, (2) invocation, (3) social comment, (4) history, and (5) funeral commemoration, with more specific subdivisions. From a more generative perspective, Yai (1989, 63) highlights the "pre-performance criticism" and social production of Efe songs during the *igbalè* sessions of the Gelede society, which are off-limits to noninitiates. Ideally, I would provide comparable insights into the production of Oroyeye texts, but I had no access.

8. It is likely that Oro Efe and Oroyeye represent varieties of the Oro cult more generally, which is commonly known as a bull-roarer cult reserved for men and which is associated with the Osugbo (Ogboni) society among the Ijebu (Abraham 1962, 484–85). That Oroyeye represents a "female" voice in a male ritual complex brings the gender contrast into bold relief. Flynn (1997), however, reveals that women traders are in fact significantly involved with Oro cults.

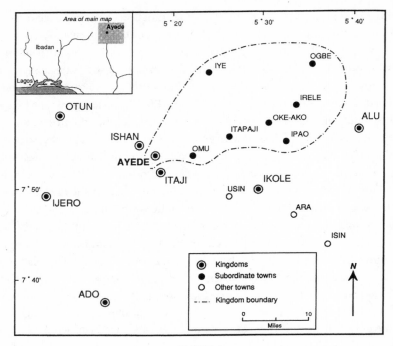

FIGURE 4
The Kingdom of Ayede

status of female elders who are honored and feared for their secret knowledge and hidden, self-contained powers.[9] "Oroyeye," I was told, thus means "festival [orò] of the grandmothers [yeye]," referring quite literally to the elderly women of the festival itself. But there is more to the grandmothers than meets the eye. Their very bodies are repositories of àṣẹ—the concentrated power of lifeblood and verbal command that motivates all ritual activity. Describing the "mothers" of Gelede ritual, Drewal and Drewal (1983, 75) explain, "Elderly women, those past menopause, are most likely to possess this power, not only because of their cool, covert, secretive characters but also because they retain blood that possesses àṣẹ, vital force. A praise name for the aged mothers is 'the one with the vagina that turns upside down without pouring blood.'" As we shall see, it is precisely this power of elderly women, congealed in the blood of their wombs and unleashed by their speech, that sanctions the discourse of Oroyeye and invests it with such concentrated àṣẹ. But if yeye refers to

9. Although Abraham (1962, 678) glosses yèyé as "mother," my assistants in Ayede insisted on "grandmother," emphasizing women beyond their childbearing years. In Ekiti dialect, yeye is pronounced with two midtones, as unmarked throughout the text.

the performers of this discourse, it also extends to the figure of their deity, Iyeye, the spiritual grandmother of the cult, who is described by some as an orisha. Iyeye is thus grandmotherhood deified, a righteous and vindictive guardian spirit who harnesses the powers of unbridled witchcraft to punish offenders and protect the community. In this sense Oroyeye signifies "festival of Iyeye," in honor of the deity herself. This semantico-pragmatic slippage between devotees and deity is of course ritually coherent since, during the festival, the priestesses become possessed by Iyeye, serving as vehicles of her voice.[10]

The deictic dimensions of ritual speech—more specifically, the grammatical shifting of speaking subjects between devotees, deities, and various social actors and categories—are a critical component of the language of àṣẹ, which I have explicated elsewhere in some detail (Apter 1992, 117–48). As we shall see, the "I," "you," and "we" of Oroyeye texts are in constant motion, not only remapping the "participation structure" (Irvine 1996, 132–36) of speech events but also sustaining multiple possibilities of discursive implication within a given utterance.[11] For now, I will emphasize the most basic consequence of the shifting grammatical subject for the priestesses themselves, which is to provide them with immunity and place their judgments beyond appeal. The priestesses, I was told, can never be challenged. They are incapable of error, not only because they know the details of each case but because their discourse belongs to their omniscient deity (Iyeye), who communicates *through* them. To illustrate the binding authority of the cult's pronouncements, I was told of an incident in 1975 when a woman in Ayede was abused by Oroyeye for using witchcraft against her husband, his second wife, and their son (fig. 5). Challenging the allegation by the son, the woman called the police, and the

10. Barber noted that Oroyeye may represent a generic praise-name for the female ritual power found in many festivals and orisha cults, rather than a specific cognomen as such: "I wish to query the name of this cult. Clearly the Ayede people refer to it as Oroyeye, but this strikes me as an oriki/adura-like epithet or invocation rather than a real name for an *orisa* such as Shango, Moremi, or Yemoja. During the Oshun festival in Oshogbo, for example, one could always hear the recurrent refrain of *orò yèyé o . . . !* chanted by the women who went to draw sacred water from the river. The same invocation could be heard also at the annual festivals of the river goddess Otin in Inisha, Okuku, or Oyan" (Karin Barber, personal communication, April 1997). Indeed, even in Ayede the priestesses of Orisha Iyagba sing the same epithet under similar conditions. I can only reply that indigenous testimony in Ayede repeatedly asserted that Oroyeye was the festival of grandmothers and treated Iyeye as a deity. It is possible that the priestesses are allied with the Olua cult of Owaiye quarter.

11. For rigorous theoretical reformulations of the linguistic processes involved in the discursive *production* of context, see the editors' introduction to Duranti and Goodwin 1992, with special reference to the essay by Hanks (1992). See also Silverstein 1976b, 1993.

(1)   (2)

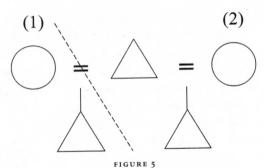

FIGURE 5
The witchcraft of lineage segmentation and fission

case was brought before the Àtá (Ayede's king). The police were abused by the "grandmothers" and the Àtá told the police to go.

The unilateral power and immunity of the Oroyeye cult, which during the festival extend over the king, are all the more significant in the context of Ayede's dynastic history. Like many Ekiti kingdoms of northeastern Yorubaland, Ayede developed from a refugee settlement of relatively decentralized villages and village clusters—what Obayemi (1971, 205–9) calls "ministates"—that were sacked by Nupe, Ilorin, and Ibadan invaders during the nineteenth-century wars and reorganized under strongmen who were then recognized as kings. Founded circa 1845 by the Ekiti warlord Eshubiyi (Johnson 1921, 308, 403), who led a core of refugees from the town of Iye to resettle between the older kingdoms of Ishan and Itaji, Ayede was augmented by an influx of immigrants who together regrouped into the four "original" Iye quarters of Owaiye, Isaoye, Ejigbo, and Ilaaro and two additional "stranger" quarters of Odoalu and Egbe-Oba. Although there is much disagreement over particulars, since dynastic history always involves a contest of political claims, local historians generally agree that the former Olú of Iye lost his crown to Eshubiyi, who tricked the Iye people into subjection by proclaiming himself the Àtá of Ayede, thereby founding a new ruling dynasty.[12] Eshubiyi's suppression of the Iye chiefs and his usurpation of the kingship not only bear directly upon the history of the Oroyeye cult, which was brought to Ayede from Iye, but, more important, underlie the active role performed by the cult in opposing Eshubiyi's rise to power and in alluding to the repression and potential restoration of Iye kingship in its songs.

The Oroyeye cult would hardly have a neutral voice in dynastic affairs, since it was (and remains) vested in the very lineage—that of Imela in Owaiye quarter—which owned the title of Olú in Iye. In other words, Imela was the

12. For details of the ritual mechanisms by which Eshubiyi effected this dynastic usurpation, see Apter 1992, 45–69.

former royal lineage of Iye, and its Oroyeye cult took an active role in protecting the kingship from outside claims. The late Michael B. Ayeni, who served as the magistrate of Ayede's first customary court under the British and became a recognized authority on Iye history, told of a struggle before the rise of Eshubiyi, when three factions sought to rotate the kingship between three additional lineages: Abudo of Owaiye quarter, Ilaa of Isaoye quarter, and Ilesi of Ejigbo quarter. During the festival, the cult members of Oroyeye came out, singing:

> Onímẹ̀là,
> Ẹ̀yin mọ̀n la ṣe Olú Ìye.

> You people of Imela,
> You [alone] make the Olú of Iye.

Although Michael Ayeni quoted the song to illustrate a historical struggle over dynastic succession, the text also illuminates the cult's very engagement within that struggle, voicing its opposition to rival political claims. Given the Oroyeye cult's proprietary interest in the crown, it is hardly surprising that the cult expressed alarm over the rise of the warlord Eshubiyi, anticipating his eventual usurpation of the kingship in the following warning song:

> Onímògún, alákoto,
> Ó ńṣèrù bà Ìye.

> Onimogun, owner of the calabash crown,
> He is threatening the people of Iye.

The text plays on the ambiguity of *alákoto*, which doubles as "owner of a deep calabash" (or "calabash crown") and as a type of military helmet worn in battle.[13] The "calabash crown" refers to the ritual calabash of the Orisha Ojuna cult in Ayede,[14] which Onimogun brought to Iye and bestowed upon his son, Eshubiyi, who used it to consolidate ritual control and build up his power base in Iye and later in Ayede, where the Orisha Ojuna cult became a major town cult. Thus, the primary meanings of *alákoto*, as "calabash crown" and

---

13. *Alákoto* also means "girl no longer a virgin" (Abraham 1962, 383), suggesting a possible third reference to the scandal of Eshubiyi's adulterous paternity, barring him from royal office as an illegitimate son of a civil chief. Mr. Michael B. Ayeni adduced the text while recounting the story of Onimogun's impregnation of the Obasakan's wife (who, because she was married, was no longer a virgin) and the subsequent birth of Eshubiyi, the future king (personal interview, March 1984). I do not know if Mr. Ayeni intended to convey this meaning of *alákoto* in the text.

14. For a video clip of this calabash crown during Ayede's Orisha Ojuna festival, 19 August 1993, see www.international.ucla.edu/africa/yra/.

"helmet," signify the dangerous potential of Orisha Ojuna as an external source and sign of Eshubiyi's growing military power.

A related Oroyeye song dating from this period warns against the political dangers of the calabash crown in order to mobilize opposition against Eshubiyi's emerging political agenda:

> Olú Ìye kì í dé akoto.

> Olú of Iye never wears a calabash crown.

The song responded to Eshubiyi's effort to bring Iye within the ritual field of Orisha Ojuna by demanding that the Olú pay tribute and express obeisance to its festival, which was owned by the *bàálè* of Otunja in Ikole.[15] By rejecting the calabash crown the Olú of Iye would reaffirm his politico-ritual autonomy. Hence an expanded form of this text (which was provided in English):

> *Bàálè* Otunja is sending to inform you that the festival of *otèmúrù*
> [the sacred water of Orisha Ojuna in Ikole] is near.
> The Olú of Iye never wears a calabash crown.
> Are you not preparing for a fight?[16]

The struggle that followed is alive and well in the historical memory of the Iye "core" of Ayede's citizens, lurking beneath the surface of many contemporary chieftaincy disputes. The Iye settlers eventually lost their fight against Eshubiyi, who developed a military autocracy in Ayede and initiated the Eshubiyi ruling line. But if the Oroyeye cult failed, in the last instance, to thwart the ambitions of the infamous warrior king, it was not for lack of trying. Nor was the struggle completely in vain. Following a common Yoruba pattern, what it forfeited in political authority was retained within the ritual domain, in the cult of Oroyeye itself. Although the Imela lineage lost control over the kingship, its cult remained, as a sort of religious compensation for political dispossession, invoking the memory of the Olú dynasty in its annual crusade against internal enemies. As we shall see, in more recent texts, repressed claims of former kingship are repeatedly insinuated in Oroyeye songs, motivating their metaphors and animating their rituals as a continuous historical "subtext."

15. A *bàálè* is like the king of a town, but he cannot enjoy the privileges of kingship because his town is subordinate to a capital town with its proper *oba*. Thus, the *bàálè* of Otunja is subordinate to the Elékòlé of Ikole.

16. The text was recited by the late Michael B. Ayeni (personal interview, March 1984) to discredit the legitimacy of the Eshubiyi dynasty. An Iye native, Ayeni was ever loyal to the Olú ruling dynasty.

As the cult's historic struggle against Eshubiyi reveals, Oroyeye's political warnings and directives are not always heeded, and it would be incorrect to assume that the binding authority asserted in principle is always achieved in practice. The cult's pronouncements are always articulated within a competitive political field, and if those abused are sufficiently powerful, they can prevail against the voice of the grandmothers, although failed accusations remain as a rhetorical resource that can be resurrected as evidence in subsequent conflicts. In this respect, Oroyeye texts constitute a public record of popular opinion which accumulates over time and resurfaces in other discursive genres when embedded or alluded to in *oríkì* (praise-poetry) and in *itàn* (history).[17] During the festival of Orisha Oniyi which I attended in Ejigbo quarter (in 1984), for example, the celebrants were "praised" with an Oroyeye song that warned against cult fission:

> *Ọmọ Èjìgbò,*
> *Ẹ má pin òrìṣà ṣe ẹta.*

> Children of Ejigbo,
> Do not split your orisha into three.

When I initially inquired about this text, I was told that it was simply a praise for Orisha Oniyi, but eventually I learned its "secret": it was a veiled attack against Chief Ọbásùn, who was elevated above Chief Ọbasalo by the Àtá Eshubiyi to represent the Ejigbo quarter in the king's council of civil chiefs. Since Chief Ọbásùn originated from Obo Ora, he was not considered a bona fide Iye native and was resented by the more "senior" Iye chiefs, who saw their power bypassed by a "stranger" in collusion with the new Àtá. To consolidate his local power base, Chief Ọbásùn claimed a title in Orisha Oniyi through his mother, thereby "splitting" the cult into a third lineage segment (fig. 6).[18] The Oroyeye text was thus produced as a warning against Eshubiyi's political strategy of imposing "stranger" chiefs over Iye quarters, but in concrete terms the warning failed, and today Chief Ọbásùn ranks first among the civil chiefs. Resurrected as a "praise" during the Orisha Oniyi festival of 1984, the text registered the political resentment of the displaced chiefs in Ejigbo quarter and could resurface again if Chief Ọbásùn loses his grip and is subject to attack by powerful rivals.

---

17. For an illuminating analysis of the gendered associations of *oríkì* with women and *itàn* with men, see Barber 1990, 330–34.

18. The cult of Orisha Oniyi was already divided between Obasalu and Oloso segments of Ilewa lineage.

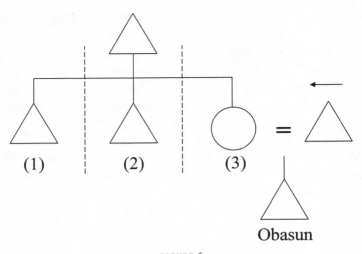

Obasun

FIGURE 6
Fissiparous consequences of complimentary filiation

Such strategies of indirection are not typical of all Oroyeye texts but seem to occur when their recommended outcome is uncertain. The songs of warning against Eshubiyi and Chief Ọbásùn do not identify their culprits by name but refer to the ritual icons and associations through which they accumulated power, as in the calabash crown of Orisha Ojuna and the cult of Orisha Oniyi in Ejigbo quarter. The songs thereby objectify ritual as the medium of power competition, as if to stake their challenge and retreat within the interpretive ambiguities which ritual sustains. But not all Oroyeye texts work that way, and when political conditions are right, direct accusations hit their mark like the verbal arrows of incantations (*ọfọ*). For example, when Ayede's infamous Àtá Gabriel Osho began to rule autocratically—intimidating his chiefs and punishing his critics—local constituencies and subordinate towns within the district turned against him in a historic power struggle which he eventually lost; he was deposed and exiled in 1935 (Apter 1992, 78–81). During this struggle, when the townspeople assembled in the marketplace to voice their grievances against the king, Gabriel Osho was accused of stealing goats, a charge of heinous antisociality, since goats roam freely in Yoruba towns, unattended for days. The theft of such goats is thus a serious breach of community trust, and when such an accusation is directed against a king, it signals public disaffection.[19] Soon afterward, the Oroyeye cult amplified this

19. On a basic structural level, the theft of a goat by a king inverts the royal ritual imperative of supplying a goat to the town for collective sacrifice and protection. In Ayede, the Àtá must supply such a goat during the Orisha Ojuna festival, whereas during the Yemoja festival he must

accusation in a song of abuse which devotees sang at the palace and throughout the town:

> Ìkokò t'ó ńkẹran kó adìyẹ.
> Ínijilẹ̀.
> Ọdẹ wọ̀nyí ẹ máa kiyèsí.
> Wọ́n ńkó kèbukẹ́bu.

> Spotted Hyena steals goats and chickens.
> It is serious [lit., "deep"].[20]
> You hunters take notice.
> He takes indiscriminately.

In addition to its general defamatory thrust, several features of the song text warrant special consideration. First, the cognomen "Spotted Hyena" comes from the praise-name (*oríki*) of the first Àtá, Eshubiyi, the original, infamous warrior king who usurped the kingship to inaugurate his ruling dynasty. Since the praise-name, with high office, devolves down the royal lineage, it also denotes the ruling incumbent. Thus, if "Spotted Hyena" refers historically to the first Àtá, who "stole" the crown from the Iye dynasty, it also refers more immediately to his patrilineal descendant Gabriel Osho, who "stole," as it were, from the public trust. This double interpretation is supported by the fact that the song—like all Oroyeye songs—was sung in Iye dialect, as indicated by *ínijilẹ̀* ("it is serious" or, lit., "deep"), which uses a high tone /í/ rather than a high tone /ó/ to mark the third-person singular, literally invoking the Iye quarters in Ayede. As such, the song recuperates the cult's previous, if unsuccessful, campaign against Eshubiyi's encroaching "calabash crown," thereby framing the struggle against Osho within an original struggle against the Eshubiyi ruling house. Furthermore, the hunters who were advised to take note of the theft were of course the armed guardians of the community, and their invocation raises the threat of armed insurrection against Osho. Moreover, reference to the thief as 'Wọ́n' (followed by the continuous present tense

---

provide a ram for Shango. It is interesting to note that when the Resident of Ondo Province investigated the allegations against Gabriel Osho, the theft of goats was recorded as a literal civil offense: "a delegation of Ayede title holders spoke on behalf of all and accused the Ata of the theft of goats and stated that they did not wish to acknowledge him any longer" (Carr 1934, 1).

20. The song's assertion that the matter surrounding the king's theft of chickens and goats is "deep" (*jinlẹ̀*) offers a valuable glimpse into a more general property of deep knowledge in Yoruba hermeneutics, which is its capacity to challenge authority structures and, when conditions are right, break out into open articulation. The truth of the cult's accusation—against none other than the king himself—is of course predicated on its access to the deep knowledge of the grandmothers.

marker /ń/) employs the formal or distanced style of third-person address in Yoruba (in a sense, the royal "he" becomes "they"), indicating in no uncertain terms that the present incumbent is the target of attack. And finally, since the grandmothers (*yeye*) sang the song, the accusation was ritually sanctioned and de facto true, beyond dispute.

The eventual deposition of Gabriel Osho does not illustrate the ultimate efficacy of Oroyeye songs as media of political action, since many other factors (including the judgment of the district officer) were involved in the power struggle, and the king might have survived the crisis had he played his cards differently. What is illustrated, however, is how such songs of abuse brought a repressed past (the usurpation of the Iye chiefs) to bear upon the present (the political crimes of Gabriel Osho) through a poetics of shifting references and revelations that channeled and articulated collective action against the king. Not all targets, however, are so lofty, and not all songs so serious. To grasp Oroyeye's broader discursive field, we can focus on the festival itself, as celebrated in April 1983.

Sexual Politics

The Oroyeye festival began after sundown in the marketplace, where Ayede's youths convened beneath the darkness of a new moon.[21] No light was allowed. The kerosene lamps of the night market were extinguished, and flashlights were banned. It was the opening ceremonial Àjàkadì, or wrestling match, when the young men of Ayede's junior age-sets divide the town into two "sides," one called Isaoye, representing the four "original" Iye quarters which migrated under Eshubiyi's protection to their present location during the nineteenth-century wars, the other called Odoalu, representing the quarters of "strangers" who emigrated to Ayede from the Ikole and Yagba areas (including Alu) farther east (table 2). The town was thus organized into two wrestling teams of indigenes and strangers. Each side was stratified by equivalent age-sets, which carry the same name but meet on alternating fortnights during the year. The wrestling would last for fourteen nights, ascending from younger to older contestants. The atmosphere was jovial but tense as reputations rose and fell with each match. While the young men fought with their bodies, the young girls of Isaoye and Odoalu fought with words, praising the winning

---

21. The festival described began on 25 April 1983. All the texts in this section were recorded by me in situ. The songs of homage and incrimination in the next section were recorded over the following seven days.

TABLE 2
Ritual remapping of Ayede's quarters

Ayede quarters	Town "sides"	Associated subordinate towns
1. Isaoye	"Isaoye"	Iye, Omu, Itapaji
2. Ejigbo	(indigenes)	
3. Owaiye		
4. Ilaaro		
5. Odoalu	"Odoalu"	Ipao, Irele, Oke-Ako
6. Egbe-Oba	(strangers)	

wrestlers with flattery (*ìyìn*) and insulting the losers with abuse (*èébú*).[22] Their stated goal was to provoke the anger of the loser, although such abuse is always cast in the spirit of a joke (*afè* in Iye dialect, *èfè* in standard Yoruba).

The Ajàkadì opened with the young women of Odoalu hurling general insults against their female counterparts from the Isaoye "side":

> Ọni ìyà bí a pa
> Ìsàoyé rí a lọ
> Ìsàoyé súę́!
>
> Alábę̀ riró tótó,
> Akó fáńsì okó.   5
> Ojo iń ṣe yín ni,
> Àbę́rù í bà ín?
>
> Éè éè!
> Ìsàoyè ró dọ́kọ lọ́jà,
> A dòbò dé'lę pi.   10
> Èpípá òbò rę́ ṣíjo lọ́jà.
> Òkúrú ń mú yèyé,
> Elékò bêè kó adìẹ.

Only someone who will die in poverty
Will go [and join] Isaoye.
Isaoye bullshit!

22. The term *ọmọgé*, which I am glossing as "young girls" and "young women," has no precise equivalent in English. It denotes the specific status and attributes of an attractive unmarried young woman, presumably without children, who is, as Edmund Leach (1958, 133) would say, "fair game for a love affair." Unmarried young women with children are sometimes referred to by their female age-mates as "after one" (child) or "after two" (children) in Nigerian English slang.

You with dripping vaginas,
Victims of penis dirt.   5
Are you ashamed,
Or do you feel afraid?

No way!
It is the [women of] Isaoye who are promiscuous
    in the marketplace,
Dragging the earth with their vaginas.   10
The scabs of your vaginas have scaled off in heaps
    in the marketplace.
Lady victims of scabies,
Your mouths are like chicken beaks.[23]

The insults are transparent enough. The Odoalu girls are putting the rival side down as disgraceful and impoverished, implying that no Odoalu girl in her right mind would marry into Isaoye (given virilocal residence patterns). Isaoye girls, moreover, are debased and polluted—sleeping with unclean men, their vaginas drip from infections. Rather than feel shame or fear, these girls spread their venereal contagions in the marketplace, where their vaginal scabs form "heaps" from their excessive promiscuity. To top it off, Isaoye girls are ugly, with mouths like chicken beaks.

Following these general sexual insults, the song texts become more specific, cursing an individual male wrestler—named Taye—from Isaoye so that he will fall:

> Bírí gbe.
> Òyì gbe.
> Táyé elétù ń'ńu,
> Ìbàjẹ́ a ba tẹre jẹ́,
> Ìbàjẹ́.[24]

Let him be carried by the wind.
Let him be carried by dizziness.
Taye, whose stomach is full of gunpowder,

23. I would like to thank Dr. 'Dejo Michael Afolayan for the initial transcription and translation of my Oroyeye tapes, and Mr. Olusanya Ibitoye (of Ayede) for correcting specific translations and interpretations according to his intimate knowledge of the town and cult.

24. This curse exemplifies one of the morphosyntactic features that characterize àṣẹ (power, performative efficacy) in ritual speech, namely, the transposition of noun forms (in this example, ìbàjẹ́) into verb forms (in this example, bà . . . jẹ́) within the same utterance. For further discussion and permutations of this grammatical device, see Drewal and Drewal 1987, 226; Olatunji 1984, 152–64.

> May all that is yours be spoilt,
> May it be spoilt.

Taye, as it turned out, did lose the fight, in a battle that echoed men's agonistic struggles against visible and invisible enemies. His defeat was not only personal but seemed to bring Isaoye down with him as the chorus of insults shifted its attack:

> *Adé ró di,*
> *Bí ọní kọyìn.*

> The crown has thumped down,
> Like a bunch of palm kernels.

In this historically layered insult not only has Taye been deposed like a king but, more seriously, he has let his "side" down. Hailing from an Iye lineage in Isaoye, his failure not only recalls the historic failure of the Iye ruling dynasty to keep the crown from Eshubiyi but also echoes Gabriel Osho's shameful deposition in 1935, which was led largely by "big men" in the Odoalu quarter of Ayede and in the Yagba subordinate towns.[25] Finally, as the past is brought to bear upon the present, the fallen wrestler reminds Isaoye's side that even the current ruling house is vulnerable from attack by Odoalu wrestlers and warriors.[26]

If such humiliations are painful, however, they are temporary. In the next match, Isaoye's chorus turns to taunt their tormentors:

> *Odòàlù,*
> *Bèèmbẹ́ níkù,*
> *Abọgán wo mọ́ 'yán.*
>
> *Ọmọdé é gun'gi ọ̀gẹ̀dẹ̀*
> *A yọ́ báárá, aṣe wì.*   5
>
> *Ẹ bá ti mọ́n jà, ẹ wí sí a.*
> *Iwòwò so un gbó lóko?*
>
> *Odòàlù sí kọ́ o?*
> *Gbogbo wọn ló ti dókó lọ.*
> *Odòàlù d'òúkọ.*   10

25. The Yagba towns within the kingdom of Ayede, which are Oke Ako, Irele, and Ipao, played a decisive role in the deposition of Àtá Gabriel Osho.

26. The same rebellious theme is ritually expressed in Ayede's Orisha Iyagba festival, when the Balógun Àòfin's warrior priestesses carry spears and cutlasses decorated with palm fronds. See Apter 1992, 156–60, for details.

B'alẹ́ bá lẹ,
À fọn fèrè polókó.

Odòàlù pa tírà sí bèbè,
Jínginní-jínginní.
Okó ló a dànù poo.   15

Ó nírun é nìrun,
Odòàlù dídó ni pọ̀nkí!

Ó ń sè kuru,
Òbò Àjàyí ń sẹ kuru wọ̀wọ̀.

Òní è m'óbò s'ahun,   20
Àfẹni okó rẹ bá rọ.

Ìsápá toro mọ́'yán,
Odòàlù toro m'ókó gbọnin.

Odòàlù kòì tẹra pọ̀,
Ọní lóyún sí gègè,   25
Owèlèwélé elékó béekó adìẹ.

[People of] Odoalu,
Protruding stomach like the *bẹ̀ẹ̀mbẹ́* drum,
One whose fangs hold fast to the pounded yam.

A child who climbs the banana tree
Will slide down and fall from it.   5

You shouldn't have attempted bashing us with chants.
Naked ones, can you hear us on the farm?

Where is Odoalu?
All of them have gone whoring.
Odoalu has become a he-goat.   10

When the evening comes,
The owner of a penis is beckoned with a whistle.

Odoalu girls add amulets to their waist beads,
Jinginni-jinginni.
It is the penis that breaks it away.   15

With or without [pubic] hair,
The vaginas of Odoalu are meant for constant copulation!

Giving out hot steam,
Ajayi's vagina is giving out hot steam profusely.

Oni is generous with her vagina,   20
Only one whose penis is impotent [cannot have
    intercourse with her].

[Just as] The sorrel soup clings to the pounded yam,
[So do] Odoalu girls cling to the penis.

Odoalu is never united,
People with pregnant necks [i.e., goiters],   25
Mouths like chicken beaks.

Isaoye's reply is reciprocally obscene and direct. Comparing their stomachs
to the *bèèmbé* drum casts a double insult to the people of Odoalu, since the
bèèmbé is basic to Odoalu's festival of Orisha Iyagba, symbolizing its ritual
power and easterly provenance.[27] Thus, the people of Odoalu, and their ritual,
are ugly. They are furthermore greedy gluttons, devouring pounded yam with
their "fangs." And if Isaoye's crown falls down the palm tree like a bunch of
palm kernels, the children of Odoalu cannot even make it to the top of the
banana tree but slide down trying. Lines 6–7 introduce a metapragmatic warning not to fight with speech, relegating Isaoye's opponents to the margins of
society and earshot, naked on their farms, deprived of agency. Odoalu girls are
accused of similar promiscuity, whistling at night for any man who walks by,
using medicines in their waist beads to attract sexual partners, and copulating
before puberty. Lines 18–21 target specific girls reputed to be "flirts," while the
charge that Odoalu as a whole is "never united" attacks the quarter's political
integrity.

In what was a gendered division of ritual labor, young men of Isaoye and
Odoalu fought each other to defend the reputation of their respective sides,
while young women abused each other to defame the reputation of the opposing side. The sanctioned obscenities were clearly uproarious, the vulgarities
unthinkable in any other public context, yet the game was played for real sta-
kes. For the young men, victory meant a bigger reputation and better chances

27. For a detailed discussion of the distribution of this drum throughout Yorubaland, in
many cases following Nupe migrations and festivals, see Thieme 1969, 146–72.

with the eligible young women.[28] Meanwhile, the young women could vent
their tongues and curse their rivals while surveying the available male talent.
By overstating female sexuality, by permitting the impermissible in hyperbolic
ritual discourse, and by disclosing that which is "normally" repressed, young
men and women could initiate sexual liaisons in that dangerous twilight zone
of premarital experimentation. What are the limits of the game? Clearly, the
voiced parodies of women's unbridled sexual appetites establish a collective
limitation, but these remain abstract. The images of rampant sexuality are hi-
larious because they are absurd. But personal attacks make the abstract concrete, and the absurd suddenly serious. We saw how two young women of
Odoalu were singled out by name and humiliated. For them the message was
more than just a warning not to overstep the limits of acceptable romantic
circulation. It constituted a social sanction, a text for the archive of collective
memories that could actually hurt their chances of a desirable marriage.[29]

In the larger context of Oroyeye as a whole, the Àjàkadì wrestling remained
fun and games. It provided a nocturnal backdrop for the real business of the
festival, which belongs to the "grandmothers" of Oroyeye, who target specific
malefactors and bring their misdeeds into the light of day. What concerns us at
this preliminary point in the festival is the construction of a basic parallelism
between male political competition through wrestling and female sexual competition through song, or, more simply, between the return of the politically
repressed and the return of the sexually repressed. These two modalities of
"permitted disrespect" displace the repressed desires of the sociopolitical col-
lectivity onto specific individuals in the community. If at night the sexual subtext dominated the discourse, in the daytime the political subtext took over.

Poetic Justice

"Anybody can join the Oroyeye cult, but the real people doing it are from
Owaiye" was the reply when I asked how members were recruited. Given
the layers of secrecy surrounding Yoruba ritual associations, it is never entirely clear to those on the outside (or even to some on the inside) who all
the members are. Oroyeye is reserved exclusively to women, yet I eventually
learned that their real leader was the Àró, an elderly man from the Imela lineage in Owaiye who also held the second-highest post within Ayede's senior

28. And to some extent, which I am unable to determine in any statistical sense, the young
men who fight each other will marry each other's classificatory "sisters."

29. As it turned out, the young woman here referred to as Ajayi became second wife to a
much older, illiterate farmer, a match that, according to her age-mates, suited her promiscuity.

age-set (called Erokesin). The connection between male age-sets and Oroyeye during the wrestling matches thus extends up the generational ladder through a hidden set of overlapping memberships or points of articulation that become clear only when mapped within the kingdom's entire sociopolitical organization and compared with the less centralized village clusters surrounding Ayede, including the now-subordinate town of Iye itself.[30] In its basic contours, the Oroyeye cult of women intersects with that level of the senior male age-set which includes the four Iye quarters (called *iye-merin*) of the Isaoye "side" but excludes the "stranger" quarters of Odoalu and Egbe-Oba, which form the Odoalu "side." This is why the Àró of Oroyeye is the number 2 man in Erokesin. The number 1 elder of Erokesin stands at the apex of the entire age-set system of the whole town (and kingdom, since he heads all age-sets of Ayede's subordinate towns), including the Odoalu side.

In addition to age-set stratification, the Oroyeye cult also articulates with lineage organization, through a very simple form of ancestor worship called Àà̀wọ. In this fairly low-key sacrifice, the lineage or household head places handfuls of pounded yam with some meat and melon seed (*ègúsí*) soup on the grave of an apical ancestor, adding palm oil, kola nut, and the blood of a cock while asking for protection. The ceremony is consciously associated with Oroyeye, since the two are performed together and form part of a greater ritual complex that not only distinguishes Ayede's Iye indigenes from immigrant "strangers" but extends the division throughout the historic kingdom at large. Of Ayede's subordinate towns, Iye, Itapaji, and Omu perform Àà̀wọ and celebrate Oroyeye, whereas the Yagba towns of Irele, Oke Ako, and Ipao do not.[31] The important point is that Ayede, Iye, Itapaji, and Omu perform the Àà̀wọ sacrifice and celebrate the Oroyeye festival at the same time in their respective ritual calendars, bringing the protection of ancestors to bear upon local events while mobilizing an Iye-centric ritual field within the wider kingdom. As we shall now see, the historic allusions of Oroyeye songs resurrect the former glory and unity of Iye in idioms of common descent, while the cult's indictments appear to focus on lineage fission.

The inner core of Oroyeye priestesses were eight in number during the first festival that I attended, but not all were present, since some were too old to make the rounds. With the two senior representatives dressed in the

---

30. See, for example, the politico-ritual patterns found in Ishan and its subordinate town of Ilemesho (Apter 1995).

31. It is interesting to note that Omu may well be the same town that Barber (1991b, 21) identifies in the *oríkì orílè* of *ilé* Elemeso in Ikole as performed in Okuku. This correspondence demonstrates the utility of *oríkì* as historical records of lineage migrations.

white cloth of purity and death—as elderly "grandmothers," they are already
entering the otherworld—the cult took possession of the town, proceeding
from household to household for seven days of ritualized evaluation.[32] I was
told that they proceed to the king's palace and abuse him first, after which
they abuse Yeye, the deity herself, but I was unable to confirm that this
actually occurred. What I did record during several festival outings was a
variety of discourse styles or genres, ranging from a relatively fixed stock of
ritual refrains to contingent, context-specific accusations and curses against
named malefactors. In ethnolinguistic terms, the priestesses sang a special type
of song called ìjúbà, which includes oríkì (praises) of individuals, to propitiate
the ancestors and pray for prosperity. As they approached each house with
ancestral propitiations, their praises were repaid with money, which in turn
triggered prayers that the household would prosper. There is perhaps an element of ritual blackmail in this, since a household head could be seen as
bribing the priestesses to register a positive report. But the logic of investment
and returns is more complex, since by recognizing the power of the cult, and
investing in its ritual protection, the addressee's name and status are effectively validated. Such payments are understood as thanks to the ancestors
for keeping the household free from scandal—a literal payment of homage.[33]
Moreover, when an addressee is indicted by the cult, there are no praises to
repay, and hence no opportunities for buying protection.

In more formal terms, the ìjúbà follows a parallel structure of four-line
stanzas, the first two lines of which are fluid and variable, indexing the addressee with the appropriate oríkì, flattery (ìyìn), or prayer (àdúrà); the second two lines are fixed and repetitive, paying homage to the cult's founding
ancestor from Iye. As such the ìjúbà is a double homage, the first to the living,
the second to the dead, bringing the former into the protective custody of
the latter through the very speech act itself, as well as through the subsequent reciprocal payments. The following stanzas illustrate this pattern with
paradigmatic simplicity:

> A-ti-Kékeré j'ológun,
> Mo mò a kan ní rẹ o.

32. Most major orisha festivals are preceded by fund-raising visits of priestesses to households
throughout the town. What distinguishes Oroyeye's visits is the explicit threat of ostracism. The
seven-day "outing" of the Oroyeye priestesses is identified in an announcement song: "Oròyeye
ó dé ò, / Olórò àrí simi kèje." (Oroyeye has arrived, / Owners of the festival that brings anxiety
for seven days.)

33. Hence, the Oroyeye text "I pay homage because the child that pays homage will not suffer
or go astray." For the first penetrating analysis of "paying" for homage as status validation in
Hausa society, see M. G. Smith 1957.

Aá júbà Àró onílẹ̀,
'Mọ aṣẹ̀jẹ̀ 'ye.

Ọmọ tilé olórí-Ilésì,   5
Orí dára àbo.
Aá júbà Àró onílẹ̀,
'Mọ aṣẹ̀jẹ̀ 'ye.

He who becomes a commander from childhood,
I am bowing low to you.
We shall pay homage to Àró Owner-of-the-land,
Offspring of Iye by blood.[34]

Child of the head of Ilesi [lineage],   5
May you have a good destiny [lit., may your head be good].
We shall pay homage to Àró Owner-of-the-land,
Offspring of Iye by blood.

In these typical, if ordinary, examples, the first two lines of each stanza reward specific individuals—and by extension their lineages—for correct behavior toward the cult and in the community. Thus, in lines 5–6, the Ilesi lineage in Owaiye quarter is praised through one of its sons. The text combines an *oríkì* ("Child of the head of Ilesi") with a prayer ("May you have a good destiny"), which simultaneously identifies the "head" of the Ilesi lineage with the destiny ("head") of the addressee. This fluid, contingently variable couplet contrasts with the fixed refrain of the second couplet, the "homage" to Àró, owner of the land, which identifies the important founding ancestor from Iye and, by extension, all descendants "by blood."[35] The allusions here are "deep." Àró

34. This translation is idiosyncratic, since *aṣẹ̀jẹ̀* can be more literally rendered as "one who bleeds," as well as "which is the blood." The "descent" translation comes from Mr. Olusanya Ibitoye, who, in correcting the original translation by Dr. 'Dejo Afolayan, consistently wrote, "offspring of Iye by blood." Dr. Afolayan, for the record, wrote, "Offspring of he-who-pays the vow and lives," according to a very different morphosyntactic parsing that also makes sense in the sociolinguistic context of paying homage. Since Mr. Ibitoye is an Ayede indigene with intimate knowledge of ritual-language idioms, I have gone with his translation. This does not mean that Mr. Ibitoye is right or even that both translations are mutually exclusive. But I do remain confident that Mr. Ibitoye's version represents the spirit, if not the "letter," of the dominant local meaning.

35. In a sense, the figure-ground distinction in the semantics of deixis (Hanks 1992, 60–71) extends here to the paradigmatic Oroyeye textual stanza, in which the first, fluid (variant) couplet focalizes a figure (usually a living person in the community), while the second, fixed (invariant) refrain relates this figure to the (indexical) ground. Is it by chance that Àró is also "Owner-of-the-earth/ground"?

is identified as the founder of Oroyeye, who brought the cult from Ife to Iye, from which it traveled to Ayede. As "Owner-of-the-land" he may be related to the deity (Onílè) of the Ogboni secret society, associating him with the collective authority to judge cases of incest, witchcraft, and crimes against the earth (Morton-Williams 1960b). This is supported by the fact that Abraham (1962, 65) glosses "Aro" as "one of the Ogboni Titleholders" and that the Morgan Report for Ondo State identifies "Aro" as first in rank among Iye's five "traditional" kingmakers (afòbajẹ), which are chiefly offices invested with ritual power to install, depose, and bury the king. Given the "ministate" structure of northeastern Yoruba village clusters, with kingmakers vested in age-sets (Forde 1951, 79–80; Krapf-Askari 1966, 5–9, 12–13), it is likely that the Àró was the senior title of Iye's complex age-set organization. (For details see Apter 1992, 40–45.) In any case, line 8, "Offspring of Iye by blood," refers to the first Àró, who was born in Iye, but implicitly alludes to the "original" Iye core within Ayede. Taken together, the fixed refrain of lines 3–4 and 7–8 ground the power and authority of Oroyeye's discourse in a historical charter of Iye kingship and kinship, a grounding in the sanctified power of the earth itself as protector of one blood.

Thus, even the simplest Oroyeye songs deploy complex discursive strategies. If the first flexible couplet tags specific individuals through their family names, implicating them in wider social groups, the second fixed couplet brings them into Iye's politico-ritual community, to which they must "pay" homage. Not all Oroyeye homage follows this strict pattern, since the first couplet can expand into multiple lines, depending on the length of the oríkì prayer or proverb chanted. In some songs, deities such as Shango, Ogun, and Orisha Iyagba or spiritual classes like the beings of earth or heaven are addressed, while in others the town as a whole is implored to cooperate (which, given the mounting tensions of the imminent 1983 elections, was no casual command).[36] At times, the Oroyeye singers address themselves and foreground their verbal art:

> Olórin máa gbọ,
> Aláfè ní i rónìkèje.
> A á 'júbà Àró Onílè,
> 'Mọ aṣèjè 'ye.

---

36. Thus, e.g.: "Ẹ Sà jùmọ̀ rìn, / Bí 'mọlèè jùmọ̀ rẹ yè. / A ájúbà Àró-Onílè, / 'Mọ aṣèjè ye." (You should all walk together, / Just as the deities walk together. / We shall pay homage to Àró Owner-of-the-land, / Offspring of Iye by blood.) For details of the election riots that followed, and their underlying ritual logic, see Apter 1992, 179–91.

Àfẹ̀rẹ́ bí somi-yín,   5
Ìsọgbé-ta'kùn-yan.
A ájúbà Àró Onílẹ̀,
'Mọ aṣẹ̀jẹ̀ 'apye.

Listen, singers,
Aláfẹ̀ has sent us to deliver these
messages for seven days.
We shall pay homage to Àró
Owner-of-the-land,
Offspring of Iye by blood.

Wind [that is] like knocking out teeth
    [i.e., a force to be reckoned with],   5
Have you forgotten? Let me quickly remind you
    [lit., mark it with a rope],[37]
We shall pay homage to Àró Owner-of-the-land,
Offspring of Iye by blood.

In these two stanzas the singers signal a coming shift from "homage" to
accusation, as they identify themselves as incriminating agents (line 2) whose
forceful speech, capable of knocking out teeth (line 5), not only punishes the
guilty but also polices collective memory (line 6). By drawing attention to
the danger of their speech in this warning, the Oroyeye priestesses prepare
the indexical ground for highlighting negative "figures" in the community.

In the Oroyeye festival of 1983, public enemy number 1 was identified as a
man named Oladiran. True, the Àtá of Ayede was mildly rebuked for his poverty and political impotence, but the real vindictive drama focused on the
heinous crime of a money-magic murder. As the priestesses reached the
culprit's house, their homage (ìjúbà) switched to curse (èpè):

Ọldìran,
Tilé ria raí bèrè rẹ̀ o.
Ilé ò kọ́ sílé rian lógbọ̀n-ọ́n Òkè-Òdò.
Ọmọ ò bá bá ṣiré,
Wọ̀ ọ́ bẹ̀ ẹ́ dàjùlé ọ̀run.   5

Ọdẹ ò perin lóko
O mọ́ járù 'a 'lé o.

37. These translations of lines 5 and 6 are rather free, based on Mr. Olusanya Ibitoye's
rendering of local idioms, which may not be found in standard Yoruba but which ring clear to
Ayede indigenes. The song is basically a warning to beware of the cult's power.

Ọládìran, ò-gbé-ni-pa,
Ó mọ̀ d'Èṣù ṣ'ọ̀rùn rẹ
Èwù rẹ ṣe'pọ́n 'á 'lé.   10

Ọládìran,
Ọrẹ o gbé a mú ṣ'owó,
Mọ̀ ró d'Èṣù ṣọ́rùn rẹ,
Ó-wẹ̀wù-èjè-á-'lé.

Oladiran,
All of us are asking for you.
The house you built in their compound
     at Oke-Odo.
The child you should have been playing with,
You instead sent to heaven [i.e., killed].   5

The hunter does not kill an elephant
Without [at least] bringing its tail home.
Oladiran, One-who-kidnaps-to-kill,
Eshu is on your neck [you are in trouble/
     stigmatized]
Your cloth is stained with blood on your way
     home.   10

Oladiran,
Ore, whom you used to make money
[for moneymaking jùjú medicine],
Has become the Eshu on your neck,
One-who-wears-bloody-cloth-on-his-way-
     home.

In contrast to the homage, the curse identifies the addressee by his personal name
only, conspicuously avoiding his oríkì-orílè (lineage praise-name). In effect,
Oladiran is nominally isolated from his kinsmen and all other social relations. His
house is identified by its place-name (Oke-Odo, or the lower hill; lit., "near
the river") but not its lineage name, which remains suppressed. He is then
accused of killing his kinsman (identified as Ore in line 12) for the egregious
crime of money-magic. The story was explained to me with alacrity.[38] What

38. Anybody who has tried to interview Yorubas about family and genealogical history will
know how reluctantly they provide information, since family history is a private affair, full
of disputes and secrets. Even simple household survey questions ring alarm bells over dubious
paternities, unofficial wives, land tenure, even lineage depth and span. Normally, at least in a small

follows is a free translation of the recorded explanation that was narrated in situ:

> Oladiran had an elder brother [ègbón] named Ore, born of the same father but of different mothers. Ore lived in Ayede, whereas Oladiran had moved to the town of Idanre. One day Oladiran came to Ayede and invited the elder brother to return to Idanre with him. When Ore refused, Oladiran compelled his elder brother to accompany him. Four days after they left, Oladiran came back home [to Ayede] and started asking for Ore, saying, "Where is my elder brother?" Then those who saw them leave Ayede together replied, "Haven't you driven him away for the last four days?" Thereafter, the relatives sent people to go with him in quest of his brother at Idanre. After getting there, Oladiran took the search team to track the forest. After searching the forest without success, they returned home.
>
> When these relatives gave the report of their abortive effort to locate Ore, the family decided to send a new group to Idanre. These men were sent as emissaries to the king of Idanre himself. They were instructed to tell the king that an Ayede native was lost in Idanre and that he must be found. The king gave them a cheerful welcome and told them that human beings would never get lost in his domain without good cause. Oladiran was therefore summoned to confess where he kept his elder brother. The elder brother's son went ahead with the police and arrested Oladiran. They did everything possible, but his whereabouts remain a mystery to this day. Oladiran now lives in Ayede, and, it being the time of Oroyeye's festival, he has become a target of Oroyeye's castigating songs. They have gone to his house at Oke-Odo [above the stream, north of the river, down the hill area, the southern part of town]. They are also singing in the homes of the members of his family.

I have quoted this passage at length because it provides an illuminating, example of how a subtext is glossed by ritual speech. (See also Barber 1990, 1991a, for subtexts glossed by oríkì.) In this performative context, the full story (itàn), normally known only to insiders, was freely proffered, since Oroyeye's task is to bring such misdeeds into the light of day. Oladiran is accused of leaving no trace of his brother. He is accused of kidnapping Ore and killing him for moneymaking medicine. Oladiran is in big trouble; indeed, Eshu is on his neck. His cloth is stained with the blood of his kinsman. In lines 8 and 14 of the Oroyeye song, Oladiran is effectively renamed. His lineage name is

---

town like Ayede, people will never discuss the affairs of other families, replying that, if you want to know about X's family, then go and ask them yourself. The zeal with which Oladiran's story was narrated to me by onlookers is itself ethnographically significant, illustrating a suspension of "normal" discursive constraints.

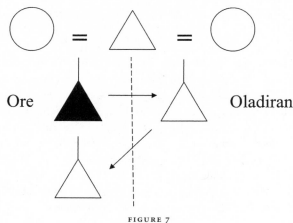

FIGURE 7
Fratricide and aborted devolution

replaced with the incriminating aliases One-who-kidnaps-to-kill and One-who-wears-bloody-cloth-on-his-way-home.[39] Soon afterward, his house was confiscated by the Àtá of Ayede, and Oladiran was jailed.

Returning to the subtext, we can see that there is more in this case than meets the eye. The fact that Oladiran and Ore were paternal half brothers may be significant because it is precisely between sons of the same father and different mothers that Yoruba lineage segmentation and fission occur (Lloyd 1955). The money-magic crime thus appears motivated by a structural drama of lineage dynamics, since, whatever actually happened, Ore's disappearance and Oladiran's return home would have shifted the lineage headship (and some of its corporately entailed property) to Oladiran, weakening Ore's lineage segment and possibly transferring Ore's house to Oladiran, since Yoruba family titles and properties can move "sideways" before moving "downward" (Lloyd 1962, 306; Goody 1970). In this respect, the fact that Ore's son arrested Oladiran can be seen as an act of filial vengeance which preempted the lateral transmission of Ore's lineage title and property to Oladiran and rerouted it vertically to the son himself (fig. 7). As for Oladiran, we can only conjecture. Perhaps he did kidnap and murder Ore to make money-magic with his head and body parts, and got caught. Or perhaps he killed Ore to gain his title and property, a crime that was configured in the idiom of money-magic. Maybe he was innocent, the victim of a terrible plot or of misfortune. One thing is certain. After Oroyeye's verbal strike, Oladiran was considered guilty by the town,

39. This image is particularly charged, since it inverts the sartorial idiom of family sociality in "family cloth" (aṣọ ẹbí). Instead of wearing the cloth of his kinsman, Oladiran wears a cloth that is stained by the blood of his kinsman.

despite the fact that he was acquitted in court, owing to lack of evidence. Banished from his house, he rented a room in another part of town, gradually lost his mind, and, according to popular reports, dropped dead at a crossroads ten years later in 1993.

Conclusion

To address the broader significance of the Oroyeye festival, I have tried to relocate its abusive texts in their historical and performative contexts. Within the historical context of Ayede kingdom, we have seen how the cult has had an active "voice" in important political affairs, including the negotiation of dynastic succession and the deposition of Gabriel Osho. In this respect the voice of the "grandmothers" has not been exactly neutral but has consistently championed the political claims of the displaced Iye chiefs. By resurrecting a repressed history—the usurpation of the Iye ruling line by the Àtá Eshubiyi—the cult reproduces a historical template of Ayede's founding which is brought to bear on contemporary events in order to explain and shape them. Part of the power of Oroyeye in Ayede, I would argue, is the return of the politically and historically repressed, in that the desire of the Iye order to reestablish its preeminence is ritually mobilized and discursively "canalized" (to return to Evans-Pritchard's original term) by the cult's very shifting from homage (ìjúbà) to abuse (àfè, èébú). If the priestesses protect the town by disclosing the crimes of specific scoundrels, they also protect a specific definition of the town, as "offspring of Iye by blood." When the Oroyeye priestesses take possession of the town, they therefore remake it in the image of Iye, the sanctified "ground" of the cult's more personalized invective.

If the old women of Oroyeye sing for the old Iye order, restoring it rhetorically if not politically in Ayede, the younger girls represent both "sides" during the nocturnal wrestling contests. In the event the town is ritually remapped into Isaoye and Odoalu, terms that, as we have seen, normally refer to two of Ayede's six quarters but are here extended to embrace Iye "indigenes" (four quarters) and Yagba and Ikole "strangers" (two quarters) as organized by age-sets. As the young men wrestle to promote their names and protect their ground, the young women sing jocular obscenities to defend their side and defame their rivals, both collectively (as Isaoye versus Odoalu) and personally by name. The "political" contest between indigenes and strangers is thus explicitly sexualized by sanctioned obscenities. Political and sexual contexts (competition) and subtexts (desire) are reciprocally encoded to augment the power of Oroyeye with the return of the sexually repressed. And, as we have seen, this power is not merely displaced into harmless palliatives through collective catharsis but is effectively channeled onto targeted culprits through the pragmatics of ritual speech.

This interpretation of Oroyeye can be further developed by framing it within more culturally coherent terms, as a regionally and historically specific expression of Yoruba female power and agency more generally. As I have argued elsewhere, Yoruba women are distinguished from men by two inversely related powers: the procreative power of fertility and the deadly power of witchcraft. If it is according to their "secret" that women give birth, it is also with their "secret" that they take life, by consuming the life essence of their kinsfolk, be they co-wives, collaterals, or even their own children, although it is more common for a witch to attack the child of a co-wife. The Yoruba witch is technically a cannibal, since she transforms herself into a witch-bird and sucks the blood of her victims until they die. Wealthy women are sometimes accused of exchanging their victims for financial gain, offering a child to a coven in return for illicit profit. All this is, of course, copiously documented by a fairly extensive scholarly and popular literature and emerges as a common concern among diviners (*babaláwo*) and medical specialists (*oníṣegùn*), in newspapers and in elite households,[40] and among Christians, Muslims, and politicians. Since witchcraft, like fertility, is endemic to Yoruba womanhood, all women are potential witches, and a woman becomes a witch and joins a coven (*egbẹ́*) when her witchcraft power is activated. Usually it will happen after menopause, when the woman's procreative fluids have been exhausted and her blood congeals inward. Thus, if fertility and witchcraft are antithetical female powers, each may dominate the other at different times in a woman's life. This diachronic dimension of fertility and witchcraft corresponds clearly to the two basic components of the Oroyeye festival—the nocturnal wrestling match (Àjàkadì) and the daytime procession of the "grandmothers." In the former, unmarried girls at the height of puberty and fertility sing songs of excessive sexuality, whereas in the latter old women past their childbearing years wreak havoc on public offenders. The two categories of singers exemplify the antithetical powers of fertility and witchcraft, and, with these powers in mind, the "canalizing" logic of abuse can be spelled out more clearly.

Foregrounding the female voice, as Oroyeye does, we might say that the unmarried girls displace male power competition into explicit idioms of female sexuality, which they celebrate and control, and thus effectively transform male power into socially sanctioned powers of social reproduction. By allowing

40. For some representative discussions, see, e.g., Beier 1958; Belasco 1980; Morton-Williams 1956, 1960a; R. Thompson 1976; Drewal and Drewal 1983; Idowu 1970; Hoch-Smith 1978; Prince 1961; Matory 1994; Makinde 1988; Bastian 1993; Apter 1993.

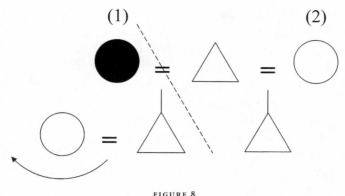

FIGURE 8
Land claims and lineage optation

sexual images to run amok while identifying actual "flirts" in the town, the
singers direct potentially rampant sexuality and unbounded desire toward "legitimate" fertile unions. The homology between male wrestling and female
sexual competition can be seen as a ritual transformation, a conversion of male
violence into female sexuality and fertility. Nor is such a transformation "purely"
symbolic, judging from the nocturnal liaisons that occur during the festival.[41]

As for the grandmothers, they can be seen as powerful witches who convert
their infertility and malice into socially recognized punitive sanctions. By routing
out evildoers they use their witchcraft to protect the town from its enemies
within. In this respect, the case of Oladiran is revealing, not only of the dire
consequences of ritual abuse but of the cultural logic that motivates it. During my investigations I was struck by the large proportion of Oroyeye songs
that focus on individuals implicated in lineage fission. One man who was
accused of stealing land from his brother had moved away from his patrilocal
compound to set up house on his wife's family land (fig. 8). Although the
"crime" concerned farmland, was he guilty of lineage fission? Recall the Oroyeye song warning Orisha Oniyi not to split its cult into three by generating
a third lineage matrisegment. These and many other examples suggest that
the "witchcraft" that normally focuses on the position of women in lineage

---

41. I do not mean to suggest that this ritual transformation explains the Àjàkadì wrestling
and singing as some cathartic carnival (which it is not), only that within "the play of tropes"
such a series of displacements is effected, perhaps through such "syllogisms of association"
as Fernandez notes for Asturian deepsong (1986, 102–29). Many other readings are of course
sustained, although partial corroboration comes from Parkin (1980, 57), who notes that "sex
entails marriage" is one of the three elementary propositions of joking.

segmentation and fission—since, following Lloyd (1955), it is children of the same fathers but different mothers who generally divide—is transformed by the grandmothers of Oroyeye into the crimes of men.[42] In this respect, Oladiran's crime is paradigmatic. He not only initiated lineage fission but did so by killing his half brother and using his body for making money, thereby mirroring the cannibalistic appetites of witches, who are believed to profit by consuming their kin. Oladiran was, in effect, a male witch. For this crime against society, isolated and broken, the man died.

For whom, then, do the priestesses of Oroyeye speak? I have identified a number of localized answers, ranging from young girls and old women to the old Iye order and the kingdom of Ayede at large. I have argued that, as a specific ritual genre, Oroyeye songs encode a particular historicity, a template of dispossession and repression which maps onto all sorts of contemporary relations, and is itself a historical consequence of Iye's experience in the founding and development of Ayede. And it is to this local level of embedded meanings and con/textual strategies that the exegesis of oral literature and ritual discourse in Africa should attend, if we are to grasp the critical agency of linguistic practices.[43] Following Evans-Pritchard's lead, I have shown how the "canalizing functions" of obscenity and abuse can be discursively contextualized in relation to homage and praise, and locally historicized in the repressed social memory of lineage fission and "sexual" politics. If relocating ritual texts in their performative contexts illuminates how they work, however, we need not remain in the local particularities of specific speech communities, and, with this in mind, we can reflect on the more general relationship between Oroyeye texts and female power. Within the broader sociocultural contexts of fertility and witchcraft, the young girls and old grandmothers of Oroyeye speak—with impunity—for all Yoruba women.[44]

42. See also Schwab 1955 for an insightful, if overly mechanical, discussion of matrisegments and lineage segmentation in the town of Oshogbo.

43. In a pathbreaking study, Parkin (1980, 47) identifies "politeness" and "abuse" as contrastive dimensions of greetings which are deployed to negotiate status relations. In many ways these dimensions map onto authority and power, praise and dispraise, hierarchy and solidarity, avoidance and joking. In Parkin's analysis, the "creativity" of abuse refers to its transformative potentialities. See Gal 1991, 178, for a comparative formulation of the relations between gender, speech, and power, advocating "studies [that] attend not only to words but to the interactional practices and the broader political and economic context of communication in order to understand the process by which women's voices—in both senses—are routinely suppressed or manage to emerge." It is my hope that this examination of Oroyeye songs represents a step in that direction by emphasizing the critical agency of women's ritual speech.

44. In this broader connection, Yai (n.d.) argues for an emancipatory focus on the Yoruba goddess Nana as a paradigm for theorizing and analyzing female literary genres and voices.

5

Griaule's Legacy

Few Africanists, indeed few anthropologists, remain as controversial as Marcel Griaule. Hailed as a hero of French Africanist ethnography, with a prodigious output and prestigious "school," and assailed as an antihero whose sympathy for Africa masked deeper forms of colonial violence, Griaule embodies—as we saw in chapter 1—the best and the worst of our disciplinary history. Lecturing in his aviator's uniform, badgering his informants,[1] seizing the Parisian limelight, using aerial photography, embarking on missions, collecting for museums, and eventually "becoming" a Dogon elder, Griaule remained a curious combination of nineteenth-century adventurer and twentieth-century colonial commandant, at once an agent of the French government and a liberal advocate of African cultural sophistication. Through the extended critique of Lettens (1971), the signal essays of Jamin (1982b) and Clifford (1988), and Hountondji's attack against ethnophilosophy (1983), Griaule became a favorite target, personifying the violence and duplicity of colonial ethnography and its mystification of cultural traditions.[2] With his substantive research on Dogon deep knowledge questioned on empirical grounds (van Beek 1991a), his interpretive focus on secrecy and hidden meaning (what he called "*la parole claire*") has become iconic of the colonial imagination at large (Mudimbe 1988). How, then, do we read Griaule's oeuvre and assess its ethnographic legacy? What can we gain from his ethnophilosophical project? To answer these questions,

1. Whereas Griaule's favored fieldwork metaphor was that of "juge d'instruction" (Jamin 1982b, 87; Clifford 1988, 74–75), Leiris would write, in *L'Afrique fantôme*, "Je continue mon travail de pion, de juge d'instruction ou de bureaucrate.... Pourquoi l'enquête ethnographique m'a-t-elle fait penser souvent à un interrogatoire de police?" (quoted in Jamin 1982a, 205).

2. For a critical reappraisal of Hountondji's position, refer back to chapter 1. For an extended tribute to Griaule's life and work (bordering on hagiography), see Fiemeyer 2004.

I propose a critical rereading of his Dogon ethnography and a new model of the esoteric knowledge that he purported to reveal.[3] My aim is neither to defend nor to dismiss Griaule's ethnography on political grounds but to grasp the inner connections it manifests between language, secrecy, and agency.

My rereading is based on two methodological moves that recast Griaule's exegetical project in more socially dynamic terms. The first move, based on my Yoruba research in Nigeria, is to recognize that esoteric levels of African philosophical systems are actually indeterminate and unstable, and that this capacity to contradict or subvert official or exoteric knowledge renders secret knowledge transformative and thus powerful. Following Griaule, we can acknowledge the significance of what he called "*la parole claire*"—the deepest level of secret knowledge—as an important domain of social knowledge and power, but contra Griaule, we will maintain that its content is fluid rather than fixed. As we shall see, this perspective vitiates van Beek's "discovery" that the Dogon today do not recognize the secret myths and cosmogony documented in Griaule's later work, since we need not presume that deep knowledge possessed a fixed content in the first place. If Dogon esoterica are like Yoruba deep knowledge, they are context specific, not stable and timeless.

The second methodological move, developing out of the first, shifts the Griaule school's elaborate analysis of Dogon language and symbolism—and, more importantly, of Dogon ideas *about* language and symbolism—to the level of pragmatic analysis, locating dominant symbols, schemas, and ritual-speech genres in their contexts of production. Focusing on speech acts, locatives, and pronominal shifting, as well as Dogon ideas about linguistic performance, we can return to the rich Dogon material in terms of its situated pragmatic functions. In so doing, the central figure of the body in Dogon symbolic classification emerges within an interactive framework of linguistic practice, what Hanks (1990, 1992) calls a "corporeal field" establishing "the indexical ground of deictic reference."

I will begin by returning to Griaule's "initiation" into the realm of Dogon esoterica, for it is here that his "deep-knowledge" paradigm is introduced and developed through conversations with Ogotemmêli, the blind Dogon sage. It is not my intention to endorse Griaule's self-proclaimed induction, which has become a textbook case of ethnographic mystification, but to identify the model of knowledge he proposes and relate it to my Yoruba material. From here I will turn to Leiris's formidable study *La langue secrète des Dogon de*

---

3. For more specialized research and discussion of Griaule and his ethnography, see Amselle 2000; Bouju 1984; Ciarcia 1998, 2001; Doquet 1999; Jamin 1982b; Jolly 1998–99, 2004; Lebeuf 1987; Lettens 1971; Michel-Jones 1999; Piault 2000; van Beek and Jansen 2000.

Sanga, focusing on the pragmatic dimensions of Dogon ritual language that his research brought to light and that also appear in the ethnolinguistic investigations of Marcel's daughter, Geneviève Calame-Griaule (1986). I will then extend this communicative framework to Griaule's symbolic codifications, arguing that the dominant Dogon cosmological configurations are better seen as generative schemes for orienting the body in social space, coextensively with broader domains of the habitus. How these configurations developed dialogically, and in what senses they could be politically transformative, involve fresh considerations of political context and agency that Griaule himself so assiduously repressed.

La Parole Claire

The famous *Conversations with Ogotemmêli*, first published in 1948, represents a turning point in Griaule's research, away from the objectivist documentation of his earlier *Masques dogons* ([1938] 1983) and into the rarefied domain of secret meaning and knowledge. After fifteen years of energetic inquiry into the manifold activities of Dogon custom and culture, Griaule was "initiated" into the inner sanctum of what he would call "*la parole claire*," the deepest level of knowledge. Or so the story goes in its various versions. Unbeknownst to him, the Dogon elders of Ogol and Sanga held a special meeting and decided to reveal the mysteries of their religion. Griaule was summoned to Ogotemmêli's inner sanctum, where he would return for the next thirty-three days to receive instruction, acquiring the interpretive keys to Dogon culture and society through the wisdom of the ancestors. From that point on, the Griaule "school" became a scholarly cult, investigating the world of words, signs, and mythopoetic correspondences throughout the Dogon and Bambara regions of the French Sudan.[4]

However contrived this famous mise-en-scène in establishing his ethnographic authority, Griaule was onto something interesting. Whatever the status of these privileged conversations, and the dialogical text that has come to represent them, Griaule sketches a system of symbolic connections represented by a stratified series of restricted "words." Never mind that the three words or levels in *Conversations*, and in his shorter essay *Descente du troisième Verbe* ([1947] 1996), would later be extended to four (Griaule 1952), or that the

---

4. In addition to Griaule 1983, 1965, see also Griaule and Dieterlen 1951, 1991; Calame-Griaule 1986; Dieterlen 1942, 1951; Ganay 1942; Leiris 1992; Paulme 1940; Rouche 1960; Zahan 1960, 1963. Despite their self-distancing from Griaule's "school," Leiris and Paulme produced their work through his "missions."

ordinal series in other contexts collapsed into a binary "simple" versus "deep" contrast, recapitulated as "exoteric" versus "esoteric" knowledge, or as *paroles de face* versus *la parole claire*. Whatever fictions he deployed or illusions he held in his quest for the secrets of Dogon cosmology, Griaule clearly demonstrated the importance of language as its central organizing principle. Indeed, Geneviève Calame-Griaule (1996, 14–15) would later note the Dogon predilection for reflecting on language, proclaiming that, through Ogotemmêli, "Dogon civilization revealed itself as a civilization of the Word." Where father and daughter went wrong, I shall argue, was not in their linguistic formulation of deep knowledge but in their approach to its meaning and content.

Griaule was convinced that *la parole claire* represented a highly restricted and specialized body of knowledge, consisting of myths, codes, signs, and classification systems—that is, of philosophical ideas, symbolic associations, and ritual techniques and procedures that together formed a sophisticated ethnophilosophy, one that structured and ordered the Dogon world. As his classic *Conversations* reveals, together with his collaborative research with Germaine Dieterlen, this knowledge took the form of creation myths—including those of the Nommo Twins, of the cosmic egg, and of the pale fox or divinatory jackal—and their symbolic analogues in the material world, particularly granaries, homesteads, villages, and fields, all variably mapped onto the human body. Part Cartesian rationalism, as with Dogon zoological classifications, and part symbolist poetics, resonating throughout social and celestial domains, this knowledge was compared with ancient Greek philosophy as a precolonial African tradition that was equally rich and worthy of investigation. Indeed, for Griaule and his intimate group, the pursuit of *la parole claire* became an end in itself, an almost exegetical *mise-en-abîme* that became increasingly unreadable the deeper it went. But however obscure its myths, graphic signs, and secret languages, such deep knowledge was for Griaule a coherent tradition, a fixed corpus of hidden insights and connections shared by initiated elders of the highest order. Griaule actually estimated the distribution of such specialized knowledge numerically as ranging between 4 and 15 percent of the population depending on the relative "word" or level of depth. Bracketing the question of their quantitative accuracy, these figures framed *la parole claire* in the form of empirical documentation.

It is just such an account that van Beek (1991a) has disputed, subjecting Griaule's entire corpus of ethnophilosophical investigations—the period following his putative "initiation"—to sustained empirical and theoretical critique. So devastating is van Beek's attack, a deconstruction in the literal sense of the term, that it warrants reconsideration to see if any of Griaule's *paroles* survive.

Van Beek's essay made quite a splash in the pages of *Current Anthropology*, where, following the journal's format, it appeared with responses from a range of prominent scholars to whom he then replied. Presented as a restudy, it offers a "field evaluation" of Griaule's Dogon ethnography, raising a host of interesting questions about secrecy, method, and the reproducibility of ethnographic findings. After an admirable synopsis of Griaule's two "initiatory" texts—*Dieu d'eau* and *Le renard pâle*—van Beek seeks to demonstrate that most of the deep knowledge elicited by Griaule was actually a "hybrid" product of his creative and fertile imagination, generated in dialogue with a few idiosyncratic informants who did not represent Dogon culture at large. Attending to what Pels (1994) calls the *préterrain* of the ethnographic situation, van Beek convincingly argues that the "courtesy bias" of the Dogon toward powerful figures of colonial authority, as Griaule clearly was, with his pith helmet, whites, and indomitable style, would have led them to endorse what he wanted to find. For example, van Beek's discussion of how Griaule neglected the tonal system in his etymologies (van Beek 1991a, 151–52), and how he badgered his informants into producing ad hoc names for twenty-four types of dung beetle (154) without appreciating the inventiveness involved, reveals systematic distorting mechanisms (if not shades of Kafka!) at work. Equally misleading was Griaule's commitment to a pristine precolonial model, one that blinded him to the way Dogon culture incorporated the foreign within its horizons—a process that included ideas, values, and techniques of neighboring peoples but also extended to biblical and Qur'anic episodes at the center of his esoteric creation myths. Indeed, as van Beek points out, Sanga was an important market and administrative center, "and the earliest Christian and Muslim influence radiated from it" (143). These and other examples of Griaule's interpretive excesses and limitations are indeed important and well established, but the bulk of van Beek's negative commentary comes from his literal-minded understanding of what deep knowledge should be.

Van Beek's most devastating evidence against Griaule is lack of corroboration. When confronted with the contents and contours of Griaule's esoteric writings, the Dogon whom van Beek interviewed were bewildered: "The Dogon know no proper creation myth; neither the version of Ogotemmêli nor that of the *Renard pâle* is recognizable to informants," adding that "Dogon society has no initiatory secrets beyond the complete mastery of publicly known texts" (1991a, 148). More important than Griaule's misleading emphases on ancestors, the Nommo spirit, and classificatory schemes is the total absence of *la parole claire* within a socially restricted set of ideas. Van Beek found that the concept of *nyama*, or "vital force," is irrelevant to Dogon religion; that body symbolism is not isomorphic with house plans, fields, or villages; and that "no sign systems or hierarchical ordering of different *paroles* (*so*) or levels of knowledge can be found" (148). What secret knowledge there is, he argues, pertains to witchcraft, sorcery, and those skeletons in the closet that cast shame upon specific persons and groups whose unbridled ambitions generate conflict and rivalry to undermine the public good.[5] As he concludes, "The tendency towards the creation of increasingly 'deep knowledge' shows itself much more towards the end of Griaule's life, with a decreasing amount of 'Dogon-ness' marking the text" (157). Thus, the deeper we go, the more we get of Griaule and the less of the Dogon themselves.

Van Beek's findings were embraced by Griaule's critics and detractors and provide an important corrective to his lack of historicism and sociopolitical grounding, but I will argue that the negative thrust of the article is misguided. Contra his claim that Griaule's Dogon present a "paradigm anomaly" in the regional ethnography, owing to the lack of comparable deep knowledge in West African societies (1991a, 142), a glance at the relevant literature shows otherwise. Many of Griaule's original team did provide comparable evidence among Bambara, Bozo, and Mande peoples, as did Leiris among the Dogon. Certainly, research on African ritual associations and secret societies reveals a broad distribution of such "gnostic inner circles of knowledge," as Douglas (1991, 162) points out in her critical response. It is precisely because Griaule's deep-knowledge formulations resonate with my own Yoruba research that I have continued to take them seriously—not in terms of a dogma to be mastered but as a rhetorical resource to be deployed.

When I began my research on Yoruba religion and politics, or what I now call the hermeneutics of power, I immediately ran into serious barriers. My project seemed straightforward enough—to examine the politics of orisha worship as a space of contesting political authority—but even my most preliminary inquiries were blocked from the start. In the kingdom of Ayede-Ekiti, where I conducted my fieldwork, I was allowed to record and photograph public festivals and visit the dominant town shrines, but discussion of ritual symbols and practices, and virtually anything relating to the priests and priestesses, was extremely limited at best. Over the months and years, I built up enduring relations with ritual specialists and devotees of Yemoja, Orisha Ojuna, and Orisha Iyagba as well as with members of the Ogboni secret society, but I never once experienced any running exegesis of sacred symbols and their secret meanings. Direct questioning would provoke such responses as "*Aṣáa ni*" (it is tradition), "*Mi ò mọ̀*" (I don't know), and only eventually "*Awo ni*" (it is a secret), as if the very acknowledgment that there was a hidden

5. See Bouju 1991 for corroboration on this point.

meaning was a major concession to my intrusive requests. Even when my interviews were prepared with schnapps and kola nuts, further demands for money often followed from those who did not know me well, based on the understanding that deep knowledge, called *imọ ìjinlẹ̀*, was restricted, scarce, and had extraordinary value. If I protested such demands—and they could be quite exorbitant—I was asked whether or not specialized education was free in America and, furthermore, if I had any idea what initiates invested over the years to acquire their secrets. Why would I presume that such secret knowledge should be given freely to me? Didn't I know that if its secrets were leaked, an orisha would lose its power?

While invoking their orisha during sacrifices and festivals, devotees often pray not to leak any secrets, requesting ritual assistance in sealing their lips. An elder devotee is much like a vessel, filled with the *omi*, or "water," of the orisha's power, which must not leak, spill, or fall—mirroring the vessels of *ọtun*, or revitalizing water, that they carry on their heads to ritually reproduce the kingdom. When I began my research on Yoruba ritual and politics, a neighboring chief with a university degree laughed as he told me: "No matter how much time you spend with them, the priestesses will never tell you their secrets—they will never reveal anything!" And indeed, in terms of overt disclosures, he was right. Formal initiation would not solve the problem since it was predicated on a blood-oath (*imùlẹ̀*) not to reveal cult knowledge to outsiders. Indeed, secrets were equally protected within the shrines, distinguishing degrees and grades of elderhood within. If I were formally initiated, my lips too would be sealed. Pondering my predicament with the help of palm wine, I experienced something of an ethnographic epiphany. The very barriers that so effectively blocked my access to deep knowledge should not be seen as a problem to overcome but were themselves part of the ethnographic solution, to be documented as socially significant data. If the secrets remained forever out of reach, the mechanisms protecting them were not.[6]

With my research perspective thus radically readjusted, my fieldwork took a productive turn. I no longer asked inappropriate questions unless seeking the limits of discursive disclosure. As I spent more time with the devotees and was brought into the protected groves and inner chambers of their shrines, I came to appreciate how secrecy operated in practice, as a mode of drawing boundaries, setting agendas, and discussing controversial affairs. From this method of prolonged osmosis—very different from Griaule's concentrated instruction—I received insights about deep knowledge in fragments, with respect to prior conflicts in the kingdom, in relation to specialized passwords

6. This methodological insight was already developed by Jamin (1977).

and handshakes, regarding witchcraft and fertility, or pertaining to "true" histories (*itàn*) not publicly acknowledged, and sometimes danced rather than spoken. In the more general terms of everyday use by uninitiated Yoruba townsfolk, deep knowledge was associated with powerful people with access to the original secrets of the first ancestors—incantations like *àyàjó* that were uttered by the first people, true histories proclaimed in the heteroglossic arenas of *ìjalà* chants and in curses (*èpè*) and incantations (*ofò*) that could kill, and invocations of ancestral spirits of humans and deities alike, as in *oríkì* and *ègún pípè*, not to mention the enigmatic secrets (*awo*) of Ifa divination. Applied to issues or events, however, the qualifier "deep" denoted political disruption and moral violation, as in the usurpation of a royal dynasty by the Eshubiyi line, the murder of a kinsman for making money-magic (as in chapter 4, this volume), or the nefarious activities of the once-ruling National Party of Nigeria (NPN), which rigged gubernatorial election results in 1983.

Two aspects of such secrets are especially relevant to van Beek's reassessment of Griaule. The first concerns their subversive character as icons and indices of sociopolitical revolt. The dominant symbol of the royal Yemoja festival in Ayede, for example, is the calabash (*igbá*) of concentrated ritual potency (*àṣẹ*) that is carried—balanced on the high priestess's head—from the bush to the palace, where it empowers the king's person and revitalizes the body politic. Like any dominant symbol, it embraces a span of meanings ranging from explicit normative blessings ("it brings children and wealth; it keeps the king healthy") to implicit, forbidden themes of division and bloodshed, and it is this latter pole that is powerful and deep. Yemoja's fructifying calabash represents the womb of motherhood, the head of good destiny, the crown of the king, the integrity of the town, even the cosmological closure of sky and earth. But its surfaces are decorated with signs of a deadlier power within, indicated by red parrot feathers (*ìkó odídẹ*)—signs of ritual negation. Evoking the witchcraft of the priestesses and their mechanism for deposing the king, red parrot feathers on the calabash simultaneously assert a broken womb, miscarried delivery, bad destiny, a decapitated (and crownless) king, as well as political fission and a cosmos out of control. Such negative themes are rarely voiced in public, but they nonetheless constitute a repertoire of potential interpretations that under certain conditions can be invoked to mobilize opposition against the status quo. The deep knowledge of royal ritual actually involves the king's sacrifice and rebirth, whereby his icons of personal power and royal authority are literally taken apart and reassembled by authorized priests and priestesses, culminating in the crowning moment, as he receives the calabash, when the king is recapitated, reinstalled, and reproduced. In the case of nonroyal festivals, the orisha's calabash serves as a potential crown to remind the king that his chiefs can always rise up and usurp the ruling line. Such themes are enhanced by various genres of ritual speech, which invoke repressed histories and veiled warnings of former kings and warriors who can prevail again (Apter 1992, 117–48). The dominant visual and verbal tropes that express these themes include those of inversion (e.g., in the image of a capsized canoe), reversal (e.g., from right to left), and mimetic appropriation (e.g., of European crowns). The latter symbolic function is particularly relevant to bringing outside icons of power within local fields of ritual command, absorbing symbols of foreign value and authority through metaphoric and metonymic associations.

But if this aspect of deep knowledge invokes fission, usurpation, and even militant dismemberment, it does so through mechanisms of formal opposition to received historical and genealogical charters. The deeper one goes, in a sense, the less fixed and determinate the character of the secret, and the more formal the mechanisms of reversal and inversion. This second aspect of secrecy as interpretive revision is captured by what I have called the central axiom of Yoruba hermeneutics: "Secret surpasses secret; secret swallows secret completely" (*Àwó j'awo lo; awo lè gb'áwo mí torí torí*). Following this axiom to its logical conclusion, the secret behind the secret is that deep knowledge has no content at all but derives its power from context-specific opposition to the authoritative discourses that it implicitly challenges. Like Griaule's discussion of Dogon esoterica, a salient distinction between exoteric (*paroles de face*) and esoteric (*la parole claire*) knowledge is here at play (see also Griaule and Dieterlen 1991, 55), but unlike Griaule, I maintain that the deeper modes have no fixed content into which all ritual elders are eventually initiated. *If the ideology of deep knowledge asserts a fixed corpus of secrets, then this should not be taken at face value but should be understood as a screen that allows its pragmatic functions to masquerade as sanctified wisdom and learning.* As such, deep knowledge is powerful because it is revisionary, sustaining possibilities of political transformation through the revaluation and reversal of established orders. In the sociocultural contexts of historic Yoruba kingdoms, the political lines of contestation and division are formed around kings in relation to their civil chiefs and to the dominant lines of political segmentation into quarters, lineages, and households.

If we assume, for the sake of argument, that Dogon deep knowledge works in similar ways, not as a fixed corpus of meanings and myths but as an interpretive space of reconfiguration, van Beek's lack of corroborative evidence poses no real threat to *la parole claire*. For if it is paradigmatically context specific, changing over time and space to fit local political groups and relations, we would not expect to "find" the same content at all. Of course, van Beek's critique goes further than this, denying even the formal organization of knowledge into levels of restricted access, but here we can read him against himself. The deep secrets he did receive, pertaining more to sorcery, witchcraft, and skeletons in the closet than to cosmic eggs and primordial foxes, are in fact consistent with the divisive, fissive, and subversive dimensions of deep knowledge as a political—and as we shall see—illocutionary force. They form part of the repertoire of resources that can be mobilized to challenge the status quo. And the fragmentary manner in which such data were disclosed is indeed consistent with their mode of dissemination to noninitiates. I am not implying that van Beek lacked crucial insight into the deeper levels of Dogon symbolism and meaning—his essay on the *dama* masquerade is a masterpiece of ritual exegesis, linking gender transformations between men and women to the dangerous secrets of social reproduction (van Beek 1991b). That he does not see such meaning as "deep" is more a consequence of his methodological orientation: if people do not tell him it is deep, or recognize deep knowledge in overt declarations, then in effect it does not exist for him. I would argue that his Dogon informants could not tell him because they did not know or could not say, given the discursive restrictions against its disclosure.

To substantiate this countercritique, and extract the pragmatic kernel of *la parole claire* from its socially sanctioned mystical shell, I will attend more closely to language itself: first in the more contemporaneous work of Griaule's ambivalent secretary archivist, Michel Leiris, followed by the subsequent investigations of his loyal daughter, Geneviève Calame-Griaule.

Ritual Language

By the time *La langue secrète des Dogon de Sanga* was published in 1948, Deborah Lifchitz—of Griaule's Africanist circle—had died in Auschwitz, and it is to her memory that Michel Leiris dedicated this extraordinary study of ritual language. Published the same year that Griaule's *Entretiens* (*Conversations*) first appeared, it presents a complex counterpoint to the French master's voice, at once derivative of Griaule's first documentary tome, *Masques dogons* ([1938] 1983)—given its extensive focus on *sigi* ritual texts—and yet uneasy with the colonial situation in Africa and the German occupation of France.[7] To what extent *La langue secrète* voices a muted indictment of Griaule in this broader context is difficult to say, since Leiris's debts cut in both directions: not only to the 1931 Dakar-Djibouti expedition, during which he recorded the bulk

7. That the Vichy regime was uneasy with Leiris is evident in their burning of *L'Afrique fantôme* on the pyre (Jamin 1982a).

of his linguistic material, as well as the more "sociological" groundwork first established by Griaule (1983), but also to the "lamented" Deborah Lifchitz, acknowledged in the foreword, with her comrades-in-letters Denise Paulme and André Schaeffner.[8] I am not suggesting that Leiris collected his material with a radical political project firmly in place, however haunted he was by the manifold forms of colonial alienation in *L'Afrique fantôme*; but in Paris, at least, he was writing in the basement of the Musée de l'homme, the headquarters of one of the founding cells of the resistance movement.[9] The issue remains unclear, in part, because the politics of secrecy sustains ambiguous interpretations in shifting contexts.

Ambiguity and unstable content are in fact diagnostic of *sigi* ritual texts, which are marked more by simplified syntax and morphology than by complex metaphors and poetic associations. *Sigi* texts are paradigmatically vacuous, posing difficulties of translation because their shifting meanings so closely relate to their performative contexts. As Leiris (1992, xv) explains: "The nature . . . of secret language, with its much reduced vocabulary and rudimentary grammar, where things are suggested, indicated more than described, and where the same phrase, the same locution is sometimes understood very differently following the context or circumstances to which they apply, even the character of this language which proceeds hastily, by large and brief allusions, lends itself poorly to rigorous translation."[10] These difficulties of capturing ritual meanings highlight the relevance of indexicals in relating texts to their contexts, thereby foregrounding the pragmatics of ritual speech. The improvisational scope around texts and their variants also suggests contextual sensitivity to fixed liturgical segments, which resonate with implications that

8. Leiris (1992, 25) even referred to their fieldwork in Sanga as "la mission Lifschitz-Paulme," as if to further accentuate their differences with Griaule. See also Paulme 1992.

9. For a poignant account of how the resistance movement originated, to a large degree, in the Musée de l'homme, see Blumenson 1977. Although Leiris himself "lacked the temperament" to join (Jean Jamin, personal communication, January 2001), the cell was led by the anthropologist-linguist Boris Vildé and included anthropologists Germaine Tillion and Anatole Lewitzky. On 19–20 May 1942, Leiris had a nightmare about Lewitzky's execution, dreaming that Lewitzky's memories would be published (Ghrenassia 1987, 239). Leiris also dreamed that he saw Boris Vildé in a café, lifting his glass to German officers and crying out "Heil de Gaulle!" in an act of parodic resistance (Lelong 1987, 333).

10. "la nature . . . du langage secret, au vocabulaire très réduit et à la grammaire des plus rudimentaires, langue où les choses sont suggérées, indiquées plutôt que décrites, et où la même phrase, la même locution doivent parfois être entendues de façons très différentes suivant le contexte ou suivant les circonstances auxquelles elles s'appliquent, le caractère même de cette langue qui procède sommairement, par larges et brèves allusions, la fait se prêter assez mal à une traduction rigoureuse."

extend beyond the meanings of the word themselves. Indeed, Leiris complains in his preface of the hermeneutical circularity that bedeviled his translations. Returning to previous *sigi* transcriptions in order to check or improve their accuracy, his "informant" would never review "point by point" the same text but instead would produce a new text—"analogous, certainly, but not identical"—as if to underscore the deconstructive joke that every decoding is simultaneously a recoding (1992, xv). Such resistance to definitive philological documentation, however, needs to be seen, not as a problem to be solved, but as a critical characteristic of ritual language itself; that is, as part of the object of description and analysis. From this more inherently dynamic perspective, suggested to me by the indeterminacy of Yoruba deep knowledge, the goal of achieving definitive translation shifts to that of grasping Dogon interpretations as situated in their social and ritual contexts. What counts from this more "indigenous" perspective is not an authoritative translation but the plurality of meanings in the public domain.

In its broadest sociopolitical context, the secret language of *sigi so* belongs to an exclusive men's society organized by age-grades and associated with the primordial ancestor Awa, from whom the secrets of *sigi* descended. Represented by masked dancers in red fiber skirts, the spirit of Awa embodies the complementary principles of death and rebirth underlying the perpetuation of age-graded generations. At the apex of the hierarchy is an inner core of *olubaru* elders, initiated into the highest grade during the full *sigi* ceremony, performed every sixty years at the completion of the full generational cycle and following a coordinated itinerary throughout villages and regions.[11] Of course, not all *sigi* elders make it to this highest grade, since a man's date of birth determines his point of entry into the overarching cycle. Hence, this elite body of elders—the oldest of the old—are recognized as the highest ritual experts, who mingle with the ancestors and the dead and thus are referred to as "people of the bush," deemed socially powerful and impure. These ritual elders are considered the "official depositories" of *sigi so*, and it is through them that the language was differentially disseminated to the lower grades in accordance with their levels. Building on Schaeffner's 1935 survey of iron gongs associated with *olubaru* dignitaries, Leiris estimated their total number at around fifteen ("*une quizaine*") in the entire Sanga region, representing a highly restricted inner circle controlling access to secret language and knowledge. Beneath this specialized elite, the remaining elders represent the next level of deep knowledge, acquired through long association with the

11. For a discussion of this itinerary over a five-year period, see Griaule 1983, 174–75. See also Dieterlen 1971.

dama rites and funeral ceremonies connected with the *sigi* festival complex. Following this group are individuals of varying ages who study the *sigi* language with specialists, shortcutting, as it were, the initiation hierarchy for the conventional fee of 33,003 cowries—a figure signifying a considerable cost rather than a precise amount (Leiris 1992, 17). Not only is the effect of this more direct route to the language financial, providing additional funds for the mask society, but it also broadens the social range of ritual-language competence and performance. More conventionally, however, instruction begins with male circumcision as the first initiation into the men's society. While being prepared and doctored in the bush, the novices receive millet beer, sesame oil, black pepper, and medicines to help them "hear" the voice of Awa, and they begin an instruction in *sigi* language and mythology that increases as they advance up the hierarchy.

The content of such esoteric instruction, which increased with elderhood, remains both sketchy and charged in the work of the Griaule school: curiously displaced by each account into shifting mythic figures and linguistic forms. The initial *sigi* teachings involve greeting formulae, benedictions and propitiations, myths of origin, the secret names of foods and drinks used in initiation, and a new lexicon for parts of the body. In addition, initiates learn the exhortations that enhance the *nyama*, or "vital force," of the masked dancers, with specific calls linked to particular masks. Mythically located in the realm of the bush with *ginn (gyinu)* spirits and souls of the dead, the *sigi* language evokes earlier historic migrations by mixing Mande and Voltaic terms and archaisms together with Dogon lexemes.[12] The mythic origins of the *sigi* festival itself, and the presiding Grand Awa mask at the center of the ritual complex, trace back to an eponymous ancestor who, after becoming a snake, as all old people did in that time, broke a taboo against speaking ordinary vernacular to humans and thereafter ushered in death and mortality, but also regeneration. Building on Griaule's documentary foundation by providing alternative versions and variants of the origin myth recorded in *Masques dogons*, Leiris introduced a subtle but significant shift in perspective. Unlike Griaule, who operated under the philological tradition of a mythic urtext at the heart of the *sigi* complex, Leiris recognized the inherent heterogeneity built into the corpus of *sigi* founding myths. In an extended footnote to Griaule's "definitive"

12. For a discussion of different *sigi* "dialects" in the villages of Banani, Oro Sono, Kunnu, and Kabage, see Leiris 1992, 33. As a combination of Mande and Voltaic elements, the *sigi* language involves complex considerations of origins, migrations, and borrowings from Mossi, Malinke, and Bambara language areas, as well as possible Arabic influences in articles like *al-*, reflecting the past through linguistic forms and archaisms as well as the problematic genealogy of the Dogon themselves (Leiris 1992, 25–44, 404).

version, Leiris (1992, 146n2) explains his variations with the insight that "there exists no unique tradition but several traditions; thus it is not surprising that they are contradictory on certain points."[13] Through this important interpretive move, Leiris locates contradiction within a corpus of deep knowledge, not as a problem to be eliminated through philological ratiocination, but as a feature that makes sense in relation to changing social and performative contexts. Indeed, his investigations into *sigi* syntax and morphology highlight the critical relationship between meaning and context.[14]

I have already noted that the *sigi* language is limited and impoverished in comparison with ordinary spoken Dogon, but the direction of its grammatical reductions reveals a significant retreat, as it were, into the body—not as a transcendental symbolic scheme, but as a corporeal field of indexical functions. *Sigi* texts are not fixed, Leiris often reminds us, but are rooted in their contexts of ritual production, calling on particular masks, singling out dancers' movements and body parts, saluting presiding spirits, shifting subjects and objects, merging singular with plural, voicing changes of action, shaping points of view, merging past with present, and, above all, activating the *nyama*, or efficacy, of Awa and his avatars. To illustrate this dynamic interaction between *sigi* texts and performative contexts, I will focus on the corporeal dimensions of ritual speech with reference to verbs, pronouns, and locatives.

Verbs in *sigi* are few in number and mainly express movements of dancers or spectators within the ritual arena. The most frequently used are *dyenunu*, glossed "to go, enter, or introduce," and *sagya*, "to place, place oneself, or be placed" (Leiris 1992, 416). Common utterances exhort dancers to realize and maximize their actions, as in moving those body parts at once protected by the spirits (ostensibly to protect the masked dancer from falling) and activated by being called into motion:

> That God protects [your] legs!
> That Mouno protects [your] legs!
> That Mounokanna protects [your] legs!
> That all the Sigui protect [your] legs!
>
> [Your] arms are activated,
> [Your] legs are activated,
> [Your] eyes are activated,

13. "il n'existe pas une tradition unique mais plusiers traditions, dont il n'y a pas s'étonner qu'elles soient, sur certains points, contradictoires."

14. For extended discussions and studies of the textual status of Mande and Cameroonian epic genres, see Austen 1995, 1999.

[Your] head is activated,
[Your] entire body is activated.[15]

As the activation of the eyes suggests, these exhortations shape visual, as well as choreographic, frames, interposing acts of seeing and being seen within performance arenas. Verbs are further reduced in terms of tense and mood. Limited to the present indicative, they represent a condition of "permanent actuality" that for Leiris, citing Leenhardt, quite technically points to the "here and now" (Leiris 1992, 53). Within this condensed communicative field, only the attitude and tone of the speaker distinguish imperatives from ordinary indicatives. In the *sigi* command "*wana boy*" (come!), the urgency with which the addressees must respond—in this case dancers made to get up and perform—is expressed and enhanced by waving the right hand (51). The dramatic qualities of *sigi* language, and its enhanced forms of bodily expression, are thus partly a function of its simplified structure.

Lack of plural and singular forms further reduces the language of *sigi* to transposable schemas of situated communication. As in many West African languages, pronouns rather than verbs indicate grammatical number in ordinary Dogon, but in *sigi*, the pronouns themselves are restricted to the two "floating" forms of first- and second-person plural. The pronominal matrix of ordinary Dogon is thereby reduced to the plural "we" (*emme*) and "you" (*ye/yo/ya*), a dyadic opposition that assimilates all singular, as well as third-person, forms, subject only to the quantifier *g'ina* specifying "all" or "totality." The effect of such pronominal reduction, combining indifference to time (in the verb system) with indifference to number, is the production of discursive schemas that work, according to Leiris, as a series of dynamic landmarks ("*repères*") bringing fixed relational categories to shape the ritual arenas of movement and participation. Within this grammar of mythic reduction, plurality and singularity merge through the very acts of exhortation, as individual persons, masks, and spirits quite literally stand up for groups, categories, and types (Leiris 1992, 55–56). But whereas for Leiris this schematic ordering is iconic of mythic templates and archetypes, we can shift his emphasis from meaning to practice and discern a transposable interactive scheme. In context, the pronominal reduction in *sigi so* to a fixed "I-We/Thou-Ye"

---

15. "Que Dieu garde [vos] jambes! / Que Mouno garde [vos] jambes! / Que Mounokanna garde [vos] jambes! / Que tout le Sigui gardes [vos] jambes! // [vos] bras ont remué, / [vos] jambes ont remué, / [vos] yeux on remué, / [votre] tête a remué, / [votre] corps entire a remué." See Leiris 1992, 198, lines 1, 4–6, 13–17. I have left out the *sigi* texts and their morpheme-by-morpheme translation because they are not necessary in illustrating the bodily orientation of verbs.

opposition assimilates all ritual participants and observers within a dyadic communicative frame.

If the pronominal system merges individual and collective bodies into binary relations of mutual recognition, *sigi* locatives anchor texts to their contexts by extending the body into a corporeal field—front and back, above and below, inside and outside, right and left, and their associated directional movements (ascending and descending, entering and exiting, etc.) within the performance arena.[16] It is thus perhaps no accident that Leiris highlights these terms as particularly confusing and ambiguous precisely because their meanings shift according to their use as substantives, representing parts of the body, or as proper locatives in postposition.[17] As he notes, in postposition they indicate spatial relations, and only context distinguishes their meanings as particles (1992, 57). The most commonly used locative in *sigi* is *dyu* (alt. *dyugu*), signifying "head" or "body" as a substantive but used in postposition to mean "on," "toward," or "above." Similarly *bin(u)* doubles as "stomach" and "in," "inside"; *poré* as "back" and "behind" and "after," as well as a cadet who is both "behind" in seniority and brings up the rear in ritual procession. Extending the body to "the various social and personal spaces of an actor" (Hanks 1990, 91), terms like *igiru*, "earth" or "ground," also signify "below" and the act of descending, contrasting with *dara*, "sky," "up above," which also signifies "ascending." In a similar contrast, *dégu* ("house," "village") and *logo* ("road") signify "inside" and "outside," respectively, in more sociocentric terms and are also used in complementary expressions of entering and exiting (Leiris 1992, 421–24).

These pronominal and locative examples represent those areas of the *sigi* language most difficult to translate because their meanings are grounded in their performative contexts. Shifting and "floating" an interactive scheme between phases and components of the ritual process, they reflect a discourse less rooted in Griaule's "mythic substrate" (Ciarcia 2001, 218) than in transpositions of person and place. *Sigi so* does invoke specialized mythic knowledge in fragments, but it does not semantically contain it. Transcribed and translated, it reveals a privileged scheme of corporeal interaction that mobilizes the *nyama* of the masked *sigi* dancers, organizes participants into interposed groups, and directs the flow of movement and energy as the festival unfolds.

16. For an analytical formulation of corporeal fields, see Hanks 1990, 91–95.

17. "Lemploi des ces locatifs prête aisément à amphibologie, aucune flexion n'indiquant le rôle joué dans la proposition par un nom quelconque qui se trouve placé immédiatement avant un locatif et, parailleurs, le sujet ou complément du verbe pouvant n'être que sous-entendu, ce qui est une autre cause de confusion" (Leiris 1992, 422).

Although the model of linguistic and symbolic analysis remained res-
olutely exegetical and "cryptological" for the Griaule school, a performative approach to language and to the indexical functions of the corporeal field
is clearly adumbrated in Leiris's observations as sketched above and nearly
takes shape in the ethnolinguistic investigations of Geneviève Calame-Griaule.
Her *Ethnologie et langage*, first published in 1965, builds upon her father's tradition of mythic documentation and symbolic classification in what Hymes
(1986, v–vi) acclaimed as a pioneering ethnolinguistic investigation. And following her father's focus on the body as an important symbolic template,
Calame-Griaule reveals an elaborate corporeal system at the center of Dogon
ideas about language, linking speech to the brain, collar bone, liver, heart,
pancreas, spleen, larynx, and mouth; relating the efficacy of the word to bodily substances like blood and oil; and associating different modes of discourse
(greeting, joking, grieving, even teaching) with bodily flows and processes.
Nor is this bodily template restricted to language and speech *sensu stricto*,
but it maps onto esoteric graphic signs as the "speech" of various mythic
figures and animals. In this broader context, Dogon ideas about speech and
the body provide an interpretive key to the symbolic world at large, and this
is the general orientation that Calame-Griaule pursues. "The word for the
Dogon," she writes, "is like a book whose message must be deciphered or
'decoded,' and man is constantly concerned to interpret the 'signs' around
him" (Calame-Griaule 1986, 9). What follows is a marvelous exposition of
verbal and symbolic associations, a decoding to be sure, but with surpris-
ingly little structural description or grammatical analysis of Dogon language
itself.

There are revealing moments, however, of pragmatic disclosure that suggest an alternative grounding of her ethnolinguistic corpus, less in the body
as an anthropomorphic cipher and more as privileged corporeal field, the
ground of socially situated discursive agency. As Calame-Griaule admits (1986,
5): "Yet, in the measure in which every social act implies a verbal interchange,
and where each act is in itself a form of self-expression, 'speaking' is at times
synonymous with 'undertaking' or 'doing' . . . to Dogon thinking, actions and
words are linked together, and this is why, in a symbolic sense, one also calls
'speech' the outcome of an action." Her two examples, "his words have gone
inside (*sò: vòmo yoá*)" and "it has now become tomorrow's speech (i.e., the
work's continuation will be postponed until tomorrow, *Né yògo sóy*)," involve
just those shifting locatives (stomach, inside) and deictics (tomorrow) that
extend the body in space and time. Characteristically, Calame-Griaule assimilates this performative dimension of language to "a symbolic sense," thereby
reducing doing to meaning. Nowhere is this limitation more clearly imposed

than in her ideas about *nàma* (*nyama*) as the mana or animating principle that is activated by speech:

> *Nàma*, the life force, is envisioned as a fluid that circulates through the body carried by blood. The idea of a *nàma* has appeared since the earliest Dogon studies where it has been defined as an "actualizing energy, impersonal, unconscious, shared by all animals, plants, supernatural beings, all the things of nature." . . . the simple act of calling someone by one of his names may produce an increase in his corresponding *nàma*. For we shall see that the mechanism of speaking is essentially an action upon the personal life force. (1986, 19–20)[18]

In this passage we see how *nàma* is linked to invoking and calling not merely by a conventional symbolic association but through the pragmatic functions of speech acts. Elsewhere, we learn that the *nàma* of a speaker determines the *nàma* of his speech and correlates with his power and authority and his ability to command (35).[19] What for Calame-Griaule remains an ideational explanation—words are linked to power and efficacy because of Dogon beliefs about language and the body—becomes from our pragmatic perspective more of a grammatical explanation, based on the very principle of linguistic performativity. *Nàma* doubles as a property of discourse and a force of nature because the social relation between both domains is grammatically constituted through illocutionary force. The body as mediator of this dynamic relation establishes a corporeal field, nothing less than the indexical ground of deictic reference through which social contexts and relations are shaped and remade.

Fragmentary evidence supports this recasting of the Dogon body as corporeal field. To begin, the truth-value of utterances is closely associated with bodily position. As Calame-Griaule explains, "'True Speech' is uttered by a speaker while sitting down. The position allows for the harmony of all the faculties: the mind is calm, the water in the collar bone is calm, and words in the same way are controlled and well-considered. Elders gathered under the 'speech shelter' to converse are always seated, and it is significant that the shelter has such a low ceiling that it would be impossible to stay under it otherwise." Conversely, speech delivered from standing or walking positions is unstable: "If a person speaks standing up, his words 'do not go down' (*sò: sùgoyele*), they 'have no path.' Such is the case with angry speech or words of the light man: he speaks standing up or walking along, for they have no 'position,' no stopping point (*ìnu sèle*)" (1986, 63–64). From this relative contrast between sitting and standing, we begin to glimpse how interactive frames of situated

18. Her own, unpaginated citation is to her father (Griaule 1983).

19. In this respect, the Bambara and Dogon notions of *nàma* are just like the Yoruba idea of *àṣẹ*.

communication structure even the truth-value of discourse systemically in relation to down and up. We also need to specify associated coordinates of front and back, left and right, intimated in a more symbolic register by the social dimensions of the naming matrix in which Dogon males are located (472, fig. 41), and which is further "superimposed" on a religious schema of ritual qualities and mystical values (536–38, fig. 43). The Dogon person is further characterized by a right-left and male-female dualism that lies "at the very core of the self" and emerges "always as an agent of imbalance" despite the best efforts to control it through male and female circumcision (33). Indeed, "we find that the whole person is made up of a material carrier or body distinct from, but in close contact with, the outside world through the constant flow of the four elements.... It is watered by the *nàma* fluid, like the land by its streams, and is the source of his vital impulse.... Thus the individual is not closed, but open, to the world, soaking it in, it could be said, through every pore" (33).

I would complement this passive or receptive view of the Dogon person with a grammatically more active voice, extending out from the body as a corporeal field to shape the interactive contexts of individual and collective agency. Thus, when Calame-Griaule asks: "How does the 'self' make contact with other, similar 'selves'? What part of himself does he project outside? How does he act upon others?" (1986, 31–32), we can look not only to the liver, blood, and collar bones of the body but also to "the spatial coordinates of bodily orientation" (Hanks 1990, 90) in situated communication.

Rereading Griaule

In what senses do the pragmatic functions of Dogon language and ritual speech extend to *la parole claire* writ large? How does *nàma* (*nyama*) as an indigenous principle of linguistic performance inform the revisionary power of deep knowledge more generally? By pursuing these questions, I will reanalyze Dogon deep knowledge as a sanctified form of critical agency, one that demands not a rigid approach to secret myths and symbolic codes but a more flexible feel for generative schemes. In this section, I use Hanks (1990) and Bourdieu (1977) to transpose the body as corporeal field into broader structures and domains of the habitus. Where Griaule saw the body as both cipher and microcosm of the Dogon world, I will treat the body as geometer, that is, as the locus of practical homologies and scheme transfers that generate the "structuring structures" of Dogon society (Bourdieu 1977, 114–24). By introducing this critical shift in perspective, we can extract the pragmatic kernel from the mystified shell of Griaule's initiatory ethnography, recognizing the importance of those formal homologies and generative schemes that his work brought to light while suspending the mystifying constraint that they hold the same content for an inner circle of elders. And in developing a more dynamic analysis of *la parole claire* as critical practice, we can further explain why its oppositional features would generate orthodox and heterodox variations—not a fixed body of wisdom but a space of critical dialogue and revision. This more dialogical approach to the celebrated "conversations" with Ogotemmêli, however, involves a return to political context and agency that Griaule seems to have repressed or ignored.

Initial evidence of a more indexical approach to *la parole claire* as a *body* of knowledge comes from a short analytical summary that Griaule published just four years before his premature death in 1956. Representing his final reflections on the organization of deep knowledge, "Le savoir des Dogon" reveals four degrees or levels of access, ranging from the most general and public to the most esoteric and specialized. The first level of *giri so*, which he glosses as "*parole de face*," provides an abridged digest of the Dogon world in which certain mythic figures are disguised or left out, episodes conflated, and references mostly limited to the realm of the visible. This preliminary level corresponds to the empirical documentation of his pre-1946 mission, Griaule tells us, representing a first stage in such works as his *Masques dogons*.[20] The second level of *benne so*, glossed as "*parole de côté*," comprises words that were left out or forgotten in *giri so*; that is, meanings that are held back until the person is ready, mainly with reference to Dogon rites and representations. Here we reach the celebrated turning point of Griaule's *Conversations*, with its privileged access to secret wisdom revealing a world of hidden insights and symbolic associations. Beyond, or perhaps we should say beneath, this level, is that of *bolo so*, or "*parole de derrière*," which completes the preceding level with still further secrets otherwise withheld but also synthesizes other domains of knowledge in relation to general, more abstract principles of classification. In this sense depth and synthetic totality go together as complementary principles of knowledge formation and acquisition. Represented by his post-1949 writings, the third level, *bolo so*, corresponds qualitatively to the still-deeper insights of *Le renard pâle*, written with Germaine Dieterlen and published posthumously in 1965, and applies quantitatively to the ethnosemiotic inventory of *Signes graphiques soudanais* (Griaule and Dieterlen 1951). And finally, capping and, in a crucial sense, containing the three levels, or "words," of Dogon

---

20. The not-so-subtle implication of this claim is that the work of his students and others on his team, such as Leiris, Schaeffner, and Paulme, remain limited to this superficial level, whereas his own *Masques* becomes the first stage of a deepening series of further studies.

knowledge is *so dayi*, or "*la parole claire*" proper, concerning the "edifice of knowledge in its ordered complexity" but also ultrarestricted insights like the ethnoastronomy of the system of Sirius. Griaule himself acknowledges a certain flexibility built into this scheme, which is subject to diverse interpretations. As he notes, *la parole claire* is conditioned by various channels of transmission: the family, age-set, occupational group, priesthood, mask society, among others (Griaule 1952, 34). And as with the language of *sigi so*, there are regional variations of its distribution among elders. Even analytically, a tension persists between qualitative form and quantitative content. *La parole claire* is at once a comprehensive inventory of secret signs and meanings and the logical predicate of an ordered triad representing the very principle by which the three preceding words or levels are organized into a framework of knowledge.[21] What is more, this very classification of levels remains one of the deepest secrets, safeguarding a hidden logic of relations for the deserving few, after years of perseverance and study.

Clearly, there is a heroic autobiography written into this schematic disclosure, a self-serving synthesis of research projects and fieldwork "missions" that further ratifies the initiatory paradigm and the privileged position of "the European" at its apex. Equally suspect is the objectivist language of its representation as a consistent and shared body of secrets differentially distributed between 5 and 6 percent of Upper Sanga at the highest level and between 15 and 20 percent at the penultimate level of restriction. But one striking feature worth taking seriously concerns the "body" of knowledge as corporeal field. In the exoteric knowledge of *giri so*, *giri* is glossed as "eye, face, in front, straight," extending the eye and face of the body into the agent's forward orientation toward other interactants, that is, into social space. The next level, *benne so*, literally refers to the "side" or "profile," extending the sides of the body and face into left and right axes of the interactive matrix. Within this emerging corporeal field, the third level, *bolo so*, extends backward from the "*derrière*" of the paradigmatic social body into a "dorsal," as opposed to a "frontal," axis, synthesizing front to back, as it were, in the acquisition of knowledge. The fourth level, "*la parole claire*," performs a logical synthesis by combining the left-right and back-forward axes into a system of corporeal coordinates, thereby framing "the body as it normally engages in movement and action" (Hanks l990, 90). What is missing from this explicit matrix is the up-down axis of above and below, but we can derive this from the corporeal field as

---

21. This logic of containment, by which a relation between elements is "counted" as an additional element, is also found in the Yoruba proverb "Two Ogboni make three" (*Ògbóni méjì ṣe ẹ̀ta*), illustrating how the "third" party in the relationship is the secret (*awo*) that binds them.

covert dimensions of embodied knowledge that remain embedded in social space and implicit in interaction.

In what sense, then, does the corporeal model of knowledge extend to the broader social contexts and domains of the habitus? Through what techniques of the body are corporeal schemes put into practice? In recasting the Dogon body as geometer, I will develop two related arguments that together account for the power of Dogon deep knowledge and its shifting, revisionary content. First, I will revisit Griaule's material on homesteads and villages to identify those "generative schemes" and "practical operators" (Bourdieu 1977, 125) serving as "structuring structures" of the habitus. Second, I will examine the political dynamics of Dogon villages and districts, for these charged arenas of competitive action produce the orthodoxies and heterodoxies of deep-knowledge claims.

If, as Bourdieu has argued, the house is a "privileged locus" for the objectification and embodiment of generative schemes (1977, 89), then the Dogon homestead should provide a rich source of symbolism for practical reinterpretation. Like the internal space of the Kabyle house analyzed by Bourdieu (90–92) and the interactive matrix of the Mayan *solar* discussed by Hanks (1990, 95), the Dogon big house (*ginu da*) represents a concentrated space of deeply embedded meanings and values. For Griaule, these meanings are of course mythic and primordial, relating the human form of "Nommo, the Demiurge, the reorganizer of the world," to the house plan, with its towers as his limbs, and further relating the heavenly placenta and its earthly counterpart (which together represent the head and legs of a man lying on his right side) to the kitchen (his head), stable (legs), central rooms (trunk and belly), storerooms (arms), and entrance (penis). The logic of the plan is explicitly generative for Griaule, in that the form and structure of the house manifest an ongoing extension of original creation. The sexualized entryway leads by a narrow passage to a workroom containing jars of water and grinding stones; these are used to crush new corn, yielding a liquid associated with male seminal fluid that is carried to the left-hand end of the entry, where it is poured on the shrine of the ancestors. Such libations are a way of "fertilizing" the ancestors, of extending their reproductive powers forward in time. Griaule explains: "Each part of the building represents an original being germinating and growing from its genitor. The whole plan is contained in an oval which itself represents the great placenta from which have emerged, in course of time, all space, all living beings, and everything in the world" (Griaule and Dieterlen 1954, 97–98).[22]

22. See also Paulme 1940, 314–20.

A practical "reading" of domestic space is structural in the sense that it identifies key oppositions, but following Bourdieu (1977, 90), the meanings are inhabited, "read with the body, in and through the movements and displacements which make the space within which they are enacted as much as they are made by it." Of central importance to this dialectic of objectification and embodiment is the practical mastery of the fundamental, generative schemes shaping everyday routines—not the symbolic oppositions themselves but their navigation and deployment by the body. Thus, from a practical perspective, inside and outside, empty and full, open and shut, left and right, are significant when activated, as "going in and coming out, filling and emptying, opening and shutting, going leftwards and going rightwards, going westwards and going eastwards, etc." (91). Like Griaule, we can focus on the body as the organizing scheme of domestic space, but with Bourdieu, it is the body in motion, in its habituating practical routines.

Returning to the Dogon house with a more dynamic approach to its corporeal oppositions, we enter from the "male" vestibule to the workroom, where the jars and grinding stones used to produce "male seminal fluid" for the ancestors are located; turning left we proceed to the central room (*dembere*), or "room of the belly," moving inside to the female center of the house: "The big central room is the domain and the symbol of the woman; the store-rooms each side are her arms, and the communicating door her sexual parts. The central room and the store-rooms together represent the woman lying on her back with outstretched arms, the door open and the woman ready for intercourse" (Griaule 1965, 94–95). Even from this minimal sketch we can grasp the implicit meaning of entering a house—from the outside door of the male sexual organ (94) to the inner "belly" of the central room—as an act of male penetration and copulation, corresponding to such oppositions as outside and inside, public and private, active and passive, above and below, that are reiterated and semantically saturated throughout the house. Thus, the ceiling is dry and male, associated with departing smoke and measured produce (red pepper, purple sorrel, yellow millet) drying on the roof and also with ancestors on the carved door and façade of the upper story. The floor inside is moist and female, with jars of water, the place of fertilization and childbirth: "When a child is to be born, the woman in labour is seated on a stool in the middle of the room, her back to the north, and is supported by women. The infant is delivered on the ground and takes possession of its soul in the place where it was conceived" (95).

Such a fundamental gendered opposition is also transposed—from right to left and left to right, and also along an east-west axis—when man and woman are lying in bed: "The man lies on his right side facing west, and the woman on her left side facing east. . . . The man lies on his right side and touches the woman with his left hand, never with his right. The woman sleeps on her left arm, and touches the man with her right. They never lie in any other position" (95–96). Notwithstanding the large grain of salt with which we should take such archetypal characterizations, clearly a set of qualitative oppositions is associated with this gendered corporeal field, one that also extends back to front, since the hearth is located at the back of the house, and the woman delivers with her back to the north, the entrance and front of the house. Moreover, the impurity of "leftness" is likely linked to the polluting powers of menstrual blood, given its charged symbolism in the men's mask society, when men in red-dyed fiber skirts dance as menstruating women (Paulme 1940, 268–70), and in the strict seclusion of menstruating women for five days in special menstruation huts (*ya punune ginu*) located at the east-west boundaries of the village (Paulme 1940, 264–68), where they figure as "hands" (Griaule 1965, 97). And finally, along a vertical axis of gender, we can discern a key opposition that figures in the larger political terms of Upper and Lower Sanga, extending from floor to ceiling. If, as Ogotemmêli tells us, "the soil of the ground-floor is the symbol of the earth and of Lébé, restored to life in earth," another reference to the earth as cosmogonic mother, then the face of the house, which "gives its name to the tallest mask," must be none other than the grand mask of Awa, the primordial male ancestor, although the name is not provided in this text. Ascending is thus associated with Awa, descending with Lébé.

A key concept of practical logic is that of scheme transfer, by which generative oppositions like those sketched above are redeployed between contexts, reproducing the same opposition within a wider or narrower social space or field. The economy of logic, in its practical applications, refers to the interchangeability of a core set of generative schemes over a wide range of social, spatial, and semantic domains. Moving, in a sense, from the inside out, from the core schematic matrix of the household to the broader arenas of the village and district, we can retrace Griaule's interpretive footsteps, recasting what he saw as a widening series of symbolic correspondences into practical homologies extending from the corporeal field. The key coordinates of body space—up-down, left-right, back-front—with their associated domestic values, are thereby transposed into coextensive political and territorial relations. For Griaule, these correspondences remained mythic and symbolic: the "body" of the house was reproduced, *pars pro toto*, in the quarter (or section) of each village, in the village at large, and in the most inclusive district. As Griaule (1965, 97) explains, "Within the village each quarter is a complete

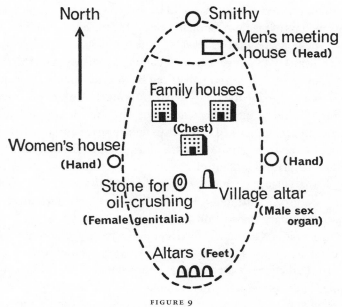

North

FIGURE 9
Dogon village scheme (from Griaule 1965, 95)

whole, and should be laid out in the same way as the village, like a separate entity." This layout is none other than the anthropomorphic template transposed from micro- to macrodomains. Like the house, the village (and each of its quarters or sections) replicates the mythic body in its layout and plan, with the iron-smelting smithy as its "head," the family houses as its "chest," the women's menstrual huts as "hands," its central altars as (male and female) genitalia, and its communal altars as feet (see fig. 9). And like the homestead "correctly sited . . . that is to say, open to the north" (94), the body of the village aligns with cardinal points: the head is north, the left and right hands east and west, and the feet south. In terms of a dynamic corporeal field, a significant egocentric and sociocentric synthesis is thus achieved, whereby north is up, south is down, east is left, and west is right. Because the body is lying down on its back, front is also celestial, and back is terrestrial. Clearly, the fixity of such schemes is problematic—as Ogotemmêli tells us, Lower Ogol is "almost right," and most of the houses of Upper Ogol face west to avoid the prevailing rains (96, 92). But again I would emphasize practical movement over static design: movement in and out, up and down, back and forth, left and right. From this more active agentive perspective, we can even "predict" certain amendments to the village scheme that find support in Griaule's text.

In Griaule's diagram, both male and female genitalia are manifest in complementary altars of the foundational shrine—the male organ in the form of a
cone, the female as a hollowed stone. This dualism replicates the bisexuality of
original twinship, with one gender dominating the other, and further suggests
that the body of the house and village can be male or female, depending on
context.[23] But if entering the village is like entering the house, with the male's
frontal penetration of interior female space, then we should find maleness
outside the village, in marked contrast to female space at the center. And in
fact we do. In a revealing footnote to the village model, Griaule and Dieterlen
(1954, 96n2) explain that "out of respect for the female sex . . . and for the
women of the village, *the male shrine is often built outside the walls*" (my
emphasis; see also Griaule 1965, 97). Whether or not this explanation is based
on ad hoc secondary elaborations, I see the discrepancy as more consistent
with the generative scheme of entering and exiting. Furthermore, following the logic of scheme transposition, the same opposition can be inverted
without contradiction, as context and circumstances dictate. Thus, from the
"assembled" perspective of normative politics, of the male regulation of public affairs, men occupy the center in the men's meeting house, while women
are marginalized in menstruation huts and the inner rooms of the domestic
domain. In this gendered distribution of male authority and order, with men
at the center and women at the margins, a further ethnographic contradiction
occurs that vanishes from a practical point of view. Again, in his normative
diagram, Griaule locates the men's meeting house at the "head" of the village,
which is above and to the north, whereas in his text, we find such structures
in the central square of the village and in each public square (presumably
those of each quarter). How can it occupy both positions at once—the northern head and the central square? In this case, Griaule is succumbing to the
synoptic illusion (Bourdieu 1977, 97–109), when practical systems of classification are abstracted into a fixed hierarchy of logical relations apart from their
context-specific validity and thus appear contradictory. The men's house can
occupy both positions at once because, according to the coordinates of body
space, "up" is male, north, dry, celestial, associated with lineage ancestors
and authority, and by implication, "down" is female, south, moist, terrestrial,
associated with childbirth. In effect, the male-female schematism "flips" between north-south, up-down, and center-periphery axes, and since Griaule
could not diagram the transpositions themselves, he privileged one location
at the expense of the other.

23. Note the male body with female parts in Griaule and Dieterlen 1954, 97–98, and the
female body in Griaule 1965, 94–95.

This latter example of scheme transposition shifts into yet another significant generative contrast that relates the words of men to the blood of women.
Returning to the men's house as centrally located in the Dogon village and
"facing north" (Griaule 1965, 98), "the elders [who] . . . confer there and take
decisions on matters of public interest" (97) are necessarily seated, as required
by the corporeal coordinates of "true speech" (Calame-Griaule 1986, 63–64)
and structurally imposed by the low roof and rafters. Such true speech, of
good words, has a straight path that is cardinally north: as Griaule (1952, 29)
reported from native testimony, "The word of the front and the word of the
back are good words . . . for the straight characteristics connote a single word,
ordered, straight, directly reaching the hearer who must understand it."[24]
In relation to the domestic matrix of gendered orientations, however, these
straight-talking elders resemble women. Like women giving birth within the
house, seated on a stool, supported by other women, so that the infant is delivered "on the ground," the men are seated at the center of the town, supported
by men, delivering good words that are "grounded" in a ground plan that
evokes the seventh and eighth ancestors, "the master of Speech, and . . . the
Word itself" (Griaule 1965, 98). But if from the vertical axis of standing and
sitting, these men are like women, from the frontal and dorsal axis of ahead
and behind, they again assert their difference: women give birth with their
backs to the north, whereas men in the speech shelter, at least in principle, face
north. It is the lateral axis of left and right, however, that extends to the most
significant contrast between men and women, purity and pollution, center
and periphery, and, finally, good and bad words, for at right angles to the
north-facing men, the women's menstruation shelters establish left and right
"hands" and east-west limits of the village. So fundamental is this schematic
opposition to the construction of gendered public space that, "in the past,
when a village was founded, the [men's] shelter and the women's houses were
the first buildings to be erected" (Griaule 1965, 97).

And it is in these primary village coordinates that we find the key to the
power of *la parole claire*. For the secret contrast to the good words of men
are the bad words of women as divisive, disorderly, polluted, and impure—
in short, transfigured as menstrual blood. According to Ogotemmêli, "the
unpleasant smell of the female sexual parts comes from the bad words heard
by the ear," adding that "bad words smell" and "affect a man's potency"
(Griaule 1965, 139, 142). Such words are not fertile but sabotage procreation,

24. "la parole de devant et la parole de derrière [sont] bonnes parole . . . car les traits droits
connotent une seule parole, ordonnée, droite, parvenant directement à l'auditeur qui doit
l'entendre."

since they are formed by unwanted blood, the result of mother-son incest when the jackal (later called the pale fox) violated the earth. Bad words thus pass out of the womb "in emanations" (142). Good words, by contrast, represent the pure water of Nummo, which is the female moisture and blood of procreation, mingling with the male seed to create new life. Since the bad words of menstruating women cause such havoc, these women are exiled to the margins of the village and, after their periods, cleanse their vaginas with *Lannea acida* oil, which, as a sweetener, works "like a good word in combating the bad smell resulting from a bad word" (142). This profound association of bad words with bad blood explains why we find, at the center of the village, the female shrine as sexual organ, made of stones "on which the fruit of the *Lannea acida* is crushed" (97), and where the bad blood of women is thus ritually converted into the good words, or straight speech, of men.

What I am suggesting is that the polluting, transgressive, nonreproductive menstrual blood of women represents the powerful efficacy of deep knowledge, as hidden and secret transformative agency in contrast to the reproductive language of "*paroles de face.*" Located at the sides and margins of the social body, these "words" have a subversive and destabilizing force as the negative dialectic of cosmological renewal—the valence that sunders and takes apart in order to remake and recombine anew, to purify through ritual reproduction. In sociopolitical terms, such deep knowledge aligns with dominant sociopolitical cleavages, emphasizing the separation and division of power competition over the administrative unity of the political body as a whole, be it the household, ward, village, or district. The secret of deep knowledge in these oppositional contexts is not found in a hidden doctrine for the privileged few but in its paradigmatic negation of the status quo associated with the relevant political authority. If the true words of men are delivered while sitting, evoking the position of women in labor, it is because their official words are socially reproductive. By contrast, the destabilizing words of the left and right are transformative, false by official standards but sanctified by deeper truth-conditions that remain impure and off bounds to the public.

To support this unorthodox rereading of Griaule, we can sketch the basic contours of Dogon government, focusing on the principal relations of segmentation between competing groups (politics) and their hierarchical inclusion within the region or district. Studies of Dogon sociopolitical organization reveal a complex tapestry of interrelated and overlapping institutions, including clans and lineages, occupational castes, various cults and mask societies, indigenes and strangers, men's and women's associations, as well as households, villages, and districts stratified by age-sets and in many cases divided between Upper and Lower sections with complementary ritual domains. Thus, in the well-worked region of Sanga, divided into Upper and Lower subregions, we find villages such as Ogol, Sangui, Ennguel, and Bongo, each in turn divided into Upper and Lower sections, as well as villages such as Barkou and Gogoli that are not divided as such.[25] As Tait's attempted synthesis of the Griaule school literature reveals, there is a lack of consensus on such key points as whether or not the entire Sanga region is led by one Hogon or two (for each division), how his council of elders and officers are recruited, whether or not the Awa men's society with its *sigi* rites recruits from Upper Sanga exclusively, and whether or not the Lébé cult belongs to Lower Sanga only (Tait 1950). But such complexities aside, we can abstract a core model of "politics" and "administration" in the Bandiagara cliffs that identifies relations of opposition and inclusion in the following terms: within the district or region, we find two main "halves" (Upper and Lower), segmented into villages, many of which are also split into Upper and Lower divisions, and which in turn break down into quarters or wards, and further into lineages and lineage segments organized by households or homesteads of the "Grandes Maisons." Headed by the Hogon as a fused political and ritual office, the system was administered through a council of elders that represented the dominant quarters and lineages of each village, and these presumably were similarly organized around a senior elder and his representative age-mates, and so forth in a replicating pattern that applied to the village quarter and even the "houses" within, each with its "*chef de maison.*" According to this ideal-typical pattern, authority relations refer to the hierarchical inclusion of houses, quarters, and villages within the Hogon's regional jurisdiction, and political relations to the divisive competition between houses, quarters, villages, even Upper and Lower divisions—that is, between units of equivalent status and rank—for the power to determine public policy and its outcomes.

From this structural framework, derived from M. G. Smith (1956, 1960), power is transformative and divisive, generating factions from below that attempt to prevail over others, whereas authority is reproductive, containing competitive politics through the execution of public policy from above, as one administrative body. As Smith points out, this dialectic of power and authority informs all levels of political organization; in the Dogon context, these would include the family and its internal sibling groups up through the ward, village, and district levels. But what I am suggesting in ritual terms is that the transgressive potency of power sui generis, opposed to authority as it violates its categories and constraints, is simultaneously manifest in menstrual blood and the unbounded powers of the bush, outside society. Denise Paulme

---

25. See Tait 1950, 176–77, for the full list of villages.

notes that the *olubaru* elders in the highest grade of the *sigi* society not only are considered impure (*inne puru*) and close to death but are also immune to menstrual blood and exempt from the taboos that otherwise apply to "*hommes vivants.*" For this reason they are designated to repair the women's menstruation huts every year and preside over the *sigi* and *dama* masks, which are both powerful and impure. In fact, the red fiber skirts, evoking the original blood of incest and women's subsequent menstrual debt to the earth, transform the powerful masked men of the bush into menstruating women, subject to the same taboos while manifesting their polluting potency: "This impure character of the masks reaches its maximum on the day the men stain red the fiber-tendril coverings (skirts, bracelets, etc.) that accompany the carrying of the masks. *Anam punia*, 'menses of men,' designates this day of coloring the fibers red, when the men will not show themselves in the village any more than menstruating women would be walking around" (Paulme 1940, 269).[26] Paulme further notes that the impure elders of the mask society are charged with the conservation and transmission of its traditions, linking the deepest power (*nyama*) of the deepest secrets to the polluting blood of women.

The complementary frame, in political terms, of the "witchcraft" of such unbridled power is the "fertility" of administrative authority: the Hogon in office, the moral order upheld, and the reproductive capacities of men and women revitalized. In ritual terms, the power of deep knowledge and menstrual blood must be domesticated and incorporated into the body politic, brought from the bush into the center of the village—in effect, cleansed and channeled into regeneration. Effective incorporation within the social order involves a cooling and freshening of the hot redness of Awa, the notion of *tawa* in *sigi so* (Leiris 1992, 72) associated with the humidity and wetness of cleansed female sexuality. Such a reading of the hot-cold ("*ardeur-fraîcheur*") opposition (73) is consistent with van Beek's interpretation of the *dama* festival as the male appropriation of female reproductive power but further identifies menstrual blood with political power and deep knowledge. I therefore identify the blood of women as a critical component of ritual reproduction (a feature that van Beek cannot really explain) and the domain of deep knowledge not as fixed esoterica (which van Beek could not find) but as a shifting corpus of generative schemes and pragmatic functions. What makes deep knowledge powerful

26. "Ce caractère impur des masques atteint son maximum le jour où les hommes teignent en rouge les vêtements en fibres de sansevière (jupes, bracelets. . . .) qui accompagnent le port des masques. *Anam punia*, 'menstrues des homme,' désigne ce jour de la coloration en rouge des fibres, où les hommes ne se montreront pas plus au village que ne s'y promèneraient des femmes menstruées."

is not only its association with the bush but its formal, pragmatic, and structural opposition to the authority structures that it enters and revitalizes.

In the broadest context of Upper and Lower Sanga, the Awa mask associated with *sigi* and *dama* clearly mediates political relations between subregional levels; between villages themselves (some perform *sigi* together, others apart); and within villages, between their Upper and Lower halves, between their quarters, and between lineages. Clearly, the crosscutting sodalities of age-sets are crucial in this process, dividing opposed sections in political competition and combining them in administrative hierarchy, and it is precisely such relations of union and separation that correspond to freshness and heat, power and authority, outside and inside, deep words and straight speech, values that are contextually situated in the dominant coordinates of the corporeal field. And clearly, the very politics of village fission and rebellion are signaled by new ritual itineraries and routines. But to finally explain how *la parole claire* relates to the semantic and corporeal schemes of the habitus, in the overt symbolic if unstable elaborations which Griaule's ethnophilosophical investigations brought to light, we need to return to the generative conditions of orthodox and heterodox discourses.

In Bourdieu's initial theory of practice, the world of the habitus—the house, the village, the farming cycle and agricultural rituals—is paradigmatically silent. Implicitly embedded in social space and time, through the practical taxonomies shaping everyday routines, practical consciousness exists in the body as a set of habituated dispositions rather than an explicit ideology or body of ideas. In an oft-quoted statement, "what is essential *goes without saying because it comes without saying*... the play of mythico-ritual homologies constitutes a perfectly closed world, each aspect of which is, as it were, a reflection of all the others" (Bourdieu 1977, 167; his emphasis). In such a field of internalized *doxa*, there can be no deep knowledge of *la parole claire*, reflecting on the secrets of empowerment and reproduction, unless either "culture contact" or class formation calls the given world into question. Bourdieu has been criticized for hypostasizing such an organic idiom for the traditional, "premodern" world, and Jean Comaroff and John Comaroff (1991) have incorporated it into a more realistic theory of hegemony; nevertheless, his insight stands as a theoretical definition of the embodied forms of practical consciousness. As such, it remains characteristically uncritical: "The adherence expressed in the doxic relation to the social world is the absolute form of recognition of legitimacy through misrecognition of arbitrariness, since it is unaware of the very question of legitimacy, which arises from competition for legitimacy, and hence from conflict between groups claiming to possess it" (Bourdieu 1977, 168).

As I have argued in a Yoruba context (Apter 1992, 228n7), the critical calling into question of doxa—the meanings and values embedded in the habitus—is not limited to "contact" or class formation but is also found in the dialectics of power and authority motivating segmentary opposition and administrative hierarchy. Competition for power seeks the revision of authority structures just as administrative authority contains power competition; thus, along the dominant political cleavages and lines of segmentation we will find heterodox challenges to the orthodoxy of the status quo. In the Dogon context, such challenges could be leveled against the household head within a homestead, between lineage elders of a quarter or village, or against the Hogon of Upper Sanga by a hunter or priest of Lower Sanga—perhaps by Ogotemmêli himself. My point is not to document such challenges, since I can only infer such relations from the data (see also Jolly 1998–99, 2004; Jolly and Guindo 2003), but to establish the political conditions in which they arise, as a heterodox field of destabilizing discourses against "the straight speech" of men. Through the ritual articulation of political competition and mediation, the critical agency of *la parole claire* destabilizes the very ground of political authority by reflecting on the generative schemes of the habitus, endowing them with explicit mythic content and shifting their meanings to remake the body politic. That such renewal is always transformative and reproductive, hot and cool, polluting and purifying, powerful and authoritative, does not detract from the power of critical agency but locates it within a dynamic arena of competitive politics and material relations.

Leach (1958, 120) has said that good ethnography sustains alternative analyses and interpretations, including those that controvert the original author. Thus, he praised Malinowski's Trobriand fieldwork while "refuting" his extensionist kinship thesis in a rival analysis of social category terms. In a sense, I have pursued a similar strategy, affirming the value of Griaule's Dogon studies and the enduring legacy of *la parole claire* in an alternative reading of its indexical functions, privileging pragmatic over semantic categories as shifting coordinates of a corporeal field. Despite the growing criticism of Griaule's colonial epistemology, his ahistoricism, the violence of his strategies and tactics, and the paternalism of his "sympathetic" quest—problems that belong to anthropology's history more generally—his investigations into Dogon deep knowledge are not so easily swept aside but provide a body of knowledge, a *corpus inscriptionum* (to reinvoke Malinowski [1961, 24]), that sustains productive reanalysis and reinterpretation.

In my own rereading of selected texts and passages, including those of Leiris and Calame-Griaule, the body of knowledge takes center stage, not as a collection of secrets or a symbolic cipher, but as the indexical ground of deictic reference, generating and transforming social space and political context through ritual performance and incantation, and thus challenging and revising authority structures through idioms of cosmological renewal. When secret knowledge is liberated from its ideology of fixed and determinate content, it can be seen as a socially sanctioned rhetorical resource that is unstable and destabilizing because it redeploys the practical homologies of the habitus, drawing on the left hand and the polluting blood of women to reshape the social and political body. In this capacity, *la parole claire* sustains a grammatical space of critical agency, which, if lost on Griaule in his search for hidden symbols, remains equally lost on his critics and detractors.

6

Decolonizing the Text

> I returned deliberately to the first I had seen—and there it was, black, dried, sunken, with closed eyelids, a head that seemed to sleep at the top of that pole, and, with the shrunken dry lips showing a narrow white line of teeth, was smiling, too, smiling continuously at some endless and jocose dream of that eternal slumber.... Rebels! What would be the next definition I was to hear? There had been enemies, criminals, workers—and these were rebels. Those rebellious heads looked very subdued to me on their sticks.
> JOSEPH CONRAD, *Heart of Darkness*

In a revealing passage of his *Races of Africa*—first published in 1930 and re-issued four times by 1966—Seligman quotes Dr. Wilhelm Junker on the African pygmy's "amazing talent for mimicry":

> A striking proof of this was afforded by an Achua whom I had seen and measured four years previously in Rumbek, and now again met at Gam[b]ari's. His comic ways and quick movements made this little fellow the clown of our society. He imitated with marvelous fidelity the peculiarities of persons whom he had once seen; for instance the gestures and facial expressions of Jussuf Pasha...and of Haj Halil at their devotions, as well as the address and movements of Emin Pasha "with the four eyes" (spectacles)...and now he took me off to the life, rehearsing after four years, down to the minutest details, and with surprising accuracy, my anthropometric performance when measuring his body at Rumbek. (Seligman 1966, 26–27)

The passage is strangely decontextualized by Seligman, with no reference to the southern Sudan, where the event took place, or even to the text in which it was originally recorded (Junker 1892, 86), and it would have reflected nothing more than a typical trope of the time—that is, the diminutive African as mimic and clown—were it not for the formidable reputations of Seligman and his collaborators, including E. Gellner, E. E. Evans-Pritchard, P. Bohannan, D. Forde, M. Fortes, P. Kaberry, S. F. Nadel, D. J. Stenning, J. Beattie, L. Mair, J. Perstiany, J. Barnes, M. Douglas, and I. Schapera, who were listed in later editions. We cannot assume that they consciously endorsed every page of Seligman's book, but the documentary use of Junker's observations, the passage itself, and its relationship to the rest of Seligman's ethnological text exemplify the "awkward relationship" of Africanist anthropology to the politics and culture of empire more generally. Treating Seligman's quotation of Junker's text as paradigmatic of the imperial palimpsest in Africanist anthropology, I review key positions and debates shaping its theory and practice today. The philological metaphor framing this review is not merely rhetorical but has significant methodological implications for navigating into and out of anthropology's heart of darkness.

This chapter thus returns to the discourse *of* Africa, and the larger challenges of writing both within and against the grain. I begin by reviewing the strongest critiques of Africanist anthropology in relation to empire because they raise fundamental challenges that must be taken into account by anyone working in the field, and they represent a growing literature that is developing in interesting ways. Somewhat polemically, in both explicit and implicit response to these challenges, I then review a range of studies that serve to recuperate Africanist anthropology from its imperial conditions of impossibility, first by examining its dialogical dimensions and then by illuminating the dialectics of imperial culture not only in Africa but "between metropole and colony" (Stoler and Cooper 1997). I focus mainly on British and French Africanist contexts and traditions and blur the boundary between anthropology and history.

Africa, Anthropology, and the Colonial Library

As we saw in chapter 1, Mudimbe's critique of the colonial library (1988) traced a genealogy of models in which representations of the African "Other" functioned not as windows into another world but as signs of imperial domination. Previous scholars had already examined the connections between anthropology and colonialism in Africa. In the important collection by Asad (1973), James (1973) could cast the anthropologist in Africa as a "reluctant imperialist" capable—like Malinowski in his better moments—of openly criticizing colonial authority and policy, whereas Faris (1973) could confirm that those like Nadel were willing coconspirators in imposing theoretical-cum-colonial order and control. In an equally important publication the previous year, Leclerc (1972) located imperial ethnocentrism at the very core of anthropological method, refined by functionalism and transformed by relativism but never transcended or erased. Indeed, the first monumental indictment of Africanist ethnography was by Leiris and first appeared as *L'Afrique fantôme* in 1934, then disappeared in 1941 by order of the Vichy regime, and reappeared in three subsequent editions (1951, 1968, 1981) as a meticulous testimony to colonial fantasy and desire (Jamin 1982a; see also Leiris 1989). In one entry, Leiris likens "l'enquête ethnographique" (the ethnographic quest/inquest) of the historic Dakar-Djibouti expedition (Jamin 1982b; Clifford 1988) to police interrogation, disclaims the possibility of ever knowing what Africans actually think, and displaces his frustrated ethnographic desire into unconsummated lust for the racialized Other: "Je n'ai jamais couché avec une femme noire. Que je suis donc resté européen!" ("I have never slept with a black woman. Thus will I remain a European!"; see Jamin 1982a, 206). Clearly, Leiris's "*fantôme*" prefigures Mudimbe's "invention" in these respects, but unlike the former poetics of documentation, the latter project is explicitly grounded in critical theory and method, posing as its central problem the location of gnosis in the order of knowledge about Africa.

As we have seen, gnosis functions for Mudimbe as a duplex sign anchoring the form and content of "traditional" African philosophies within those Western discourses that purport to represent them. In other words, gnosis is both a body of secret knowledge to be mastered and an imperial trope of authentic alterity, which, like the Holy Grail, is nobly pursued but endlessly displaced. Without denying the existence and local authority of actual African gnostic systems, Mudimbe (1988, 186) locates them within "a Western epistemological territory" where they remain colonized and thus beyond adequate representation and understanding. Of the African worlds portrayed by such scholarship, Mudimbe (1988, 186) asks: "Is not this reality distorted in the expression of African modalities in non-African languages? Is it not inverted, modified by anthropological and philosophical categories used by specialists in dominant discourses?" Although the ethnophilosophical investigations of Griaule (1952, 1965) and Tempels (1969) are most directly attacked for reproducing the politics of paternalism in their "cultivated sympathy" (*Einfühlung*) for the African sage, the critique extends beyond ethnophilosophy as such to embrace virtually all Africanist ethnography, including de Heusch's work (1982, 1985) on symbolic functions and Turner's (1969, 1981) on social dynamics and ritual mediations, not to mention that of African intellectuals who remain unwitting heirs to a colonial "philosophy of conquest" (Mudimbe 1988, 69). There are of course other readings and arguments in Mudimbe's rich study, with his multifaceted "idea" of Africa developed further in a sequel (Mudimbe 1994), but the problem of gnosis and the colonial library poses fundamental questions concerning the very limits of anthropological reason.

To illustrate, can Junker's description of a pygmy, quoted in Seligman (1966) above, be easily dismissed as a relic of an earlier ideology, or does its rupture into Seligman's discussion represent a deeper subtext in Africanist ethnography that remains hidden by various mutations and guises to this day?

On the surface, Seligman's ideological legacy among his Africanist progeny seems merely nominal. Their aforementioned names appear in a publisher's note to the third (1957) and fourth (1966) editions, together with their writings in an expanded bibliography, but can they be held accountable for the sins of their father (Kuklick 1978)? The very framework of the International African Institute's (IAI) Ethnographic Survey of Africa series emphasized the social organization and cultural life of African peoples rather than their physical characters and racial types. But here is precisely where the conceptual elisions of Mudimbe's epistemological territory take place. How is it possible that a book entitled *Races of Africa*, with its designated *diacritica* of "skin colour, hair form, stature, head shape, and certain characters of the face, e.g. prognathism, and of the nose" (Seligman 1966, 2–3), a book that also explicitly invokes the Hamitic hypothesis and the childlike simplicity of African languages, contains so much material on social organization, economy, burial, and so on? Here the racial, linguistic, and cultural domains form an integrated whole, with the classification of racial types (Bushmen, the True Negro, Hamites, Bantu, and Semites) informing the distribution of tribes and traditions, such that society and culture are effectively subsumed by race. There is no question that Seligman's students and colleagues working in Africa disavowed such subsumptions on political and intellectual grounds, but does not an implicit racial logic— cloaked in the essentializing categories of native administration and customary law—slip unnoticed through the back door? Insofar as modern Africanist ethnography has sought pristine models of social structures (British tradition) and systems of thought (Griaule school), has it not endorsed the fundamental objectifying, essentializing, and even implicit racializing of imperial science at large? Like Junker's pygmy breaking into Seligman's text, does the logic of racialization constitute the imperial palimpsest of modern Africanist research?

Supporting evidence for this radical thesis illustrates how implicit imperial/colonial logics and categories have been imposed on Africa and interpolated back into the precolonial past. This has occurred in two related registers that can be crudely labeled narrative and inventive. If evolutionism served as the dominant narrative paradigm in Victorian anthropology (Stocking 1987; Brantlinger 1986), supporting imperial ideas of racial difference, destiny, and hierarchy, it also provided the working guidelines for colonial officers and government anthropologists following Lugard's (1965) "dual mandate" in Africa—the uplifting of native peoples according to their natural (i.e., racial) capabilities while benefiting commerce and industry at home (Kuklick 1991). Within this British African context, the challenge posed by functionalism to evolutionary thinking could be developed by "pure scholars" unfettered by policy (and funded by the Rockefeller Foundation through the IAI), but methodological strictures notwithstanding, evolutionary thinking and its hidden racial assumptions were not so easily transcended. Functionalists could jettison pseudohistorical speculations about the undocumented histories of African peoples, replacing diffusionist and evolutionary origins with the more rigorous concept of "social function" (Radcliffe-Brown 1952b, 3, 12–14), but— as Fabian (1983) argued with respect to the anthropological object of knowledge at large—their societies were not only frozen in time but also functioned implicitly as living relics of the past. Lurking beneath the genealogical and political morphologies and typologies was an evolutionary assumption, still difficult to exorcise, that acephalous societies like the Tallensi, Nuer, or Tiv were structurally more primitive than the centralized "states" that formed precolonial kingdoms and empires, and hence were less advanced or capable of civilization. The tenacity of such chronotopic displacements is most clearly illustrated by the so-called Bushmen, or San-speaking peoples, of southern Africa, whose enduring image as Stone Age hunters and gatherers providing a living museum of minimal society has been perpetuated not only by cultural ecologists and materialists (Lee 1979; Lee and Devore 1976) but also by cultural anthropologists like Sahlins (1972, 1–39), who found in Bushmen "bands" a Paleolithic parable of "the original affluent society." It was not until Wilmsen's definitive analysis of such images and ideologies against the historical conditions of Kalahari political economy—based on archeological, archival, and socioeconomic data of ancient trade routes and modern relations of production—that the myth of the Bushmen could be explained and debunked as a modern fiction projected back in time (Wilmsen 1989).

In the more "inventive" register of reification mentioned above, more strongly associated with British functionalism and indirect rule (Kuklick 1984; Pels 1996), we find a variety of innovations and transformations ranging from imperial pageants to customary law (Ranger 1983). We will return to this range in due course, but here I want to focus on those colonial categories that were imposed on Africans in the name of local tradition. As Ranger (1983, 250) writes: "The most far-reaching inventions of tradition in colonial Africa took place when the Europeans believed themselves to be respecting age-old African custom. What was called customary law, customary land-rights, customary political structure, and so on, were in fact *all* invented by colonial codification." Quoting Iliffe (1979, 323–24) on the creation of tribes in colonial Tanganyika, Ranger shows how the essentialized units of indirect rule retained a racial inflection:

> The notion of the tribe lay at the heart of indirect rule in Tanganyika. Refining the racial thinking common in German times, administrators believed that every African belonged to a tribe, just as every European belonged to a nation. . . . Tribes were seen as cultural units "possessing a common language,

a single social system, and an established common law." Their political and social systems rested on kinship. Tribal membership was hereditary. Different tribes were related genealogically.... As unusually well-informed officials knew, this stereotype bore little relation to Tanganyika's kaleidoscopic history, but it was the shifting sand on which Cameron and his disciples erected indirect rule by "taking the tribal unit." They had the power and created the political geography. (Ranger 1983, 250)

No stronger demonstration of Mudimbe's thesis regarding the colonial invention of Africa can be found, and even if questions remain concerning the representativeness of the Tanganyikan case, its German colonial legacy, and, more importantly, the dialectical character of the inventions themselves, the example illustrates the implicit racial logic of tribal organization and classification as it was framed by colonialism and interpolated into the past. Of course, customary law was not invented ex nihilo, but the colonial powers fixed flexible principles into written statutes that were applied in the name of the chiefs and their traditions, thereby effecting a hidden transformation of "traditional law" itself (Chanock 1985; Mann and Roberts 1991). Similarly, Amselle examines the "hardening of identities" by colonial policy rather than their invention *tout court* and develops a more accurate perspective in which "Africa is the joint invention of Africans and Europeans" (Amselle 1998, xv). But these more historically situated approaches to the codifying forms and functions of colonial governmentality in Africa do not necessarily vitiate Mudimbe's radical critique and may in fact extend it to the very methods and models of scientific anthropology operating at the time. It takes no major effort to see the formal similarities between the administrative units of indirect rule and the ethnographic classifications of Hailey (1957) and of the classics by Radcliffe-Brown and Forde (1950), Fortes and Evans-Pritchard (1940), and Forde (1954). Less obvious, however, is the significance of the role played by kinship and descent in establishing the a priori framework of tribal structure and its "comparative morphology" (Radcliffe-Brown 1952b, 195).

Following the Tanganyikan example of Iliffe (1979), I suggest that the racial dimensions of Victorian evolutionism and imperial pseudoscience slipped into the functionalists' obsession with kinship, descent, and genealogical method, where, in a sense, function followed not only structure but also form. Despite the explicit disavowal by Radcliffe-Brown (1952b) of conjectural history in favor of social function and—more to the point—his rejection of biological for social kinship, forms of racial reasoning remained embedded in biological metaphors and matrices. Not only does the physiological model the social for Radcliffe-Brown (1952b, 188–204), it also hides within the generative matrix of kinship and the social order, masquerading beneath the axiom of amity

of Fortes (1969), infusing the extensionist thesis, and even revealing its face
in such unguarded moments as when Fortes (1969, 309) proclaims: "I regard
it as now established that the elementary components of patrifiliation and
matrifiliation, and hence of agnatic, enatic, and cognatic modes of reckoning
kinship are, like genes in the individual organism invariably present in all
familial systems." As R. T. Smith (1973, 122) observed, this view "comes dan-
gerously close to reintroducing the confusion between biology and kinship."
Does it not in fact represent Junker's pygmy popping up like a jack-in-the-
box from the depths of Fortes's text? If it does, this is not to discredit Fortes's
undeniable insights and achievements in Africanist ethnography and kinship
studies (Goody 1995) but to show that the imperial palimpsest survives in
the most unexpected places and informs the ethnographic reifications of an
Africa observed.

The Critique of Pure Colonialism

I have pushed Mudimbe's thesis (1988, 1994) in a particular direction to illustrate how a putatively precolonial and hence traditional Africa has been
invented by colonial structures and categories. The thesis contains a powerful
critique of anthropological reason in Africa, and the argument can be illustrated historically in relation to travel narrative, missionary discourse, language standardization, colonial medicine, and cartography as well as ethnography per se (John Comaroff and Jean Comaroff 1992; Fabian 1986; Fanon 1967,
121–45; Hunt 1997; Noyes 1994; Thornton 1983; White 1995). In this section, I
signpost a literature that might appear to "refute" Mudimbe's epistemological
reductions of Africanist anthropology to colonial discourse, but it need not
and in fact should not be seen contra his position. In what follows, I attempt
a synthesis of what otherwise look like counterarguments.

DIALOGICS

The simplest alternatives to the radical reductions of Mudimbe (1988) belong
to those studies that complicate the hegemonic picture with a range of ambiguous and ambivalent voices found within the colonizing discourses themselves. Cocks (1995), for example, shows how the rhetoric of science could be
invoked to undo, as well as uphold, colonial policy, focusing on G. Wilson's
(1941, 1942) criticism of the "native problem" as a case in point. Forster (1994)
demonstrates a link between functionalism and the cultural nationalism of
Kenyatta and Banda. Goody's (1995) somewhat-rambling defense of Africanist

anthropology against colonial critique takes great pains to show how the non-British funding sources and nationalities of many Africanists insulated the discipline from imperial influence and control; he also reveals how anthropologists like Fortes were suspiciously regarded as "Jews" and/or "Reds." Nor did anthropologists of Africa remain obsessed with the primitive, seeking pristine models of precolonial systems. In Britain, the Manchester school had focused on the social dynamics of colonial transformations and dislocations in both town and country since the 1950s (Werbner 1984), a perspective paralleled by Balandier's "*sociologie actuelle*" of the "colonial situation" (Balandier 1966, 1970) in Francophone Africa.

If hegemonic discourse was not exactly monolithic, neither was it monologic. Studies of resistance have redefined various colonial situations (including patriarchal and neocolonial domination) as a dialogical encounter ranging from poetic and prophetic voices of self-expression and empowerment (Abu-Lughod 1986; Boddy 1989; Fernandez 1982; MacGaffey 1983) to signifying practices in both ritual (Jean Comaroff 1985) and armed struggle (Lan 1985). These studies have developed frameworks for analyzing the dialogics of colonial discourse within localized political fields. Such "dialogues" take many forms, extending from the study of critical agency in Africa (as explored and developed in the previous chapters) to the mimetic appropriation (Stoller 1995; Kramer 1993) and political negotiation of colonial power and authority by socially situated actors. An important essay by Ranger (1983) discusses how Africans manipulated "invented custom" to promote a national culture, to prevent the erosion of gerontocratic authority by wage-laboring youth, to redefine gender relations, or simply to aggrandize political power. The strength of such perspectives is that they put Mudimbe's principles into historical practice, revealing that the fictions and inventions of colonial discourse and power are indeed social facts and, perhaps most important, how they become social facts. We can now read Junker's pygmy not simply as a relic of imperial racism but as the paradigmatic subaltern voice, commenting on the idiocy of imperial authority and anthropometry through a form of mimicry in which the master becomes the fool (Bhabha 1997).

Within this dialogical mode of capturing the colonial situation and its legacy in Africa, two "philological" approaches to the production of ethnographic texts establish a way of writing within and beyond the constraints of Africanist discourse. In a bold experimental initiative, which followed Mudimbe (1988) and Wilmsen (1989) in winning the Herskovits Award, Fabian (1990) produced a critical ethnography of a theatrical performance in which the anthropologist played a "leading" role. Working with a popular acting troupe in Shaba, Zaire, Fabian documented the production, direction, rehearsal, and performance of a play that developed in direct response to questions he asked about the saying "Le pouvoir se mange entier, Power is eaten whole" (Fabian 1990, 3). Extending the ethnography of speaking and performing to creating and fashioning through social praxis, Fabian's ethnography and the play that it in effect coproduced emerge as part of a larger communicative interaction within an evolving framework of historical, political, and cultural meanings. To a certain extent, Fabian answers the challenge of reflexive anthropology without falling into self-serving solipsism because he incorporates his interlocutors into a performance about which, but not of which, he remains the author, although many of the middle chapters—recording rehearsal takes verbatim—make for tedious reading. What is salutary in this attempt, however, is how philology recapitulates epistemology, in that the object of ethnographic knowledge as a meaning-making activity is framed by its own textual history. At the very least, Fabian has blazed a path between the historic hegemony of imperial positivism and the self-centered penitence of ethnography "degree zero" to say something interesting about popular performance and consciousness in postcolonial Zaire. Later he extended this approach to Zairian painting and historical consciousness (Fabian 1996).

Pels (1994) has applied similar philological concerns to the production of missionary and administrative ethnographies in the Uluguru Mountains of (then) eastern Tanganyika, examining the textual production of "tribal" traditions in terms of "the complex interplay of colonizing and resisting strategies and the hybrid co-production of knowledge which results from it" (Pels 1994, 345). Distinguishing three phases of these processes—the *préterrain* of power relationships in the field, the "ethnographic occasion" or socially organized encounter between observing ethnographer and natives observed, and the "writing up" of field notes into the ethnographic traditions of ethnographic texts—Pels reveals significant differences between administrative and missionary methods and genres. Whereas the former invented tribal histories and chiefs within a "pidgin politics that kept the *Realpolitik* of Luguru big men and lineages out of bureaucratic procedure" (336), the latter "aimed at the selection and transformation of assumed parts of social practice, not at the preservation of assumed wholes" (339), focusing on life cycles, economy, magic, and healing. Not only does comparison of these genres, taken as processes of textual production, complicate the colonial picture on both sides of the imperial divide, but more importantly, it shows how the *préterrain* shaped ethnographic encounters that in turn overdetermined the ethnographic "facts," and how these facts subsequently circulated to serve the interests and agendas of colonizers and colonized alike.

DIALECTICS

The colonial library acquires a new significance within such a philological turn, introducing a more socially grounded appreciation of how colonial inventions of Africa have been coproduced to become sociocultural realities. At issue is not whether the colonial figures and categories of Africanist discourse should be (or ever could be) abandoned, but how they have been indigenized, Africanized, and in some cases even nationalized through processes of ethnographic writing and representation. Whatever weight we may attribute to the role of anthropology as such in colonizing Africa, ranging from considerable (Kuklick 1991; cf. Goody 1995, 191–208) to trivial (Asad 1991, 315), its location within the larger contexts of imperial politics, science, and culture can be seen as an advantage rather than a liability. Turning anthropology on its own imperial culture introduces a measure of reflexivity that, far from undermining the discipline's knowledge claims, underscores them with self-conscious recognition. From this more object-oriented perspective, a growing body of scholarship has emerged to illuminate the development of imperial cultures and their political configurations in the colonies. In brief, colonial anthropology has given rise to an anthropology of colonialism.

Key texts that chart the course of this development (Callaway 1987; Mitchell 1991; Hansen 1989, 1992; Cooper and Stoler 1997; Jean Comaroff and John Comaroff 1991; John Comaroff and Jean Comaroff 1992, 1997) are complemented by work on imperial ritual and colonial optics (Coombes 1994; Geary 1988; Edwards 1992). These and other numerous studies of colonial cultures and encounters in Africa engage a vast historical and theoretical territory that can be characterized with reference to certain paradigmatic positions and breakthroughs in research. In a study of European women in colonial Nigeria, for example, Callaway brings together insights on "the theatre of empire" (1987, 55)—like the *durbar*, installation ceremonies, Empire Day parades, staged arrivals and departures, and more quotidian routines of dining and dressing—with the renegotiation of gender roles and relations both within and between European and African social categories, enhancing female professional autonomy among the former while diminishing it among the latter. Developing a nuanced notion of imperial culture that includes official ideologies of gender and race, male fantasies of heroic conquest, and the political cosmology of lived space, Callaway's study represents one of the first systematic anthropological approaches to social distinctions and practices among Europeans in Africa, revealing female visions and voices that tell another story of empire behind the scenes (see also Kirk-Greene 1985). This perspective is important not only because it explains how the "trappings" of power were central to establishing colonial authority but because it highlights the dynamics of domesticity in colonial life before and after World War II. If the former theme is brilliantly developed in Mitchell's (1991) analysis of imperial spectacle, illuminating how a visual ontology of colonial representation valued the exhibition above the "original," the latter is elaborated in an important collection by Hansen (1992), which reveals how gender, race, and class were historically reconfigured by ideologies and practices of domesticity that include "labor and time, architecture and space, consumption and accumulation, body and clothing, diet and hygiene, and sexuality and gender" (Hansen 1992, 5; see also Hansen 1989, 1997; Hunt 1997; McClintock 1995; White 1990, 1995; Wildenthal 1997). One of the major themes emerging from this literature is how the politics of imperial culture in Africa belonged part and parcel to politics in the metropoles, as centers and peripheries developed historically and dialectically. This theme breaks down into two significant variations: imperial spectacle and colonial conversions.

Imperial Spectacle   While research on colonial expositions and industrial world's fairs has blossomed over the past two decades, revealing how spectacular displays of commodities and racial hierarchies represented the imperial order of things (Benedict 1983; Bennett 1996; Çelik 1992; Çelik and Kinney 1990; Corbey 1993; Greenhalgh 1988; Hinsley 1991; Leprun 1986; Rasool and Witz 1993; Rydell 1984, 1993; Silverman 1977), recent studies have begun to unpack the "dialectics of seeing" (Buck-Morss 1991; Apter 2002) in relation to commodity fetishism and its value forms. We know, for instance, that anthropologists were consulted to showcase scientific knowledge in native displays, even publishing voluminous ethnographies for such events to educate the public and ratify its progressive place in the world. We can also appreciate how the metropolitan centers remade themselves in the images of their colonized Others, by way of explicit contrasts between civilization and barbarism as well as by the implicit assimilation of "the savage within" (Kuklick 1991). Indeed, the grand era of colonial expositions, from London's Crystal Palace of 1851 to the Exposition coloniale internationale of Paris in 1931, literally and figuratively staged Europe's civilizing mission in Africa, producing knowledge of the territories for domestic consumption while exporting models of trusteeship and enlightenment abroad.

But if European centers and their African colonies were so intimately imbricated in each other's images, such connections were not limited to material interest and strategic intent; they also spoke to an ontological transformation of "the real." Here Mitchell (1991) achieves an important breakthrough in analyzing colonial power and representation. Beginning with Egypt at the

1889 Exposition universelle in Paris, he identifies a revealing optical illusion whereby an exhibited Egypt produced in the West became more real and authentic than the land and people themselves. This inversion of simulacrum and original—a kind of commodity fetish writ large—has profound implications for understanding colonial power and statecraft. One implication is that imperial spectacles at home assume an active role in the construction of colonial overrule, not as supportive props or legitimating ideologies but as framing devices whereby models and plans become political realities with perceived truth-effects. A second implication is that such "techniques of the observer" (Crary 1990) produce the very split between colonial state and society, one that begins as an internal distinction and develops into an external boundary. From this perspective, the state is not assumed in advance or taken whole; it emerges from representational technologies and practices into an institutionally reified "domain." This insight helps us rethink the status of civil society in postcolonial Africa (see below), and it is relevant for understanding how inventions of Africa became African realities.

As two further "breakthrough" studies reveal, inventions of Africa became European realities within Britain and France as well. In a landmark study of museum displays as well as regional and national exhibitions in late Victorian and Edwardian England, Coombes (1994) examines the relationship of "scientific" and popular knowledge of Africa to ideologies of race and national culture within Britain (for the politics of the camera, see also Street 1992; Vansina 1992; Faris 1992; Geary 1988; Prins 1992). Bringing the rise of professional anthropology (including theories of evolution and degeneration) to bear on popular forms of ethnographic display as well as on questions of aesthetics and cultural value, Coombes argues that museums and exhibitions became temples and spectacles of empire that remade the British nation and its various publics through the images and objects of its African Others. Nor were such displays directed exclusively to a national public sphere. They also redirected didactic attention to maternal and wifely obligations in the private sphere by invoking the African woman as an object lesson against "feminist tendencies amongst white British women" (Coombes 1994, 99–100). It is within this contrapuntal development of professional knowledge and popular imagination, of British racial and cultural unification and African racial and cultural classification, that the categories of Mudimbe's colonial library were forged and refined, and the grammar of its selections and substitutions set into historical motion. Lebovics (1992) reveals a similar dialectic, although more global in its imperial scope, at work in France, relating debates and divisions between physical anthropologists and ethnologists to the location of Africans, and indeed Franks and Gauls, within the shifting boundaries and policies of nation and empire. Examining the colonial exposition as "the simulacrum of greater France," Lebovics (1992, 67) argues that it not only promoted an imperial consciousness and a new sense of national identity at home but also produced "a governing ideal" that recognized "the wrapping of cultures around a French core as a kind of mutual apprenticeship in citizenship: on the one side natives learning to be French while of course retaining their local customs; on the other European French, recalling their own apprenticeships as Gascons or Bretons, learning to welcome the new French" (79). That this ideal diverged dramatically from the realities of racism and corvée labor need not disrupt the truth-effects of the governing discourse, in that—following the insight of Mitchell (1991)—the simulacrum surpasses the original within the political ontology of imperial spectacle.

Colonial Conversions Understood as a mode of objectification and even fetishism grounded in colonial relations of production (McClintock 1995), imperial discourses and spectacles of Africa defined centers and peripheries, citizens and subjects (Mamdani 1996), through the camera obscura of class. If European class relations were mapped onto race relations abroad, projecting the dislocations of the industrial revolution onto the savagery and heathenism of the Dark Continent, class differences at home were increasingly cast in racial terms as well. Moreover, the class-race axis was further transposed into gender, religious, and national differences—and discriminations of "sexuality and sentiment" (Cooper and Stoler 1997, 26)—forming an emergent imperial culture at large. Here is where historical anthropology and anthropological history converge. Focusing on Tswana encounters circa 1820–1920 with nonconformist Christian missionaries in South Africa, Jean Comaroff and John Comaroff (1991) wrote a nuanced historical ethnography of the cultural forms of conversion and domination, showing how the "colonization of consciousness" through religious rhetoric and quotidian reform led to the "consciousness of colonization" ranging from embodied poetics to overt political struggle. Crucial to their analysis is a model of how hegemony and ideology— seen as two ends of a continuum—operate reciprocally within a cultural field, bringing implicit cultural form (which remains unconscious or dimly apprehended) and more explicit meaning or content (more consciously grasped) to bear on the symbolic and material production of the social world, not through endless mechanical reproduction, but dynamically, in relation to shifting alignments and struggles. One of the strengths of this formulation is that it opens up the gray area between domination and resistance in the ambivalent and hybrid terms with which Tswana experienced the colonial encounter, thereby accounting for how they responded, ranging from struggles over space and time to struggles over words and water. In more historical terms, the study shows how the class position of the Wesleyan missionaries on the "social margins" of bourgeois Britain engendered (in both senses of the term) a pastoral vision of the African landscape and the cultivation of its gardens and souls, placing them at odds with dominant factions of the colonial elite (Stoler and Cooper 1997, 27) and gradually giving rise, through its imposition on the Tswana, to a growing "sense of opposition between *sekgoa* (European ways) and *setswana* (Tswana ways), the latter being perceived for the first time as a *system* of practices" (Jean Comaroff and John Comaroff 1991, 212). Here we see how the colonial encounter produced the very opposition that more conventional anthropology and historiography presuppose, reifying a Tswana culture of language, law, and custom that the Tswana themselves came to recognize and appropriate (for a comparable dialectic in colonial Tanganyika, see Pels 1999).

Within the broader dialectics of center and periphery, John Comaroff and Jean Comaroff (1992) relate evangelical models of bodily and household reform—promoting nuclear homes for the more cultivated Tswana Christians—to the politics of domestic reform in Britain, where the "dangerous classes" and their squalid slums would be tamed and cleansed by enlightened social policy. John Comaroff and Jean Comaroff (1997) extend these themes to the reordering of public space through architecture and town planning (see also Wright 1997), the recasting of public and private domains, bourgeois self-fashioning, the moral and material "currencies of conversion," the commodified forms and signs of salvation, and the emerging racial and gender ideologies that characterize a bourgeois modernity not simply imposed or resisted but reciprocally determined by the imperial center and its colonial frontier. In a methodological shift that resembles the critical optics of Mitchell (1991) by revealing how internal distinctions materialize into the external boundaries of social order and meaningful space, Comaroff and Comaroff solve the problem of the colonial library by taking the development of its genres and categories into ethnographic account. If this method works for historical anthropology, does it have a place in postcolonial Africa?

Notes from the Postcolony

For Mafeje (1998) it does not. In a damning indictment of all major attempts to reinvent anthropology for a postcolonial Africa, Mafeje condemns the discipline to—at best—entropic death. Coming from a classically trained social anthropologist who produced one of the first critiques of the ideology of tribalism (Mafeje 1971), this strongly principled attack represents the most recent version of Mudimbe's more scholastic challenge and invites a serious response.

Focusing on "the deconstruction of Anthropology with reference to the excolonial world," Mafeje (1998, 1) makes the case that, whatever the pretensions of liberal apologists and revisionists from "the North," African scholars today should dispense with the discipline. Caught in the double bind of either reproducing colonial reifications or losing the ethnographic referent in self-reflexive confusion, anthropology has become a lost cause for postcolonial African scholars. Reviewing, and at times excoriating, efforts to develop an adequate postcolonial anthropology (Asad 1973; Hymes 1974; Scholte 1974; Clifford and Marcus 1986; John Comaroff and Jean Comaroff 1992; Moore 1994), Mafeje is also hard on his African colleagues who seek refuge in development or alternatives in feminism or unmodified Marxism. But his solutions underscore a more general process of indigenizing the ghosts of colonialism in Africa under the guise of decolonization.

Mafeje (1991) proposes a way out of the anthropological double bind by replacing the anthropological concepts of "society" and "culture" with revised concepts of "social formation" and "ethnography." By social formation, Mafeje departs from standard Marxian modes of articulation to specify "the articulation of the economic instance and the instance of power," a move that brings politics into the "base" to recast "kingdoms" more historically in relation to colonialism. From this perspective, what matters is "not which people were called Ba-Nyoro, Ba-Ganda, Ba-Hindi, Ba-Hutu, Ba-Tutsi, etc., but what they were actually doing in their attempts to assert themselves" (Mafeje 1998, 36). Such a perspective is useful if not entirely original, given studies of cultural ethnogenesis as a historical and sociopolitical process (Amselle 1985; Peel 1989), but more unusual is his notion of ethnography, referring to those texts authored by the people themselves in the course of their social struggles and identity politics, as well as the rules of social discourse underlying such textual production. It is up to the social scientist to relate the "ethnography" of native (and nativist) discourse to the historical dynamics of the social formation, and thus to disclose its "hidden" significance: "As I conceive of it, ethnography is an end product of social texts authored by the people themselves. All I do is to study the texts so that I can decode them, make their meaning apparent or understandable to me as an interlocutor or the 'other.' What I convey to my fellow–social scientists is studied and systematised interpretations of existing but hidden knowledge" (Mafeje 1998, 37). There are several ironies in this revisionist reversal of an ethnography without anthropology, not least of which is the nearly full-circle return to Mudimbe's model of gnosis—the hidden knowledge produced by the Other and revealed by the ethnographer—that characterized the ethnophilosophical illusion of the colonial library. Mafeje (1998, 37) actually cites Griaule for establishing an appropriate methodological precedent for his ethnographic elicitations! But what is of interest are the philological dimensions of Mafeje's solution and its logic of indigenization.

Briefly stated, Mafeje's dismissal of Africanist anthropology as inseparable from the colonial politics of knowledge actually relocates it in the historical terrain (or *préterrain*; see Pels 1994) of the social formation and in the cultural domain of what he now calls ethnography. Like Monsieur Jourdain with his prose, Africans now learn that they have been speaking ethnography all of their lives! Mafeje (1998, 37) maintains that it "is immaterial" whether these discourses are generated "through conversation, as Griaule or Dumont did, or through interviews, recordings, participant observation, oral traditions, artistic expressions, or written accounts," because these discourses constitute prima facie knowledge production as ethnographic texts unto themselves. By taking the anthropological concept of culture out of ethnography, the resulting social science is cleansed of its colonial accretions. But is it really? Has not the colonial palimpsest of the culture concept slipped into the native voice under the sign of its erasure? Mafeje has indigenized the concept of culture by displacing it into a textual model that actually remains complex, embracing both the explicit enunciations of ethnic identity politics and the implicit grammars of their production. And it is at these deeper levels of discursive and textual production that something between a social formation and an invented ethnic identity—namely, culture—resides. Junker's pygmy is still clowning around despite the most vigilant efforts to exorcise his ghost.

Mafeje's argument is particularly interesting because it represents a philological variation of the decolonization paradigm in African studies and cultural production. Variously represented by negritude (Senghor 1964; Diop 1987, 1991), Pan-Africanism (V. Thompson 1974; Esedebe 1982; Padmore 1971), or African personality and consciencism (Nkrumah 1970) and summarized succinctly by Ngugi (1986), the paradigm maintains that true liberation from colonial and neocolonial domination requires a "cultural decolonization [which] has yet to be accomplished" (Stoler and Cooper 1997, 33). My metacritique of Mafeje (1998), however, suggests that we pay close ethnographic attention to what goes on under the guise of cultural decolonization. What we find behind different strategies of cultural production and recuperation is the indigenization of colonial culture itself, such that its structures, categories, and even rituals of incorporation become Africanized as local, regional, national, or even Pan-African traditions.

For example, the *durbar* ceremony celebrated with such fanfare in Nigeria during FESTAC '77 (the Second World Black and African Festival of Arts and

Culture) actually reproduced a central ritual of colonial overrule that had developed in India and was adapted by Lugard to northern Nigerian conditions and practices (Apter 2005, 167–99). This is not to deny the indigenous dimensions of Nigerian *durbars*, like the *jafi* salute, which colonial *durbars* appropriated, but to underscore their historical development as rituals of colonial subjugation. What is interesting anthropologically is how the very decolonization of cultural tradition based on the rejection of imperialism proclaimed by FESTAC involved the nationalization of colonial tradition by the postcolonial state. Explicitly erased, such traditions as the *durbar* and regatta were indigenized through the very festivals and ministries that objectified culture for citizens and tourists (for a Francophone example of this process, see Austen 1992). Here we see in reverse, as it were, the colonial palimpsest in postcolonial Africa, mirroring anthropological history in its spectacular productions of a precolonial past. My point is not that cultural decolonization has yet to be accomplished but that it cannot be accomplished by simple negation. Rather, it is accomplished historically by the very processes of indigenization and nationalization, such as FESTAC's festivals and Mafeje's nonanthropological anthropology, in which colonial forms of culture and knowledge are appropriated and reinscribed by Africans. This is both a process for Africanist anthropology to study and a practice that African anthropologists can more critically pursue.

Conclusion

The philological exploration of anthropology's heart of darkness has traced the colonial palimpsest in the figure of Junker's pygmy to show that the discipline's imperial history unfolds through the very production of ethnographic texts and cannot be erased. In this respect, Mudimbe (1988, 1994) is correct in arguing that this history establishes important limits on the practice of Africanist anthropology. But when anthropology examines this history, as in the work reviewed above, it deepens our understanding of the colonial encounter itself, providing a dialectical perspective in which imperial centers and colonial peripheries developed in reciprocal determination. As new research is beginning to reveal (John Comaroff and Jean Comaroff 1999; Cooper 1994, 1997; Mamdani 1996; Mbembe 2001; Werbner 1998; Werbner and Ranger 1996), this approach applies to studies of civil society and the public sphere in postcolonial Africa as well, in that the very historical development of civility and publicity in bourgeois Europe was part of the "civilizing mission" in Africa, where—for better and worse—a new realm of res publica was forged that today sets the stage for democratization and political struggle.

A GRUESOME GIFT.

FIGURE 10

Human heads brought to Dr. Wilhelm Junker for his scientific collection (from Junker 1892, 161)

Returning to Junker's African exploits, however, there are other relics of an imperial history, less loquacious if no less eloquent than the pygmy at Rumbek, that are buried even deeper in the archives of colonial memory. Describing his travels and tribulations, Junker (1892) records one appropriately "gruesome" event that he experienced in the service of natural science: "I had already taught Dsumbe how to prepare skeletons of mammals, and this work was now again taken in hand.... These collections were now enriched by the gruesome present of a number of human heads. I had merely given a general order to procure bleached skulls, should the occasion present itself. But Zemio's people having once made a raid on some unruly A-Kahle people, those who fell were beheaded, and the heads not eaten, as is customary, but brought to me. I had them for the present buried in a certain place, and after my next journey prepared for the collection" (Junker 1892, 160–61). Junker's sketch (fig. 10) adds documentary force to this "gruesome gift," ostensibly illustrating African cannibalism and savagery but also implicating the European explorer in the very same crimes—framed by exchange relations and modes of accumulation—which remain the hidden hallmark of anthropology's heart of darkness. What is so remarkable about Junker's heads is not just the cavalier violence of their collection and preparation but the fact that Junker actually took them home to Europe. These heads, bearing silent testimony to European cannibalism and savagery in Africa, remind us that if anthropology's imperial subtexts are to be acknowledged, they cannot be forgotten (Trouillot 1995; Depelchin 2005).

Bibliography

Abraham, R. C. 1962. *Dictionary of Modern Yoruba*. London: Hodder & Stoughton.

Abu-Lughod, Lila. 1986. *Veiled Sentiments: Honor and Poetry in a Bedouin Society*. Berkeley and Los Angeles: Univ. of California Press.

Ahearn, Laura. 2001. "Language and Agency." *Annual Review of Anthropology* 30:109–37.

Ajayi, J. F. A. 1961. "Nineteenth-Century Origins of Nigerian Nationalism." *Journal of the Historical Society of Nigeria* 2 (2): 196–210.

———. 1965. *Christian Missions in Nigeria, 1847–1891: The Making of a New Elite*. London: Longman.

———. 1974. "The Aftermath of the Fall of Oyo." In J. E. A. Ajayi and Michael Crowder, eds., *History of West Africa*, 2:129–66. London: Longman.

Akinjogbin, I. A. 1967. *Dahomey and Its Neighbours, 1708–1818*. Cambridge: Cambridge Univ. Press.

Akintoye, S. A. 1971. *Revolution and Power Politics in Yorubaland, 1840–1893*. London: Longman.

Amselle, Jean-Loup. 1985. "Ethnies et espaces: Pour une anthropologie topologique." In J.-L. Amselle and E. M'Bokolo, eds., *Au coeur de l'ethnie: Ethnies, tribalisme et état en Afrique*, 11–48. Paris: La Découverte.

———. 1998. *Mestizo Logics: Anthropology of Identity in Africa and Elsewhere*. Trans. C. Royal. Stanford: Stanford Univ. Press.

———. 2000. "L'anthropologie au deuxième degree: À propos de 'La mission Griaule à Kangaba (Mali)' de Walter E. A. van Beek et Jan Jansen." *Cahiers d'Études Africaines*, vol. 40, no. 160, issue 4: 775–77.

Amuka, Peter S. O. 2000. "The Play of Deconstruction in the Speech of Africa: The Role of *Pakruok* and *Ngero* in Telling Culture in Dhuluo." In I. Karp and D. A. Masolo, eds., *African Philosophy as Cultural Inquiry*, 89–104. Bloomington: Indiana Univ. Press.

Appiah, Kwame Anthony. 1991. "Is the Post- in Postmodernism the Post- in Postcolonial?" *Critical Inquiry* 17 (Winter): 336–57.

Apter, Andrew. 1988. "Ritual Reinterpretations (Swazi)." *Man*, n.s., 23:376–78.

———. 1992. *Black Critics and Kings: The Hermeneutics of Power in Yoruba Society*. Chicago: Univ. of Chicago Press.

———. 1993. "Atinga Revisited: Yoruba Witchcraft and the Cocoa Economy, 1950–51." In J. Comaroff and J. L. Comaroff, eds., *Modernity and Its Malcontents: Ritual and Power in Postcolonial Africa*, 111–28. Chicago: Univ. of Chicago Press.

———. 1995. "Notes on Orisha Cults in the Ekiti Yoruba Highlands." *Cahiers d'Études Africaines*, vol. 35, nos. 138–39, issues 2–3: 369–401.

———. 2002. "On Imperial Spectacle: The Dialectics of Seeing in Colonial Nigeria." *Comparative Studies in Society and History* 44 (3): 564–96.

———. 2005. *The Pan-African Nation: Oil and the Spectacle of Culture in Nigeria*. Chicago: Univ. of Chicago Press.

Asad, Talal, ed. 1973. *Anthropology and the Colonial Encounter*. Atlantic Highlands, NJ: Humanities.

———. 1991. "From the History of Colonial Anthropology to the Anthropology of Western Hegemony." In G. Stocking, ed., *Colonial Situations: Essays on the Contextualization of Ethnographic Knowledge*, 314–24. Madison: Univ. of Wisconsin Press.

Asiwaju, A. I. 1975. "Efe Poetry as a Source for Western Yoruba History." In W. Abimbola, ed., *Yoruba Oral Tradition: Poetry in Music, Dance and Drama*, 199–266. Ife: Univ. of Ife, Department of African Languages and Literatures.

———. 1976. *Western Yorubaland under European Rule, 1889–1945: A Comparative Analysis of French and British Colonialism*. London: Longman.

Atanda, J. A. 1973. *The New Oyo Empire: Indirect Rule and Change in Western Nigeria, 1894–1934*. London: Longman.

Augé, Marc. 1979. "Towards a Rejection of the Meaning-Function Alternative." *Critique of Anthropology* 13/14:61–75.

Austen, Ralph A. 1992. "Tradition, Invention and History: The Case of the Ngondo (Cameroon)." *Cahiers d'Études Africaines*, vol. 32, no. 126, issue 2: 285–309.

———. 1995. *The Elusive Epic: Performance, Text and History in the Oral Narrative of Jeki la Njambè (Cameroon Coast)*. Atlanta: African Studies Association.

———, ed. 1999. *In Search of Sunjata: The Mande Oral Epic as History, Literature and Performance*. Bloomington: Indiana Univ. Press.

Austin, John. L. 1962. *How to Do Things with Words*. London: Oxford Univ. Press.

Ayandele, Emmanuel Ayankanmi. 1966. *The Missionary Impact on Modern Nigeria, 1842–1914: A Political and Social Analysis*. London: Longman.

———. 1970. *Holy Johnson: Pioneer of African Nationalism, 1836–1917*. New York: Humanities Press.

Balandier, George. 1966. *Ambiguous Africa: Cultures in Collision*. Trans. H. Weaver. London: Chatto & Windus. (Orig. pub. 1957.)

———. 1970. *The Sociology of Black Africa: Social Dynamics in Central Africa*. Trans. D. Garman. New York: Praeger. (Orig. pub. 1955.)

Barber, Karin. 1981. "How Man Makes God in West Africa: Yoruba Attitudes toward the Òrìsà." *Africa* 51 (3): 724–45.

———. 1984. "Yoruba *Oríkì* and Deconstructive Criticism." *Research in African Literatures* 13 (4): 497–518.

———. 1989. "Interpreting *Oríkì* as History and as Literature." In K. Barber and P. F. de Moraes Farias, eds., *Discourse and Its Disguises: The Interpretation of African Oral Texts*, 13–23. African Studies Series 1. Birmingham, UK: Centre of West African Studies, Univ. of Birmingham.

———. 1990. "*Oríkì*, Women and the Proliferation and Merging of the Orisa." *Africa* 60 (3): 313–37.

———. 1991a. *I Could Speak until Tomorrow: Oríkì, Women and the Past in a Yoruba Town*. International African Library 7. Edinburgh: Edinburgh Univ. Press; Washington, DC: Smithsonian Institution Press, for the International African Institute.

———. 1991b. "Multiple Discourses in Yoruba Oral Literature." *Bulletin of the John Rylands University Library of Manchester* 73 (3): 11–24.

Barber, K., and P. F. de Moraes Farias. 1989. Introduction to K. Barber and P. F. de Moraes Farias, eds., *Discourse and Its Disguises: The Interpretation of African Oral Texts*, 1–10. African Studies Series 1. Birmingham, UK: Centre of West African Studies, Univ. of Birmingham.

Bastian, M. 1993. "'Bloodhounds Who Have No Friends': Witchcraft and Locality in the Nigerian Popular Press." In J. Comaroff and J. L. Comaroff, eds., *Modernity and Its Malcontents: Ritual and Power in Postcolonial Africa*, 129–66. Chicago: Univ. of Chicago Press.

Bean, Susan S. 1978. *Symbolic and Pragmatic Semantics: A Kannada System of Address*. Chicago: Univ. of Chicago Press.

Beidelman, T. O. 1966. "Swazi Royal Ritual." *Africa* 36:373–405.

Beier, Ulli. 1958. "Gelede masks." *Odu* 6:5–23.

Belasco, B. 1980. *The Entrepreneur as Culture Hero*. New York: Praeger.

Benedict, Burton, ed. 1983. *The Anthropology of World's Fairs: San Francisco's Panama Pacific International Exposition of 1915*. Berkeley, CA: Scolar.

Bennett, Tony. 1996. "The Exhibitionary Complex." In R. Greenberg, B. W. Ferguson, and S. Naime, eds., *Thinking about Exhibitions*, 81–112. London: Routledge.

Bernstein, Basil. 1974. *Class, Codes and Control*. Vol. 1, *Theoretical Studies towards a Sociology of Language*. London: Routledge and Kegan Paul. (Orig. pub. 1971.)

Bhabha, Homi. 1997. "Of Mimicry and Man: The Ambivalence of Colonial Discourse." In Cooper and Stoler 1997, 152–60.

Biobaku, Saburi Oladeni. 1957. *The Egba and Their Neighbours, 1842–1872*. Oxford: Clarendon Press.

Bloch, Maurice, ed. 1975. *Political Language and Oratory in Traditional Society*. London: Academic Press.

Blumenson, Martin. 1977. *The Vildé Affair: The Beginnings of the French Resistance*. Boston: Houghton Mifflin.

Boateng, E. A. 1978. *A Political Geography of Africa*. Cambridge: Cambridge Univ. Press.

Boddy, Janice. 1989. *Wombs and Alien Spirits: Women, Men, and the Zār Cult in Northern Sudan*. Madison: Univ. of Wisconsin Press.

Bouju, Jacky. 1984. *Graine de l'homme, enfant du mil*. Paris: Société d'Ethnographie.

———. 1991. "Comments." *Current Anthropology* 13 (2): 159–60.

Bourdieu, Pierre. 1977. *Outline of a Theory of Practice*. Trans. R. Nice. Cambridge: Cambridge Univ. Press.

———. 1990. *The Logic of Practice*. Trans. R. Nice. Stanford: Stanford Univ. Press. (Orig. pub. 1980.)

Brantlinger, Patrick. 1986. "Victorians and Africans: The Genealogy of the Myth of the Dark Continent." In H. L. Gates, ed., *"Race," Writing, and Difference*, 185–222. Chicago: Univ. of Chicago Press.

Brown, Penelope, and Stephen Levinson. 1978. "Universals in Language Usage: Politeness Phenomena." In E. N. Goody, ed., *Questions and Politeness: Strategies in Social Interaction*, 56–289. Cambridge: Cambridge Univ. Press.

Brown, Roger, and Albert Gilman. 1960. "The Pronouns of Power and Solidarity." In T. Sebeok, ed., *Style in Language*, 253–76. Cambridge, MA: Technology Press of MIT.

Buck-Morss, Susan. 1991. *The Dialectics of Seeing: Walter Benjamin and the Arcades Project.* Cambridge, MA: MIT Press.

Calame-Griaule, Geneviève. 1965. *Ethnologie et langage: La parole chez les Dogon.* Paris: Institut d'Ethnologie.

————. 1986. *Words and the Dogon World.* Trans. D. LaPin. Philadelphia: Institute for the Study of Human Issues. (Orig. pub. 1965 as *Ethnologie et langage.*)

————. 1996. Préface to Griaule 1996, 11–22.

Callaway, Helen. 1987. *Gender, Culture and Empire: European Women in Colonial Nigeria.* Urbana: Univ. of Illinois Press.

Carr, F. B. 1934. "The Ata of Ayede: Allegations Against." O.P. 626/1, Communication from the Resident, Ondo Province, to the District Officer, Ekiti Division, Ado-Ekiti, 1 November. Nigerian National Archives, Univ. of Ibadan.

Casalis, Eugène. 1861. *The Basutos; or, Twenty-three Years in South Africa.* London: J. Nisbet.

Çelik, Zeynap. 1992. *Displaying the Orient: Architecture of Islam at Nineteenth Century World's Fairs.* Berkeley and Los Angeles: Univ. of California Press.

Çelik, Zeynap, and Kinney, L. 1990. "Ethnography and Exhibitionism at the Expositions Universelles." *Assemblage* 13:35–59.

Chanock, Martin. 1985. *Law, Custom, and Social Order: The Colonial Experience in Malawi and Zambia.* Cambridge: Cambridge Univ. Press.

Ciarcia, Gaetano. 1998. "Ethnologues et 'Dogon': La fabrication d'un patrimoine ethnographique." *Gradhiva: Revue d'Histoire d'Archives de l'Anthropologie* 24:103–15.

————. 2001. "Dogons et Dogon: Retours au 'pays du reel.'" *L'Homme* 157 (January/March): 217–29.

Clifford, James. 1988. "Power and Dialogue in Ethnography: Marcel Griaule's Initiation." In J. Clifford, *The Predicament of Culture: Twentieth-Century Ethnography, Literature, and Art,* 55–91. Cambridge, MA: Harvard Univ. Press. (Orig. pub. 1983.)

Clifford, James, and George Marcus, eds. 1986. *Writing Culture: The Poetics and Politics of Ethnography.* Berkeley and Los Angeles: Univ. of California Press.

Cocks, P. 1995. "The Rhetoric of Science and the Critique of Imperialism in British Social Anthropology, c. 1870–1940." *History and Anthropology* 9 (1): 93–119.

Cohen, Abner. 1982. "A Polyethnic London Carnival as Contested Cultural Performance." *Ethnic and Racial Studies* 5:23–41.

Comaroff, Jean. 1985. *Body of Power, Spirit of Resistance: The Culture and History of a South African People.* Chicago: Univ. of Chicago Press.

Comaroff, Jean, and John L. Comaroff. 1991. *Of Revelation and Revolution.* Vol. 1, *Christianity, Colonialism, and Consciousness in South Africa.* Chicago: Univ. of Chicago Press.

Comaroff, John L. 1975. "Talking Politics: Oratory and Authority in a Tswana Chiefdom." In Bloch 1975, 141–61.

Comaroff, John L., and Jean Comaroff. 1992. *Ethnography and the Historical Imagination.* Boulder, CO: Westview.

————. 1997. *Of Revelation and Revolution.* Vol. 2, *The Dialectics of Modernity on a South African Frontier.* Chicago: Univ. of Chicago Press.

————, eds. 1999. *Civil Society and the Political Imagination in Africa.* Chicago: Univ. of Chicago Press.

Cook, P. A. W. 1930. "The Inqwala Ceremony of the Swazi." *Bantu Studies* 4:205–10.

Coombes, Annie E. 1994. *Reinventing Africa: Museums, Material Culture, and Popular Imagination.* New Haven: Yale Univ. Press.

Cooper, Frederick. 1994. "Conflict and Connection: Rethinking Colonial African History." *American Historical Review* 99 (5): 1516–45.

———. 1997. "The Dialectics of Decolonization: Nationalism and Labor Movements in Postwar French Africa." In Cooper and Stoler 1997, 406–35.

Cooper, Frederick, and Ann Stoler, eds. 1997. *Tensions of Empire: Colonial Cultures in a Bourgeois World*. Berkeley and Los Angeles: Univ. of California Press.

Cope, Trevor, ed. 1968. *Izibongo: Zulu Praise-Poems*. Oxford: Clarendon Press.

Corbey, R. 1993. "Ethnographic Showcases, 1870–1930." *Cultural Anthropology* 8 (3): 338–69.

Crary, Jonathan. 1990. *Techniques of the Observer: On Vision and Modernity in the Nineteenth Century*. Cambridge, MA: MIT Press.

de Certeau, Michel. 1984. *The Practice of Everyday Life*. Trans. S. Rendell. Berkeley and Los Angeles: Univ. of California Press.

de Ganay, Solange. 1942. *Les devises des Dogon*. Paris: Institute d'Ethnologie.

de Heusch, Luc. 1982. *Rois nés d'un coeur de vache*. Paris: Gallimard.

———. 1985. *Sacrifice in Africa*. Bloomington: Indiana Univ. Press.

Deng, Francis M. 1973. *The Dinka and Their Songs*. Oxford: Clarendon Press.

Depelchin, Jacques. 2005. *Silences in African History: Between the Syndromes of Discovery and Abolition*. Dar es Salaam: Mkuki na Nyota Publishers.

Desai, Gaurav G. 2001. *Subject to Colonialism: African Self-Fashioning and the Colonial Library*. Durham, NC: Duke Univ. Press.

Diawara, Manthia. 1990. "Reading Africa through Foucault: V. Y. Mudimbe's Reaffirmation of the Subject." *October* 55 (Winter): 79–92.

Dieterlen, Germaine. 1942. *Les âmes des Dogon*. Paris: Institut d'Ethnologie.

———. 1951. *Essai sur la religion bambara*. Paris: Presses Universitaires de France.

———. 1971. "Les cérémonies soixantenaires du Sigui chez les Dogon. *Africa* 41 (1): 1–11.

Diop, Alioune. 1961. "Niam M'Paya." Preface to Tempels, *La philosophie bantoue*, trans. A. Rubbens. Paris: Présence Africaine.

Diop, Cheik A. 1987. *Precolonial Black Africa*. Trans. H. Salemson. Westport, CT: Hill.

———. 1991. *Civilization or Barbarism: An Authentic Anthropology*. Trans. Y. L. Ngemi. Westport, CT: Hill.

Dixon, Robert M. W. 1994. *Ergativity*. Cambridge: Cambridge Univ. Press.

Doquet, Anne. 1999. *Les masques dogon: Ethnologie savant et ethnologie autochtone*. Paris: Éditions Karthala.

Douglas, Mary. 1991. "Comments." *Current Anthropology* 13 (2): 161–62.

Drewal, Henry J., and Margaret T. Drewal. 1983. *Gelede: Art and Female Power among the Yoruba*. Bloomington: Indiana Univ. Press.

———. 1987. "Composing Time and Space in Yoruba Art." *Word and Image* 3 (3): 225–51.

Duranti, Alessandro. 1990. "Politics and Grammar: Agency in Samoan Political Discourse." *American Ethnologist* 17 (4): 646–66.

———. 1992. "Language in Context and Language as Context: The Samoan Respect Vocabulary." In Duranti and Goodwin 1992, 77–99.

———. 1994. *From Grammar to Politics: Linguistic Anthropology in a Western Somoan Village*. Berkeley and Los Angeles: Univ. of California Press.

———. 2004. "Agency in Language." In A. Duranti, ed., *A Companion to Linguistic Anthropology*, 451–73. Malden, MA: Blackwell.

Duranti, Alessandro, and Charles Goodwin, eds. 1992. *Rethinking Context: Language as an Interactive Phenomenon*. Cambridge: Cambridge Univ. Press.

Edwards, Elizabeth, ed. 1992. *Anthropology and Photography, 1860–1920.* New Haven: Yale Univ. Press.

Esedebe, Peter O. 1982. *Pan-Africanism: The Idea and Movement, 1776–1963.* Washington, DC: Howard Univ. Press.

Evans-Pritchard, E. E. 1937. *Witchcraft, Oracles and Magic among the Azande.* Oxford: Clarendon Press.

———. 1948. *The Divine Kingship of the Shilluk of the Nilotic Sudan.* Cambridge: Cambridge Univ. Press.

———. 1965. "Some Collective Expressions of Obscenity in Africa." In *The Position of Women in Primitive Societies and Other Essays in Social Anthropology*, 76–101. New York: Free Press. (Orig. pub. 1929.)

Fabian, Johannes. 1970. *Philosophie bantoue: Placide Tempels et son oeuvre vus dans une perspective historique.* Brussels: Centre de Recherche et d'Information Socio-politiques.

———. 1971. *Jamaa: A Charismatic Movement in Katanga.* Evanston, IL: Northwestern Univ. Press.

———. 1980. "L'enseignment de la Jamaa: Modèle ethnographique et production de textes doctrinaux." Trans. V. Y. Mudimbe. *Bulletin de Théologie Africaine* 2:55–77.

———. 1983. *Time and the Other: How Anthropology Makes Its Object.* New York: Columbia Univ. Press.

———. 1986. *Language and Colonial Power: The Appropriation of Swahili in the Former Belgian Congo, 1880–1938.* Berkeley and Los Angeles: Univ. of California Press.

———. 1990. *Power and Performance: Ethnographic Explorations through Proverbial Wisdom and Theater in Shaba, Zaire.* Madison: Univ. of Wisconsin Press.

———. 1996. *Remembering the Present: Painting and Popular History in Zaire.* Berkeley and Los Angeles: Univ. of California Press.

Fanon, Frantz. 1967. *A Dying Colonialism.* Trans. H. Chevalier. New York: Grove. (Orig. pub. 1959.)

Faris, J. C. 1973. "Pax Britannica and the Sudan: S. F. Nadel." In Asad 1973, 153–70.

———. 1992. "Photography, Power and the Southern Nuba." In Edwards 1992, 211–17.

Fernandez, James. 1982. *Bwiti: An Ethnography of the Religious Imagination.* Princeton: Princeton Univ. Press.

———. 1986. *Persuasions and Performances: The Play of Tropes in Culture.* Bloomington: Indiana Univ. Press.

Fiemeyer, Isabelle. 2004. *Marcel Griaule, citoyen dogon.* Arles: Actes Sud.

Finnegan, Ruth. 1969a. "Attitudes to Speech and Language among the Limba of Sierra Leone." *Odu*, n.s., 2:61–77.

———. 1969b. "How to Do Things with Words: Performative Utterances among the Limba of Sierra Leone." *Man*, n.s., 4 (4): 537–52.

———. 1970. *Oral Literature in Africa.* Oxford: Clarendon Press.

Flynn, Donna. 1997. "Borders and Boundaries: Gender, Ideology and Exchange along the Benin-Nigeria Border." PhD diss., Northwestern Univ.

Forde, Daryll. 1951. *The Yoruba-Speaking Peoples of South-western Nigeria.* London: International African Institute.

———, ed. 1954. *African Worlds: Studies in the Cosmological Ideas and Social Values of African Peoples.* London: Oxford Univ. Press.

Forster, P. G. 1994. "Politics, Ethnography and the 'Invention of Tradition': The Case of T. Cullen Young of Livingstonia Mission, Malawi." *History and Anthropology* 8:299–320.

Fortes, Meyer. 1945. *The Dynamics of Clanship among the Tallensi*. London: Oxford Univ. Press.

———. 1959. *Oedipus and Job in West African Religion*. Cambridge: Cambridge Univ. Press.

———. 1962. "Ritual and Office in Tribal Society." In Max Gluckman, ed., *Essays on the Ritual of Social Relations*, 53–88. Manchester: Manchester Univ. Press.

———. 1969. *Kinship and the Social Order: The Legacy of Lewis Henry Morgan*. Chicago: Aldine.

Fortes, Meyer, and E. E. Evans-Pritchard, eds. 1940. *African Political Systems*. London: Oxford Univ. Press.

Fortune, G., and A. C. Hodza, eds. 1979. *Shona Praise-Poetry*. Oxford: Clarendon Press.

Gal, Susan. 1991. "Beneath Speech and Silence: The Problematics of Research on Language and Gender." In M. di Leonardo, ed., *Gender at the Crossroads of Knowledge*, 175–203. Berkeley and Los Angeles: Univ. of California Press.

Gates, Henry Louis, Jr. 1988. *The Signifying Monkey: A Theory of Afro-American Literary Criticism*. New York: Oxford Univ. Press.

Geary, Christraud M. 1988. *Images from Bamum: German Colonial Photography at the Court of King Njoya*. Washington, DC: Smithsonian Institution Press.

Ghrenassia, Patrick. 1987. "Anatole Lewitzky: De l'ethnologie à la Résistance." *Liberté de l'Esprit: Visages de la Résistance* 16:237–53.

Giddens, Anthony. 1986. *Central Problems in Social Theory: Action, Structure, and Contradiction in Social Analysis*. Berkeley and Los Angeles: Univ. of California Press. (Orig. pub. 1979.)

Gluckman, Max. 1940. "The Kingdom of the Zulu of South Africa." In Fortes and Evans-Pritchard 1940, 25–54.

———. 1954. *Rituals of Rebellion in South-east Africa*. Frazer Lecture [1952]. Manchester: Manchester Univ. Press.

———. 1956. *Custom and Conflict in Africa*. London: Oxford Univ. Press.

———. 1963. *Order and Rebellion in Tribal Africa*. London: Cohen & West.

Goffman, Erving. 1961. *Encounters: Two Studies in the Sociology of Interaction*. Indianapolis: Bobbs-Merrill.

Goody, Jack. 1962. *Death, Property and the Ancestors*. London: Tavistock.

———. 1970. "Sideways or Downwards? Lateral and Vertical Succession, Inheritance and Descent in Africa and Eurasia." *Man*, n.s., 5 (4): 627–38.

———. 1995. *The Expansive Moment: The Rise of Social Anthropology in Britain and Africa, 1918–1970*. Cambridge: Cambridge Univ. Press.

Greenberg, Joseph H. 1955. *Studies in African Linguistic Classification*. Branford, CT: Compass.

Greenhalgh, Paul. 1988. *Ephemeral Vistas: The Expositions Universelles, Great Exhibitions and World's Fairs, 1851–1939*. Manchester, UK: Manchester Univ. Press.

Griaule, Marcel. 1948. "L'alliance cathartique." *Africa* 18 (4): 242–58.

———. 1952. "Le savoir des Dogon." *Journal de la Société des Africanistes* 22 (1–2): 27–42.

———. 1965. *Conversations with Ogotemmêli: An Introduction to Dogon Religious Ideas*. Trans. R. Butler. London: Oxford Univ. Press. (Orig. pub. 1948.)

———. 1973. "The Mother's Brother in the Western Sudan." In P. Alexandre, ed., *French Perspectives in African Studies*, 11–25. London: Oxford Univ. Press. (Orig. pub. 1954.)

———. 1983. *Masques dogons*. Paris: Institut d'Ethnologie. (Orig. pub. 1938.)

———. 1996. *Descente du troisième verbe*. Paris: Fata Morgana. (Orig. pub. 1947.)

Griaule, Marcel, and Germaine Dieterlen. 1951. *Signes graphiques soudanais*. Special issue, *L'Homme* 3.

———. 1954. "The Dogon of the French Sudan." In Forde 1954, 83–110.

———. 1991. *Le renard pâle*. Paris: Institut d'Ethnologie. (Orig. pub. 1965.)

Hailey, W. M. 1957. *An African Survey: A Study of Problems Arising in Africa South of the Sahara.* London: Oxford Univ. Press.

Hammond-Tooke, W. P. 1965. "Segmentation and Fission in Cape Nguni Political Units." *Africa* 35 (2): 143–67.

Hanks, William F. 1990. *Referential Practice: Language and Lived Space among the Maya.* Chicago: Univ. of Chicago Press.

———. 1992. "The Indexical Ground of Deictic Reference." In Duranti and Goodwin 1992, 46–76.

———. 1993. "Metalanguage and Pragmatics of Deixis." In John A. Lucy, ed., *Reflexive Language: Reported Speech and Metapragmatics,* 127–57. Cambridge: Cambridge Univ. Press.

Hansen, Karen T. 1989. *Distant Companions: Servants and Employers to Zambia, 1900–1985.* Ithaca, NY: Cornell Univ. Press.

———, ed. 1992. *African Encounters with Domesticity.* New Brunswick, NJ: Rutgers Univ. Press.

———. 1997. *Keeping House in Lusaka.* New York: Columbia Univ. Press

Harper, Peggy. 1970. "The Role of Dance in the Gelede Ceremonies of the Village of Ijio." *Odu* 4:67–91.

Harris, G. 1978. *Casting out Anger: Religion among the Taita of Kenya.* Cambridge: Cambridge Univ. Press.

Heald, S. 1982. "The Making of Men: The Relevance of Vernacular Psychology to the Interpretation of a Gisu Ritual." *Africa* 52 (1): 15–36.

———. 1989. *Controlling Anger: The Sociology of Gisu Violence.* Manchester, UK: Manchester Univ. Press; Bloomington: Indiana Univ. Press, for the International African Institute.

Hinsley, Curtis M. 1991. "The World as Marketplace: Commodification of the Exotic at the World's Columbian Exposition, Chicago, 1893." In I. Karp and S. Lavine, eds., *Exhibiting Cultures: The Poetics and Politics of Museum Display,* 334–65. Washington: Smithsonian Institution Press.

Hobart, Mark. 1990. "The Patience of Plants: A Note on Agency in Bali." *Review of Indonesian and Malaysian Affairs* 24:90–135.

Hoch-Smith, J. 1978. "Radical Female Sexuality: The Witch and the Prostitute." In J. Hoch-Smith and A. Spring, eds., *Women in Ritual and Symbolic Roles,* 245–67. New York: Plenum Press.

Hountondji, Paulin J. 1983. *African Philosophy: Myth and Reality.* Trans. H. Evans and J. Rée. Bloomington: Indiana Univ. Press.

———. 1990. "Pour une sociologie des représentations collectives." In Y. Preiswerk and J. Vallet, eds., *La pensée métisse: Croyances africaines et rationalité occidentale en questions,* 187–92. Paris: Presses Universitaires de France.

———. 2002. *The Struggle for Meaning: Reflections on Philosophy, Culture, and Democracy in Africa.* Trans. J. Conteh-Morgan. Athens, OH: Ohio Univ. Center for International Studies.

Hunt, Nancy R. 1997. "'Le bébé en brousse': European Women, African Birth Spacing, and Colonial Intervention in Breast Feeding in the Belgian Congo." In Cooper and Stoler 1997, 287–321.

Hymes, Dell, ed. 1974. *Reinventing Anthropology.* New York: Random House.

———. 1986. Foreword to Calame-Griaule 1986, v–viii.

Idowu, B. 1970. "The Challenge of Witchcraft." *Orita* 4 (1): 3–16.

Iliffe, John. 1979. *A Modern History of Tanganyika.* Cambridge: Cambridge Univ. Press.

Irvine, Judith. 1974. "Strategies of Status Manipulation in the Wolof Greeting." In R. Bauman and J. Scherzer, eds., *Explorations in the Ethnography of Speaking*, 167–91. Cambridge: Cambridge Univ. Press.

———. 1993. "Insult and Responsibility: Verbal Abuse in a Wolof Village." In Jane Hill and Judith Irvine, eds., *Responsibility and Evidence in Oral Discourse*, 104–34. Cambridge: Cambridge Univ. Press.

———. 1996. "Shadow Conversations: The Indeterminacy of Participant Roles." In Silverstein and Urban 1996, 131–59.

Jackson, Michael, and Ivan Karp, eds. 1990. *Personhood and Agency: The Experience of Self and Other in African Cultures*. Washington, DC: Smithsonian Institution Press.

James, Wendy. 1973. "The Anthropologist as Reluctant Imperialist." In Asad 1973, 41–69.

Jamin, Jean. 1977. *Les lois du silence: Essai sur la fonction sociale du secret*. Paris: François Maspero.

———. 1982a. "Les metamorphoses de *L'Afrique fantôme*." *Critique: Revue Générale des Publications Françaises et Étrangères* 37 (418): 200–212.

———. 1982b. "Objets trouvés des paradis perdus: À propos de la Mission Dakar-Djibouti." In J. Hainard and R. Kaehr, eds., *Collections passion*, 69–100. Neuchâtel: Musée Ethnographique.

Johnson, Samuel. 1921. *The History of the Yorubas: From the Earliest Times to the Beginning of the British Protectorate*. Ed. O. Johnson. Lagos: CMS Bookshops.

Jolly, Eric. 1998–99. "Chefs sacrés et chefs de guerre dogon: Deux pôles du pouvoir." *Clio en Afrique* 5. www.up.univ-mrs.fr/∼wclio-af/numero/5/thematique/jolly/index.html.

———. 2004. *Boire avec esprit: Bière de mil et société dogon*. Paris: Société d'Ethnographie.

Jolly, Eric, and N. Guindo. 2003. *Le pouvoir en miettes: Récits d'intronisation d'un hogon (pays dogon, Mali)*. Paris: Classiques Africaines.

Junker, Wilhelm. 1892. *Travels in Africa, 1882–1886*. Vol. 3. Trans. A. H. Keane. London: Chapman & Hall.

Junod, H. 1927. *The Life of a South African Tribe*. 2d ed. 2 vols. London: Macmillan.

Kagame, Alexis. 1956. *La philosophie bântu-ruandaise de l'être*. Brussels: Académie Royale des Sciences Coloniales.

———. 1976. *La philosophie bantu comparée*. Paris: Présence Africaine.

Kirk-Greene, Anthony. 1985. "Imperial Administration and the Athletic Imperative: The Case of the District Officer in Africa." In S. A. Mangan and W. Baker, eds., *Sports in Africa*, 81–113. New York: Holmes & Meier.

Kramer, Fritz. 1993. *The Red Fez: Art and Spirit Possession in Africa*. Trans. M. R. Green. London and New York: Verso.

Krapf-Askari, E. 1966. "Time and Classification—an Ethnographic and Historical Case Study." *Odu* 2 (2): 3–18.

Kratz, Corrine A. 2000. "Forging Unions and Negotiating Ambivalence: Personhood and Complex Agency in Okiek Marriage Arrangement." In I. Karp and D. A. Masolo, eds., *African Philosophy as Cultural Inquiry*, 136–71. Bloomington: Indiana Univ. Press.

Krige, Eileen. 1936. *The Social System of the Zulus*. London: Longmans, Green & Co.

———. 1968. "Girls' Puberty Songs and Their Relation to Fertility, Health, Morality and Religion among the Zulu." *Africa* 38:173–98.

Kuklick, Henrika. 1978. "The Sins of the Fathers: British Anthropology and African Colonial Administration." *Research in the Sociology of Knowedge, Sciences and Art* 1:93–119.

———. 1984. "Tribal Exemplars: Images of Political Authority in British Anthropology, 1885–1945." In G. Stocking, ed., *Functionalism Historicized: Essays on British Social Anthropology*, 59–82. History of Anthropology 2. Madison: Univ. of Wisconsin Press.

———. 1991. *The Savage Within: The Social History of British Anthropology, 1885–1945.* Cambridge: Cambridge Univ. Press.

Kuper, Hilda 1944. "A Ritual of Kingship among the Swazi." *Africa* 14:230–56.

———. 1947. *An African Aristocracy.* London: Oxford Univ. Press.

———. 1972. "A Royal Ritual in a Changing Political Context." *Cahiers d'Études Africaines* 12 (48): 593–615.

Labouret, H. 1929. "La parenté à plaisanteries en Afrique occidentale." *Africa* 2 (3): 244–54.

Lambek, Michael. 1993. *Knowledge and Practice in Mayotte: Local Discourses of Islam, Sorcery, and Spirit Possession.* Toronto: Univ. Toronto Press.

Lan, David. 1985. *Guns and Rain: Guerrillas and Spirit Mediums in Zimbabwe.* Berkeley and Los Angeles: Univ. of California Press.

Law, Robin. 1977. *The Oyo Empire, c. 1600–c. 1836: A West African Imperialism in the Era of the Atlantic Slave Trade.* Oxford: Clarendon Press.

Leach, E. 1958. "Concerning Trobriand Clans and the Kinship Category 'Tabu.'" In J. Goody, ed., *The Developmental Cycle of Domestic Groups,* 120–45. Cambridge: Cambridge Univ. Press.

Lebeuf, Jean-Paul. 1987. "Marcel Griaule." In Solange de Ganay et al., eds., *Ethnologiques: Hommages à Marcel Griaule,* xxi–xxviii. Paris: Hermann.

Lebovics, Herman. 1992. *True France: The Wars over Cultural Identity, 1900–1945.* Ithaca, NY: Cornell Univ. Press.

Leclerc, Gérard. 1972. *Anthropologie et colonialisme: Essai sur l'histoire de l'africanisme.* Paris: Fayard.

Lee, Richard B. 1979. *The !Kung San: Men, Women and Work in a Foraging Society.* Cambridge: Cambridge Univ. Press.

Lee, Richard B., and I. Devore, eds. 1976. *Kalahari Hunter-Gatherers: Studies of the !Kung San and Their Neighbors.* Cambridge, MA: Harvard Univ. Press.

Leiris, Michel. 1981. *L'Afrique fantôme.* Paris: Gallimard. (Orig. pub. 1934.)

———. 1989. "The Ethnographer Faced with Colonialism." In *Brisées: Broken Branches,* 112–31. Trans. L. Davis. San Francisco: North Point. (Orig. pub. 1950.)

———. 1992. *La langue secrète des Dogon de Sanga.* Paris: Éditions Jean Michel-Place. (Orig. pub. 1948.)

Lelong, Yves. 1987. "L'heure très sévère de Boris Vildé." *Liberté de L'Esprit: Visages de la Résistance* 16:329–41.

Leprun, Sylviane. 1986. *Le théâtre des colonies: Scénographie, acteurs et discours de l'imaginaire dans les expositions, 1855–1937.* Paris: Harmattan.

Lestrade, G. P. 1937. "Traditional Literature." In Schapera 1937, 291–308.

Lettens, D. 1971. *Mystagogie et mystification: Évaluation de l'oeuvre de Marcel Griaule.* Bujumbura, Burundi: Presses Lavigerie.

Lincoln, Bruce. 1987. "Ritual, Rebellion, Resistance: Once More the Swazi Ncwala." *Man,* n.s., 22 (2): 132–56.

Lloyd, P. C. 1955. "The Yoruba Lineage." *Africa* 25 (3): 235–51.

———. 1962. *Yoruba Land Law.* London: Oxford Univ. Press, for the Nigerian Institute of Social and Economic Research.

Lucy, John A. 1993a. "Metapragmatic Presentationals: Reporting Speech with Quotatives in Yucatec Maya." In Lucy 1993b, 91–125.

———, ed. 1993b. *Reflexive Language: Reported Speech and Metapragmatics.* Cambridge: Cambridge Univ. Press.

Lufuluabo, François-Marie. 1964. *La notion luba-bantoue de l'être.* Tournai: Casterman.

Lugard, Frederick. 1965. *The Dual Mandate in British Tropical Africa.* Hamden, CT: Archon.

MacGaffey, Wyatt. 1983. *Modern Kongo Prophets: Religion in a Plural Society.* Bloomington: Indiana Univ. Press.

———. 2000. *Kongo Political Culture: The Conceptual Challenge of the Particular.* Bloomington: Indiana Univ. Press.

MacLeod, A. E. 1992. "Hegemonic Relations and Gender Resistance: The New Veiling as Accommodating Protest in Cairo." *Signs* 17 (3): 533–57.

Mafeje, Archie. 1963. "A Chief Visits Town." *Journal of Local Administration Overseas* 2:88–99.

———. 1967. "The Role of the Bard in a Contemporary African Community." *Journal of African Languages* 6 (3): 193–223.

———. 1971. "The Ideology of Tribalism." *Journal of Modern African Studies* 9 (2): 253–62.

———. 1991. *The Theory and Ethnography of African Social Formations: The Case of the Interlacustrine Kingdoms.* Dakar: CODESRIA.

———. 1998. "Anthropology and Independent Africans: Suicide or End of an Era?" *African Sociological Review* 2 (1): 1–43.

Makarakiza, André. 1959. *La dialectique des Barundi.* Brussels: Académie Royale des Sciences Coloniales.

Makinde, M. 1988. *African Philosophy, Culture, and Traditional Medicine.* Ohio Univ. Monographs in International Studies, Africa Series 53. Athens, OH: Center for International Studies, Univ. of Ohio.

Malinowski, Bronislaw. 1961. *Argonauts of the Western Pacific.* New York: E. P. Dutton. (Orig. pub. 1922.)

Mamdani, Mahmood. 1996. *Citizen and Subject: Contemporary Africa and the Legacy of Late Colonialism.* Princeton: Princeton Univ. Press.

Mann, Kristen, and Richard Roberts, eds. 1991. *Law in Colonial Africa.* Portsmouth, NH: Heinemann.

Marwick, B. A. 1940. *The Swazi.* Cambridge: Univ. Press.

Masolo, D. A. 2003. "What Is in a Name? An Outline of Recent Issues in African Philosophy. *Florida Philosophical Review* 3 (1): 72–80.

Matory, James L. 1994. *Sex and the Empire That Is No More: Gender and the Politics of Metaphor in Oyo Yoruba Religion.* Minneapolis: Univ. of Minnesota Press.

Mbembe, Achille. 2001. *On the Postcolony.* Berkeley and Los Angeles: Univ. of California Press.

Mbiti, John S. 1969. *African Religions and Philosophy.* New York: Praeger.

McClintock, Anne. 1995. *Imperial Leather: Race, Gender, and Sexuality in the Colonial Contest.* New York: Routledge.

Michel-Jones, Françoise. 1999. *Retour aux Dogon: Figures du double et ambivalence.* Paris and Montreal: L'Harmattan. (Orig. pub. 1978.)

Middleton, John. 1960. *Lugbara Religion: Ritual and Authority among an East African People.* London: Oxford Univ. Press, for the International African Institute.

Mitchell, Timothy. 1991. *Colonising Egypt.* Berkeley and Los Angeles: Univ. of California Press.

Moore, Sally F. 1994. *Anthropology and Africa: Changing Perspectives on a Changing Scene.* Charlottesville: Univ. Press of Virginia.

Morton-Williams, P. 1956. "The Atinga Cult among the South-western Yoruba: A Sociological Analysis of a Witch-Finding Movement." *Bulletin de l'IFAN* 18 (3–4): 315–34.

———. 1960a. "Yoruba Responses to the Fear of Death." *Africa* 30 (1): 34–40.

————. 1960b. "The Yoruba Ogboni Cult in Oyo." *Africa* 30 (4): 362–74.

Mudimbe, Valentin Y. 1988. *The Invention of Africa: Gnosis, Philosophy, and the Order of Knowledge.* Bloomington: Indiana Univ. Press.

————. 1994. *The Idea of Africa.* Bloomington: Indiana Univ. Press.

Mujynya, Nimisi. 1972. *L'homme dans l'univers des Bantu.* Lubumbashi: Presses Universitaires du Zaire.

Mulago, Vincent. 1973. *La religion traditionnelle des Bantu et leur vision du monde.* Kinshasa: Presses Universitaires du Zaire.

N'Daw, Alassane. 1983. *La pensée africaine: Recherches sur les fondements de la pensée négro-africaine.* Dakar: Nouvelles Éditions Africaines.

Ngugi, Wa Thiong'o. 1986. *Decolonising the Mind: The Politics of Language in African Literature.* Portsmouth, NH: Heinemann.

Nkrumah, Kwame. 1970. *Consciencism: Philosophy and Ideology for Decolonization.* New York: Monthly Review.

Norbeck, E. 1963. "African Rituals of Conflict." *American Anthropologist* 65:1254–79.

Noyes, J. K. 1994. "The Natives in Their Places: 'Ethnographic Cartography' and the Representation of Autonomous Spaces in Ovamboland, German South West Africa." *History and Anthropology* 8:237–64.

Obayemi, A. 1971. "The Yoruba and Edo-Speaking Peoples and Their Neighbours before 1600." In J. Ajayi and M. Crowder, eds., *History of West Africa,* 1:196–263. New York: Longman.

Ogunba, O. 1982. "Yoruba Occasional Festival Songs." In A. Afolayan, ed., *Yoruba Language and Literature,* 36–56. Ife: Univ. of Ife Press.

Olabimtan, A. 1970. "An Introduction to Efe Poems of the Egbado Yoruba." In *Staff Seminar Papers and Subsequent Discussions,* 192–216. Lagos: School of African and Asian Studies, Univ. of Lagos.

Olatunji, O. 1984. *Features of Yoruba Poetry.* Ibadan: Ibadan Univ. Press.

Olupona, J. K. 1991. *Kingship, Religion, and Rituals in a Nigerian Community: A Phenomenological Study of Ondo Yoruba Festivals.* Stockholm Studies in Comparative Religion 28. Stockholm: Almqvist & Wiksell.

Opland, Jeff. 1981. "Two Xhosa Oral Poets: D. L. P. Yali-Mansini and Melikaya Mbutuma." Unpublished manuscript.

————. 1983. *Xhosa Oral Poetry: Aspects of a Black South African Tradition.* Cambridge: Cambridge Univ. Press.

Ortner, Sherry. 2001. "Specifying Agency: The Comaroffs and Their Critics. *Interventions* 3 (1): 76–84.

————. n.d. "Serious Games: Beyond Practice Theory." Manuscript.

Oruka, Odera H. 1983. "Sagacity in African Philosophy." *International Philosophical Quarterly* 23:383–93.

Padmore, George. 1971. *Pan-Africanism or Communism?* Garden City, NY: Doubleday.

Parkin, David. 1980. "The Creativity of Abuse." *Man,* n.s., 15 (1): 45–64.

Paulme, Denise. 1939. "Parenté à plaisanteries et alliance par le sang en Afrique occidentale." *Africa* 12 (4): 433–44.

————. 1940. *Organisation sociale des Dogon (Soudan français).* Paris: Éditions Domat-Montchrestien.

————. 1992. *Lettres de Sanga.* Paris: Fourbis.

Pauw, Berthold. A. 1975. *Christianity and Xhosa Tradition.* London: Oxford Univ. Press.

Peel, J. D. Y. 1989. "The Cultural Work of Yoruba Ethnogenesis." In E. Tonkin, M. McDonald, and M. Chapman, eds., *History and Ethnicity*, 198–215. London: Routledge.

———. 1995. "For Who Hath Despised the Day of Small Things? Missionary Narratives and Historical Anthropology." *Comparative Studies in Society and History* 37 (3): 581–607.

Pels, Peter. 1994. "The Construction of Ethnographic Occasions in Late Colonial Uluguru." *History and Anthropology* 8:321–56.

———. 1996. "The Pidginization of Uluguru Politics: Administrative Ethnography and the Paradoxes of Indirect Rule." *American Ethnologist* 23 (4): 738–61.

———. 1999. *A Politics of Presence: Contacts between Missionaries and Waluguru in Late Colonial Tanganyika*. Amsterdam: Harwood Academic.

Piault, Marc-Henri. 2000. "La yasigui e le renard pâle: Mythes, controverses, images . . . " *Cahiers d'Études Africaines*, vol. 40, no. 159, issue 3: 415–31.

Piot, Charles. 1999. *Remotely Global: Village Modernity in West Africa*. Chicago: Univ. of Chicago Press.

Prince, R. 1961. "The Yoruba Image of the Witch." *Journal of Mental Science* 107:795–805.

Prins, G. 1992. "The Battle for Control of the Camera in Late-Nineteenth-Century Western Zambia." In Edwards 1992, 218–24.

Quine, W. V. 1960. *Word and Object*. Cambridge, MA: Technology Press of MIT.

Radcliffe-Brown, A. R. 1952a. "On Joking Relationships." In Radcliffe-Brown 1952b, 90–104.

———. 1952b. *Structure and Function in Primitive Society*. London: Cohen & West. (Orig. pub. 1940.)

Radcliffe-Brown, A. R., and D. Forde, eds. 1950. *African Systems of Kinship and Marriage*. London: Oxford Univ. Press.

Ranger, Terence. 1983. "The Invention of Tradition in Colonial Africa." In Eric Hobsbawm and Terence Ranger, eds., *The Invention of Tradition*, 211–62. New York: Cambridge Univ. Press.

Rasool, C., and L. Witz, 1993. "The 1952 Jan van Riebeeck Tercentenary Festival: Constructing and Contesting Public National History in South Africa." *Journal of African History* 34:447–68.

Ray, Benjamin. 1973. "'Performative Utterances' in African Rituals." *History of Religions* 13 (1): 16–35.

Reay, M. 1959. "Two Kinds of Ritual Conflict." *Oceania* 29:290–96.

Rigby, Peter. 1968. "Joking Relationships, Kin Categories, and Clanship among the Gogo." *Africa* 38:133–55.

Rouch, Jean. 1960. *La religion et la magie songhay*. Paris: Presses Universitaires de France.

Rydell, Robert W. 1984. *All the World's a Fair: Visions of Empire at American International Expositions, 1876–1916*. Chicago: Univ. of Chicago Press.

———. 1993. *World of Fairs: The Century-of-Progress Expositions*. Chicago: Univ. of Chicago Press.

Sahlins, Marshall. 1972. *Stone Age Economics*. Chicago: Aldine.

Schapera, Isaac, ed. 1937. *The Bantu-Speaking Tribes of South Africa*. London: Routledge & Sons.

———. 1938. *A Handbook of Tswana Law and Custom*. London: Oxford Univ. Press.

———. 1965. *Praise-Poems of Tswana Chiefs*. Oxford: Clarendon Press.

Schegloff, Emanuel. 1987. "Parties and Joint Talk." Paper presented at the American Anthropological Association Meetings, Chicago.

Schoeman, P. J. 1935. "The Swazi Rain Ceremony." *Bantu Studies* 9:168–75.

Scholte, B. 1974. "Toward a Reflexive and Critical Anthropology." In Hymes 1974, 430–57.

Schwab, W. 1955. "Kinship and Lineage among the Yoruba." *Africa* 25 (4): 352–74.

Scott, James. 1990. *Domination and the Arts of Resistance: Hidden Transcripts*. New Haven: Yale Univ. Press.

Seligman, Charles G. 1966. *Races of Africa*. 4th ed. London: Oxford Univ. Press. (Orig. pub. 1930.)

Senghor, Leopold S. 1964. *Liberté*. Vol. 1, *Négritude et humanisme*. Paris: Éditions du Seuil.

Shaw, Rosalind. 2000. "'Tok Af, Lef Af': A Political Economy of Temne Techniques of Secrecy and Self." In I. Karp and D. A. Masolo, eds., *African Philosophy as Cultural Inquiry*, 25–49. Bloomington: Indiana Univ. Press.

Silverman, Debora L. 1977. "The 1889 Exhibition: The Crisis of Bourgeois Individualism." *Oppositions* 8:71–79.

Silverstein, Michael. 1976a. "Hierarchy of Features of Ergativity." In R. M. W. Dixon, ed., *Grammatical Categories in Australian Languages*, 112–71. Canberra: Australian Institute of Aboriginal Studies.

———. 1976b. "Shifters, Linguistic Categories, and Cultural Description." In K. Basso and H. Selby, eds., *Meaning in Anthropology*, 11–56. Albuquerque: Univ. of New Mexico Press.

———. 1993. "Metapragmatic Discourse and Metapragmatic Function." In J. Lucy, ed., *Reflexive Language: Reported Speech and Metapragmatics*, 33–58. Cambridge: Cambridge Univ. Press.

———. 1996. "The Secret Life of Texts." In Silverstein and Urban 1996, 81–105.

Silverstein, M., and G. Urban, eds. 1996. *Natural Histories of Discourse*. Chicago: Univ. of Chicago Press.

Singer, Milton. 1976. "Robert Redfield's Development of a Social Anthropology of Civilizations." In J. V. Murra, ed., *American Anthropology: The Early Years*, 187–260. St. Paul: West Publishing Co.

Smet, A. J. 1976. *Le Pére Placide Tempels et son oeuvre publiée*. Kinshasa: Départment de Philosophie et Religions Africaines, Faculté de Théologie Catholique.

Smith, M. G. 1956. "On Segmentary Lineage Systems." *Journal of the Royal Anthropological Institute* 86 (2): 39–80.

———. 1957. "The Social Function and Meaning of Hausa Praise-Singing." *Africa* 27 (1): 26–45.

———. 1960. *Government in Zazzau, 1800–1950*. London: Oxford Univ. Press.

———. 1975. *Corporations and Society: The Social Anthropology of Collective Action*. Chicago: Aldine.

Smith, Raymond T. 1973. "The Matrifocal Family." In J. Goody, ed., *The Character of Kinship*, 121–44. Cambridge: Cambridge Univ. Press.

Smith, Robert S. 1969. *Kingdoms of the Yoruba*. London: Methuen.

Spivak, Gayatri C. 1988. "Can the Subaltern Speak?" In C. Nelson and L. Grossberg, eds., *Marxism and the Interpretation of Culture*, 271–313. Urbana: Univ. of Illinois Press.

Stocking, George. 1987. *Victorian Anthropology*. New York: Free Press.

Stoler, Ann, and Frederick Cooper. 1997. "Between Metropole and Colony: Rethinking a Research Agenda." In Cooper and Stoler 1997, 1–56.

Stoller, Paul. 1995. *Embodying Colonial Memories: Spirit Possession, Power, and the Hauka in West Africa*. New York: Routledge.

Street, B. 1992. "British Popular Anthropology: Exhibiting and Photographing the Other." In Edwards 1992, 122–31.

Tait, David. 1950. "An Analytical Commentary on the Social Structure of the Dogon." *Africa* 20 (3): 175–99.

Taylor, Charles. 1989. *Sources of the Self: The Making of the Modern Identity*. Cambridge, MA: Harvard Univ. Press.

Tempels, Placide. 1969. *Bantu Philosophy*. Trans. Colin King. Paris: Présence Africaine. (Orig. pub. 1959.)

—————. 1982. *Plaidoyer pour la philosophie bantu et quelques autres textes*. Trans. A. J. Smet. Kinshasa: Faculté de Théologie Catholique.

—————. 1985. *Aux origines de "La Philosophie Bantoue": La correspondance Tempels-Hulstaert (1944–48)*. Trans. Francois Bontinck. Kinshasa: Faculté de Théologie Catholique.

Thieme, Darius. 1969. *A Descriptive Catalogue of Yoruba Musical Instruments*. Catholic University of America Studies in Music 37. Ann Arbor: Xerox Univ. Microfilms.

Thompson, Robert F. 1976. *Black Gods and Kings*. Repr., Bloomington: Indiana Univ. Press.

Thompson, Vincent B. T. 1974. *Africa and Unity: The Evolution of Pan-Africanism*. London: Longman.

Thornton, Robert. 1983. "Narrative Ethnography in Africa, 1850–1920: The Creation and Capture of an Appropriate Domain for Anthropology." *Man*, n.s., 18 (3): 502–20.

Trouillot, Michel-Rolph. 1995. *Silencing the Past: Power and the Production of History*. Boston: Beacon.

Turner, V. 1967. "Betwixt and Between: The Liminal Period in *Rites de passage*." In *The Forest of Symbols: Aspects of Ndembu Ritual*, 93–112. Ithaca, NY: Cornell Univ. Press.

—————. 1969. *The Ritual Process: Structure and Anti-structure*. Ithaca, NY: Cornell Univ. Press.

—————. 1975. *Revelation and Divination in Ndembu Ritual*. Ithaca, NY: Cornell Univ. Press.

—————. 1981. *The Drums of Affliction: A Study of Religious Processes among the Ndembu of Zambia*. Ithaca, NY: Cornell Univ. Press. (Orig. pub. 1968.)

Vail, Leroy, and Landeg White. 1991. *Power and the Praise Poem: Southern African Voices in History*. Charlottesville: Univ. Press of Virginia.

van Beek, Walter. 1991a. "Dogon Restudied: A Field Evaluation of the Work of Marcel Griaule." *Current Anthropology* 32 (2): 139–67.

—————. 1991b. "Enter the Bush: A Dogon Mask Festival." In S. Vogel, ed., *Africa Explores: 20th Century African Art*, 56–73. New York: Center for African Art.

van Beek, Walter, and Jan Jansen. 2000. "La mission Griaule à Kangaba (Mali)." *Cahiers d'Études Africaines*, vol. 40, no. 158, issue 2: 363–76.

Van den Berghe, P. 1963. "Institutionalized Licence and Normative Stability." *Cahiers d'Études Africaines* 3 (11): 413–23.

Vansina, Jan. 1992. "Photographs of the Sankuru and Kasai River Basin Expedition Undertaken by Emit Torday (1876–1931) and M. W. Hilton Simpson (1881–1936)." In Edwards 1992, 193–205.

Walter, Eugene V. 1969. *Terror and Resistance*. London: Oxford Univ. Press.

Werbner, Richard. 1984. "The Manchester School in South-Central Africa." *Annual Review of Anthropology* 13:157–85.

—————, ed. 1998. *Memory and the Postcolony: African Anthropology and the Critique of Power*. London: Zed Books.

Werbner, Richard, and Terence Ranger, eds. 1996. *Postcolonial Identities in Africa*. Atlantic Highlands, NJ: Zed Books.

White, Luise. 1990. *The Comforts of Home: Prostitution in Colonial Nairobi*. Chicago: Univ. of Chicago Press.

—————. 1995. "'They Could Make Their Victims Dull': Genders and Genres, Fantasies and Cures in Colonial Southern Uganda." *American Historical Review* 100 (5): 1379–402.

Wildenthal, L. 1997. "Race, Gender and Citizenship in the German Colonial Empire." In Cooper and Stoler 1997, 263–83.

Wilmsen, Edwin N. 1989. *Land Filled with Flies: A Political Economy of the Kalahari.* Chicago: Univ. of Chicago Press.

Wilson, Godfrey. 1941. *An Essay on the Economics of Detribalization in Northern Rhodesia.* Part 1. Rhodes-Livingston Paper, no. 5. Livingstone: Rhodes-Livingstone Institute.

———. 1942. *An Essay on the Economics of Detribalization in Northern Rhodesia.* Part 2. Rhodes-Livingston Paper, no. 6. Livingstone: Rhodes-Livingstone Institute.

Wilson, Monica 1959. *Divine Kings and "The Breath of Men."* Frazer Lecture. Cambridge: Univ. Press.

Wright, Gwendolyn. 1997. "Tradition in the Service of Modernity: Architecture and Urbanism in French Colonial Policy, 1900–1930." In Cooper and Stoler 1997, 322–45.

Yai, Olabiyi. 1978. "Théorie et pratique en philosophie africaine: Misère de la philosophie speculative." *Présence Africaine* 108:65–91.

———. 1989. "Issues in Oral Poetry: Criticism, Teaching and Translation." In K. Barber and P. F. de Moraes Farias, eds., *Discourse and Its Disguises: The Interpretation of African Oral Texts*, 59–69. African Studies Series 1. Birmingham, UK: Centre of West African Studies, Univ. of Birmingham.

———. n.d. "Nana versus Ogun: Affirming the Female Voice in Yoruba Oral Literature." Manuscript.

Zahan, Dominique. 1960. *Sociétés d'initiation bambara.* Paris: Mouton.

———. 1963. *La dialectique du verbe chez les Bambara.* Paris: Mouton.

Index

Abraham, R. C., 70n9, 88
abuse, 79; shift from homage to, 93; songs of, 76–79
Afolayan, Michael ('Dejo), 80n23, 87n34
Africa: colonization of, 9, 135, 139; Europeans in, 139–40; gnosis in, 17, 21–22, 29, 30, 132, 144; invention of, by West, 15; as joint invention with Europeans, 135; misrepresented worldviews of, 17; realities arising from invention of, 141; self-determination of, 24
Africanist anthropology, 14, 131–47
African philosophy, 16, 17; *Bantu Philosophy* and, 20; genuine, 23–24; gnosis of, 17, 21–22; of Hountondji, 16; of Mudimbe, 17
African Philosophy: Myth and Reality (Hountondji), 22
African Studies Association (ASA), 15
agency, 4–6, 9, 10; critical, 2, 3–4, 12, 13, 32–49, 128
age-set stratification, 84–85
Ahearn, Laura, 3, 4, 5, 9
Ajasin, M. A., 28
Aladura church, 29
alákoto, 73
alliance, 61; Ekitiparapo military, 26
Althusser, Louis, 16
Amselle, Jean-Loup, 98n3, 135
anthropology, 50; Africanist, 14, 131–47; deconstruction of, 144; without ethnography, 144; reflexive, 138
Appiah, Kwame Anthony, 15, 28n17
Aristotle, 54
Àró of Oreyeye, 84–85, 86, 88
ASA. *See* African Studies Association
Asad, Talal, 131
Asiwaju, A. I., 69n6

Àtá (king), 8–9, 72
"Attitudes to Speech and Language among the Limba of Sierra Leone" (Finnegan), 11
Augé, Marc, 58
Austen, Ralph A., 110n14
authority relations, 5, 35, 46
avoidance, 65
Awa, 108–9, 110, 120, 126
Ayede kingdom, 8–9, 27, 68–78, *70*, 93; indigenous testimony of, 71n10; ritual remapping of quarters, *79*
Ayeni, Michael B., 73, 73n13, 74n16

bàále, 74n15
Babopi, 39
Balandier, George, 137
Balógun Eshubiyi, 27
Bambara, 20
Bantu Philosophy (Tempel), 18, 19, 22; propositions of, 19–20
Barber, K., 67, 71n10, 75n17
Barnes, J., 130
Bastian, M., 94n40
Beattie, J., 130
Beidelman, T. O., 13, 50, 51, 53–54; Gluckman critiqued by, 57–58; on Ncwala, 50, 56
Beier, Ulli, 94n40
Belasco, B., 94n40
Belgian colonialism, in Africa, 19
Bernstein, Basil, 36
Bhebhe, 43
bible, of anti-ethnophilosophers, 22
bifunctionality of praise, *49*
biography, personal, 35
black ox symbolism, 56–57
blowing-off-steam hypothesis, 55